Paul has always been a great competitor. Personally he is a good friend and Christian brother. Paul is a wonderful example of courage, strength, and most important, a person who loves Jesus Christ.

Bernhard Langer
Golf Professional

Paul's heart is as strong as his grip. This champion's visit with mortality is a reminder of who we are and what we can be.

Tom Watson
Golf Professional

A great friend, who displays courage and faith that people should strive to imitate.

Payne Stewart
Golf Professional

Paul's story is truly an inspiration to all of us. He experienced pain, frustration, and disappointment, yet he was determined to come charging back. He is a shining example of grit and perseverance.

Dan Quayle

Paul Azinger is a true inspiration to all golfers. He plays with his heart as well as his mind. If Norman Rockwell had painted a family man/golfer, he would have done a portrait of Paul.

Dave Stockton
Golf Professional
1991 Ryder Cup Captain

From the fabric of legends comes the story of Paul Azinger. Having never broken 80 until he was a junior in college, this young man bursts onto the golfing scene with a zest for life and a zeal for the game. On the heels of his greatest triumph came his greatest challenge. Uplifted by the strength of his faith, the stability of his family and the support of his fans, Paul returns to us having recovered from cancer and having reevaluated life. Whether faced with accolades or adversity, Paul displays the heart of a champion.

Larry E. Moody
President, Search Ministries,
PGA Tour Chapel Leader

Paul Azinger is an inspiration to us all, having faced the greatest confrontation, in the public eye, with the utmost grace and ability.

Robert Earl
President, Planet Hollywood, Inc.

I know Paul as an avid fisherman, fierce competitor, loyal friend, loving father, and devoted husband. On the golf course he's a colossal winner. But cancer showed us how great a winner he is, and the real secret to his winning.... Christ is his caddy!

Mickey Callanen
President, Guess Watches

Paul Azinger's determination, courage, and triumphs—in the world of professional sports, and in his personal battle with lymphoma—are inspirations for all of us.

Dwayne Howell
President and CEO
Leukemia Society of America

Paul has been a friend of mine for many years, and we have shared some great moments together, especially on the U.S. Ryder Cup teams. Paul's determination and strength have never been more evident than during the last year, when he faced the struggle to battle a life-threatening disease. Paul is a great competitor, and I am happy he is healthy, playing golf, and enjoying life again. I look forward to many more years together with Paul on Tour.

Fred Couples
Golf Professional

On a golf tour full of sameness and clones, Paul Azinger is a truly unique and exciting personality. Everything he does breaks the mold—the grip, the swing, the indomitable spirit, the need to win, the intensity, the honesty. The man's a walking storyboard.

Johnny Miller
Golf Professional

When the dark demon of adversity met Paul face to face, we saw a man stand firm for what he believes ... his faith in God. Paul exemplifies characteristics to which we all aspire, too. I applaud a good friend who is a shining star to all.

Morris Hatalsky
Golf Professional

... in one year Zing went from the Michael Jordan look to a Forrest Gump hairstyle.... I would visit Paul when he would come home from chemotherapy, and I would think about how I could cheer him up, and every time I would walk away inspired! He would pick me up—the guy is, flat-out, the most determined individual I have ever been around. He's a fighter—he's a winner—and that is what makes Zinger special.

Bob Delaney
NBA Official, Friend and Neighbor

I was very worried when I first heard the news of Paul's illness. The great competitiveness that Paul has shown on Tour for so many years was confirmed in his year-long battle with cancer, and his faith strengthened as a result.

Corey Pavin
Golf Professional

Paul was a relatively young man who had everything and seemed to have it taken away. Instead of turning to self-pity and bitterness, his faith in God and his love for his family grew as a result of his fight with cancer. Paul helped me realize the tremendous possibility to turn negatives into positives.

Scott Simpson
Golf Professional

Over the years, Paul Azinger has proven that he is a true champion on the PGA Tour. Now Paul has shown that he is a true champion both on and off the golf course. He has been a great inspiration to me through all of this.

Larry Mize
Golf Professional

Paul has overcome a lot of obstacles in his life, from struggling to keep his card on the Tour, to beating cancer. Because of his strong family values and his never-give-up attitude, he's come out on top again.

Dave Stockton, Jr.
PGA Tour Pro

All my life I have believed in the power of prayer. Paul has reinforced my beliefs. God bless him!

Vin Scully
Golf Analyst

Paul plays with exuberant determination and bears the heart of a lion. But most importantly—he is a man after God's own heart.

Lanny Wadkins
Golf Professional
1995 Ryder Cup Captain

I admire Paul as a friend and golfer. He practiced the same courage, faith, and tenacity in his battle with lymphoma as he displays on the golf course. He is truly a champion in both arenas and an inspiration to young and old.

Orel L. Hershiser
Professional Baseball Player

Paul Azinger exemplifies the natural qualities of leadership that arise from a strong moral foundation. His strength of character, shown repeatedly during intense competition, and more recently through facing down one of life's most dreaded diseases, is a beacon to us all. Many times on my show I get calls from people who lament that the country is lost. In Paul, you can find what makes this country great.

Rush Limbaugh

Having the privilege of sharing the infamous John Redman with Paul allows me the opportunity to hear much more than the average golf fan about this young champion. He's exceeded his mission without knowing how much we all have been affected by his plight. We continue to admire his ability and his courage and covet his friendship.

Julius Erving
President, The Erving Group

Several years ago I had a similar problem with cancer, so I know what Paul has gone through. He has dealt with it admirably, and has shown great courage. Paul has been an inspiration to me, as well as thousands of others.

Gene Littler
Golf Analyst

ZINGER

ZINGER

A Champion's Story
of Determination, Courage,
and Charging Back

Paul Azinger
with Ken Abraham

ZondervanPublishingHouse
Grand Rapids, Michigan

HarperCollins*Publishers*
New York, New York

Zinger
Copyright © 1995 by Paul Azinger

Requests for information should be addressed to:
Zondervan Publishing House
Grand Rapids, Michigan 49530

Library of Congress Cataloging-in-Publication Data

Azinger, Paul, 1960–
    Zinger : a champion's story of determination, courage, and charging back / Paul Azinger with Ken Abraham.
       p. cm.
    ISBN: 0–310–49760–4 (hardcover)
    1. Azinger, Paul, 1960–   . 2. Golfers—United States—Biography. I. Abraham, Ken. II. Title.
GV964.A95A3 1995
796.352'092—dc 20   95–7678
[BS]   CIP

Edited by Jim Ruark and John Sloan
Interior design by Joe Vriend

Printed in the United States of America

95 96 97 98 99 00 / ❖ DH / 10 9 8 7 6 5 4 3 2 1

This edition printed on acid-free paper and meets the American National Standards Institute Z39.48 standard.

CONTENTS

ZINGER

CHAPTER ONE
A "MAJOR" PROBLEM

I sensed trouble the moment the telephone rang in our hotel room. It was Friday evening, around eight o' clock, after the second round of the 1993 PGA Championship. We weren't expecting any calls. My wife, Toni, picked up the receiver.

"Hello?" Toni answered tentatively. Then her tone brightened. "Oh, hi, Dr. Jobe!"

Hearing Dr. Jobe's name immediately got my attention. Dr. Frank Jobe is a well-known orthopedic specialist, one of the most highly regarded sports doctors in the world. He had been treating me for pain and discomfort in my right shoulder as far back as 1987. He had operated on the shoulder in 1991, and the pain had gone away for a while.

Now it was back again.

As Toni talked with Dr. Jobe, my thoughts were churning. Why was Dr. Jobe calling me from California now, in the middle of the PGA Championship in Ohio?

"Yes, Dr. Jobe, Paul is right here. You can talk it over with him. Nice talking to you," Toni said lightly, as if she were chatting about the weather.

Toni handed the receiver to me. "It's Dr. Jobe" was all she said.

I spoke as calmly as I could. "Hey, Dr. Jobe. What's up?"

Frank Jobe has a wonderful demeanor for a doctor. He is a consummate professional, but he has a kind, grandfatherly manner. He is always calm and steady, with just the right touch of down-to-earth wisdom to make a patient feel comfortable.

On this night, however, I detected an urgency in Dr. Jobe's voice. He came straight to the point. "Paul, I have been examining the results from some of the tests we've done on your shoulder, and I am concerned about the abnormalities in the bone. I would like to do another biopsy on it. Soon. Let's try to do it Tuesday or Thursday next week."

I thought to myself, *Are you kidding? I'm right in the middle of a tournament. I'm in contention here! I have the Ryder Cup coming up in a few weeks. I'm supposed to play in Greg Norman's Shark Shoot-Out, the Skins Game in Palm Springs, the Tour Championship—I don't want to be bothered with a biopsy right now!*

That's what I wanted to say. But out of respect for the doctor, I gently protested, "Dr. Jobe, I'm playing so well right now. I'd really like to put the biopsy off a little while longer." I had already won the Memorial Tournament and the New England Classic. Now my sights were set on the Wanamaker Trophy, the award given to the winner of the annual PGA Championship.

Dr. Jobe was insistent, but a man with a stethoscope is no match for a man on the leader board. I finally persuaded him that I was feeling well enough that we could wait a few weeks. The doctor relented. He instructed me to stay on anti-inflammatories and antibiotics, in case of infection. He promised to get back in touch with me soon.

I hung up the phone and breathed a sigh of relief. For the next two days I could forget about shoulder pain, hospitals, and biopsies. I could get back to what really mattered: golf. I was in a position to win my first "major" tournament, and besides the $300,000 first-place prize money, I had at least three other reasons why I wanted to win this PGA Championship: Nick Faldo, Greg Norman, and—most of all—me.

● ○ ●

Nick Faldo is undeniably one of the world's greatest golfers. When he gets his towering six-foot-four-inch frame behind a ball, you know that little white sphere is headed toward the pin. Nick is always an awesome force on a golf course, but he is not always the most tactful person on the course. For example, in a magazine interview Nick was asked to comment on the playing forms of various pros, including me.

"Paul Azinger? Can you imagine introducing Paul Azinger as a great champion?" Nick chortled as he imitated my grip and swing. Nick suggested that my swing would never hold up under the pressure of a "major" tournament, that I have "a homemade grip and a hatchet swing."

Thanks, Nick.

By Friday night, midway through the '93 PGA, Nick Faldo's remarks seemed a distant memory, although it didn't escape my notice that his name was sitting atop the leader board. Nick had won his first major tournament, the 1987 British Open, at my expense, when I bogeyed the last two holes, giving Nick the victory by one stroke. A PGA Championship for me would be all the sweeter if I could knock off Nick Faldo in the process.

My competitive tension with Greg Norman stretched back to 1987 also. In May of that year, during the week of the Memorial Tournament, my father was hospitalized to have open heart surgery, his second valve bypass within a short time. I decided not to play in the Memorial so that I could be with Dad during his surgery. I did, however, watch parts of the tournament on television.

During a rain-out at the Memorial, CBS television commentator Gary McCord was interviewing Greg Norman in the locker room. McCord was asking such "softball" questions as, "Tell us, Greg, what kind of a guy are you, anyhow?"

Greg was unusually mellow. "Oh, I'm just happy-go-lucky, Gary. Nothing really bothers me."

As I watched and listened, I chuckled to myself, *Yeah, right! If there is anything Greg Norman is not, it is easygoing, at least not on the golf course. The guy is a fierce competitor.*

At one point McCord asked Greg about the European players' recent dominance over the American players. Why were the foreign players doing so well, McCord wanted to know.

In his best Australian brogue, Greg answered, "Oh, Gary, I just think the European players . . . you know . . . are better ball strikers. We play under different conditions, and . . . you know . . . on different kinds of courses that are not in as good of shape as the American courses . . . and I just think the foreigners are better ball strikers."

I was on the edge of my seat by now. *Better ball strikers! Who does this guy think he's kidding?*

A few weeks later, I went to the British Open feeling as though I needed to prove something about American golfers. I had already won three times in 1987—at the Phoenix Open, in Las Vegas, and in Hartford. I came close to winning the British, too, until I fouled up and allowed Faldo to beat me. I was disappointed, but confident that I had proved my point—namely that we Americans were pretty good ball strikers, too.

Back in the United States, I consented to an interview with a reporter at my home course, River Wilderness, near Bradenton, Florida. The interview went well, and I answered the questions about the British Open as best I could. After the formal interview, we were still talking casually. "Yeah," I laughed. "How about that Greg Norman saying that the Europeans are better ball strikers than the American players? If that is true, why has Greg only won five tournaments?"

The next day, a headline in the *Orlando Sentinel* read, NORMAN WHIPS AZINGER INTO FRENZY! Greg lived near Orlando at the time, and when he saw the newspaper, he got hot.

Greg confronted me a few weeks later on the putting green at the 1987 PGA. He planted himself right in front of me, nose to nose: "I understand you have a problem with me."

I stepped back, stung by the venom in Greg's voice. "Greg, I don't know what you are talking about."

Greg moved close again. "I read where you want a piece of me."

"I never said that—"

"Yes, you did. You said you wanted some of me!"

"Greg, I never said that! Where did you hear that?"

"I have an article from the *Orlando Sentinel*. I'll put it in your locker."

"Okay, Greg. You do that. I just need to see the article, and I'll be able to tell you what I really said." Norman stormed away, and as I watched him go, I couldn't help thinking, *Sheesh! Is this the same guy who earlier in the year said, "I'm a happy-go-lucky guy. Nothing really bothers me"?*

True to his word, Greg put the article in my locker. As soon as I saw the headline, I regretted ever trusting the reporter with my off-the-record comments. Reading my unguarded words in print, I instantly realized that I needed to apologize to Greg Norman. Although the article did not specifically quote me as saying, "I want a piece of Greg Norman," I could understand Greg's aggravation.

Greg and I have very different personalities and different styles as players. I consider myself a meat-and-potatoes type of golfer. I like to play the game, do whatever press interviews are necessary, then get home to my wife and kids. Until recently I attempted to maintain a low profile both on and off the golf course. I like being able to go out to dinner in a restaurant without spending most of the meal signing autographs.

Greg, by contrast, is much more visible. He is constantly on camera, flashy, and flamboyant and makes for "good TV." His charisma and pizzazz account for much of his popularity. And while he and I have never been the best of friends, we have never been enemies, either. I consider him a pretty likable guy. Before this incident we always got along fine. I would never intentionally say anything publicly to mar Greg's image, but now as I read the article in the *Sentinel,* I knew it sounded derogatory. I sought him out and apologized.

"Greg, I am really sorry. Some of this stuff was taken out of context. I did say some of these other things. But you definitely said that the Europeans are better ball strikers than the Americans, and I don't agree with you."

Greg accepted my apology like the gentleman he is, and as far as he and I were concerned, the matter was over. A few years later, some members of the press tried to resurrect the episode when Greg holed a twenty-four-foot chip shot at Doral on the first hole of a four-way sudden-death playoff. As Greg's outstanding chip trickled into the hole to beat me, I raised my wedge overhead and slammed it into the ground, burying it neck-deep in the soft Florida turf. My frustration that day, however, was not with Greg Norman. I was angry with myself for squandering the lead and allowing myself to get into a playoff situation in the first place.

By August of '93 my conflicts with Nick Faldo and Greg Norman seemed all but forgotten. Coming into the PGA, Nick and Greg were ranked the number one and number two golfers in the world, respectively. Naturally, seeing their names atop the leader board at the PGA got my competitive juices flowing, but the most intense struggle I faced at that tournament was not between Nick and me, or between Greg and me. My biggest battle at the 1993 PGA was with myself.

I had inherited the dubious distinction of being known as "The Best Player in the World Never to Win a Major." The "majors" in the world of professional golf are four tournaments that have greater significance than any others: the U.S. Open, the British Open, the Masters, and the PGA, the official championship of the Professional Golf Association. Besides drawing the lion's share of attention in professional golf, these premier tournaments are invested with enormous prestige. Winning a "major" is now the standard of greatness by which all professional golfers are gauged. In golf, it is not good enough to win tournaments; you have to win at the right time and place if you want to be considered among the greats.

Ironically, some of the finest golfers ever to play the game have not had rousing success in majors. Tom Kite is a notable example. Tom is the all-time leading money winner in professional golf. The congenial gentleman has earned nearly nine million dollars in prize money during his career and is still counting. He has won at least nineteen titles and has received almost every trophy golf has to offer. Yet until he won the U.S. Open in 1992, Tom had been labeled "The Best Player in the World Never to Win a Major." For most of his first sixteen years on the Tour, that media tag dogged Tom wherever he went.

As the 1993 Tour progressed, the press apparently felt I had earned Tom's label. I won the Memorial in May and the New England Classic in July. I accumulated ten top-three finishes during the year, the most on the Tour since Tom Watson had achieved that in 1980. So the "crown" was placed upon my head. Paul Azinger became known as "The Best Player in the World Never to Win a Major."

The needling about not winning a major was unceasing. After the Memorial, for instance—a tournament that I won by holing a bunker shot on the eighteenth green to beat my buddy, Payne Stewart—I went to play at the Westchester Classic. In the press room I was expecting members of the media to ask me about my lie in the bunker—a sand trap—at the Memorial or some other details about what was sure to become a signature shot for me. Instead, the first question asked of me was, "Paul, since you have won the Memorial, you probably are now the best player in the world who has never won a major. What do you need to do differently to win a major?"

I was stunned! I was caught so off guard I didn't know how to respond. I mumbled something like, "Gee, I thought winning the Memorial was a good thing, something to be proud of, but if you want to turn it into that, there's nothing I can do about it."

Throughout the summer of 1993, the question kept coming: "Paul, what do you need to do differently to win a major?"

Do differently? I thought. *Why would I want to do anything differently? I'm playing some great golf. What could I possibly do differently, even if I wanted to . . . which I don't!*

Several times in my career I had come close to winning a major. There was the British Open in '87 in which I was only one swing away from a major championship. But I finished bogey-bogey, and the trophy went to Nick Faldo. The following year, at the PGA Championship at Oak Tree in Edmund, Oklahoma, I was leading the pack after fifty-four holes. I played well under the pressure of the last round, but Jeff Sluman scorched the field by firing a sizzling 65 on Sunday. Again, I came home without a trophy.

After the Memorial in Columbus, Ohio, I had three opportunities to win a major in 1993. In June I played well in the U.S. Open at Baltusrol in Springfield, New Jersey, although the pain in my shoulder was really beginning to bother me. I played patiently all week long, hoping to peak on the weekend. I hit some beautiful, long putts that missed by inches. Had they gone in, I could have won—but they didn't. I finished tied for third.

In the British Open I didn't play particularly well, and Greg Norman did. Greg won his second British Open title by two shots while achieving a record for four rounds, which included a remarkable 64 in the last round. I was glad for Greg, but I still had not won a major.

A few weeks later, I won the New England Classic in Boston by four shots. I was striping the ball, hitting it as well as I could, but the victory did not come easily. The pain in my shoulder was growing more intense each passing day. I took ten Advil tablets on Saturday morning before I teed off for the third round. I usually have a high threshold for pain, but on that day my shoulder hurt so badly, I couldn't even reach far enough behind me to put my scorecard in my back pocket.

Ironically, the shoulder did not hurt when I swung my golf clubs. I had what the doctors describe as "arc pain." As long as I didn't bring my right arm up into the arc where the pain resided, I could swing without a great deal of discomfort. My shoulder didn't hurt at impact, when the club struck the ball. Instead, the worst pain came at night, long after I was off the golf course. The pain was there when I went to sleep, and it greeted me when I awoke. On that Saturday morning at the New England Classic, I could hardly raise my arm due to the pain. Somehow I shot a 64.

Although I was elated with the way I was playing, I still wanted a major, and there was only one chance left in 1993. That was the PGA Championship in August at Inverness Club near Toledo, Ohio. On this Friday night, I was only two rounds away.

● ○ ●

Nick Faldo was even closer to the title than I was. Nick had never won a PGA title, and despite the cool reserve he displayed externally, it was obvious to all that he dearly wanted the Wanamaker Trophy.

Greg Norman was close, too, fresh from his win at the British Open. Greg had suffered a stunning loss at Inverness seven years earlier when Bob Tway made a sensational bunker shot on the final hole to figuratively snatch the trophy from his grasp. Now Greg was playing some of the greatest golf of his career and, in many people's minds, was the emotional favorite to win. Like Nick and me, Greg had never won a PGA Championship.

And we all wanted it badly.

CHAPTER TWO

The Championship at Inverness

Inverness Club is a golf purist's delight. The course was designed by the great Scottish architect, Donald Ross, in 1919. Ross believed a golf course should maintain its natural beauty rather than importing vegetation, rocks, and railroad ties the way many modern courses are designed. Ross wanted to challenge a person's golfing expertise, not his ability to run an obstacle course. Consequently, Inverness imparts a sense of regal sophistication without being ostentatious. Its long, narrow fairways lead to some of the smallest greens you will ever see on a tournament-quality golf course. Those tiny greens are tightly guarded by cavernous bunkers, with water hazards looming close by to scare you, whether or not they enter into play.

Inverness has a rich golf history. It has hosted seven championships over the years. One of the first professional tournaments played there was the 1920 U.S. Open, featuring an upstart eighteen-year-old named Bobby Jones. Jones was paired with the legendary Harry Varden. Neither Jones nor Varden won that tournament, but the tradition of attracting great players to the Toledo course continues to this day.

Maybe part of the reason the pros like Inverness is that it was one of the first clubs to admit professional golfers into membership. Unlike most country clubs today, which actively solicit pros as members, many clubs in the early part of the twentieth century viewed professional golfers with disdain. Pros were tolerated on the course, but not allowed inside a club's locker room or clubhouse.

Inverness changed all that. As a token of appreciation, Walter Hagen presented to Inverness a stately grandfather clock that still stands in the clubhouse. The inscription accompanying the clock reads:

> God measures men by what they are,
> Not by what they in wealth possess.

This vibrant message chimes afar,
The voice of Inverness.

Before the 1993 PGA Championship began, I had a feeling I would play well. I knew the course because I had competed in the Dana Pro-Am at Inverness several years in a row. My caddies for the Dana were always local youths, and they really helped me gain insight into how the course plays. I had also played a major there, too—the 1986 PGA—although I missed the cut.

Strangely, I was more nervous on the first tee at the 1993 PGA than at any other time in my career. I just knew I was going to be in contention. I *felt* it.

Of course, I was not the only player who was feeling something special about the seventy-fifth PGA Championship. Greg Norman had just recently scored his stunning victory at Royal St. Georges in the British Open. He was hoping to become the first player to win the British and the PGA in the same year since Walter Hagen did that in 1924. The odds were against him, however. The last player to win any majors back-to-back was Tom Watson, who accomplished the feat in 1982.

Tom, like Greg, arrived at Inverness with a sense of destiny. He had won the British Open five times, the Masters twice, and the U.S. Open once. The PGA was the only major title that had eluded him. He came to Toledo playing extremely well, and he unabashedly declared the '93 PGA as "the most important tournament of my life." It was obvious from the start that nobody was going to walk away with the Wanamaker Trophy without a fight.

Early on, Inverness presented the players with surprises. It rained on Tuesday, making the ground soft and the greens slow and accessible. This meant the balls would more likely stay on the small greens and not run off the edge, as they were prone to do in dry weather. Then on Thursday, in the first round, Darryl Kestner, a club pro from Manhassett, New York, scored a rare double eagle, making a 2 on the par-5 thirteenth hole. And he wasn't the only one hitting spectacular shots that day. Fifty-seven players broke par in Thursday's opening round—a PGA record.

For a while, Lanny Wadkins, who would be one of my teammates at the forthcoming Ryder Cup, looked as though he was going to take us all to the cleaners. Lanny holed a 9-iron shot from the rough for an eagle on the eleventh hole. He shot a 65, a great score on any day—but not good enough at Inverness. Thursday's low score was achieved by Scott Simpson, who tied the course record of 64, set by Bob Tway on the final hole of the PGA Championship in 1986. But Scott's moment in the limelight did not last long.

On Friday, Vijay Singh replaced Scott's name in the record books by shooting a blistering 63, matching the lowest round ever shot in the PGA Championship—or in any major—and joining an elite group of only fifteen players in the history of the game. Vijay's outstanding play positioned him at the top of Friday's leader board, two shots ahead of Wadkins and Steve Elkington.

I had played well on Thursday, shooting a 69, so on Friday I was just trying to stay cool, stay smart, and stay patient. Earlier in the week I had talked with Byron Nelson. Byron had been the club pro at Inverness during the 1940s, and he could play that course with his eyes closed. I asked Byron what advice he had for me, if there were any tricks to this course.

"Just aim for the middle of the greens," Byron said. "Because the greens here are so small, you will usually have a makeable birdie putt anytime you are on them." I decided to take Byron's advice. Rather than shooting at the pin, I would try to lay my shots anywhere near the center of the green.

I had a good day on Friday. Because I was sure I was going to be in contention, I tried to pace myself so I could peak on the weekend. My mind was focused on winning. Right from the beginning I talked about winning to my caddie, Mark Jimenez. Mark had caddied for Bob Tway at the PGA in 1986, so we jokingly agreed that I was a lock to win this year.

By the time I made the turn after nine holes on Friday, I was hoping to maneuver myself into good position for the two weekend rounds. I knew the course conditions would not be favorable much longer. The ground was drying out and getting harder; the greens were getting faster; and as in any tournament, divots and spike marks were playing a greater role as the week progressed. I decided to get more aggressive.

I began charging on the back nine, making seven birdies on the last nine holes, five of them in a row. I finished with eight birdies for the day, shooting a very respectable 66, and went back to my hotel excited about returning to the course on Saturday. No wonder Dr. Jobe's phone call on Friday night failed to faze me. I was focused on only one thing: the Wanamaker Trophy.

● ○ ●

Some people say that the third and fourth rounds of the '93 PGA were two of the greatest rounds of golf ever played. I don't know about that, but I know they were among the most exciting I have ever been a part of. There were enough incredible shots hit on Saturday alone to fill a golf highlights video. For instance, Greg Norman holed a forty-five-foot pitching wedge shot on the tenth green. Jeff Sluman stuffed a 6-iron for an eagle on the fourteenth. Lanny Wadkins laid another one in from the fairway for an eagle. Tom Watson chipped in twice and dropped in several long putts as well. Tom finished the day only one stroke behind the leader. People were thinking that Tom might get his PGA title at last.

But Tom was not alone. By the end of the day, twelve players were within three shots of the lead. Seventeen players were only four behind.

The leader was Greg Norman, who, after fifty-four holes of golf, was 10-under-par. Right behind him at 9-under were Watson, Singh, Wadkins, Bob Estes, Hale Irwin, and me. Faldo was only one shot further back, having ended his third round with a pair of birdies. Nobody was counting Nick out yet. He had won at least one major every year since 1989. Few golf prognosticators dared predict that Nick would be shut out of the '93 majors. Besides, the way things were going at this tournament, anything could happen Sunday during the final round.

Sunday dawned a hot, humid, hazy day. The temperature hovered in the high eighties, but on the golf course it felt like 110 in the shade. The muggy air was stifling. My shoulder was bothering me again, but I was too excited and too nervous to give it much attention. I took my "normal" dose of Advil before teeing off around noon. Bob Estes and I teed off just in front of the last pair, Hale Irwin and Greg Norman.

The leader board looked like a "who's who" of golf, but before long the numbers were changing. Maybe it was the heat, maybe the tension, but things began to happen early in the round. Tom Watson, who had been struggling of late with his putter, three-putted the first hole. Then he missed a four-footer for par on the third. In this tournament that was enough to knock a guy out of contention. Tom never seriously threatened Norman's lead again. Similarly, Lanny Wadkins played well but couldn't find a birdie all day long.

By contrast, Norman got off to a super start by sinking a long birdie putt at the third hole. Visions of St. Georges, where Greg's final round had made history, haunted the other leaders. By the fifth hole, Greg was sitting at 11-under. But on the sixth he stumbled. He found a bunker and took two strokes to get out. That cost him a double bogey and allowed Faldo, Estes, and Singh to take the lead by one shot.

Meanwhile, I had gotten off to a slow start and by the fifth hole had dropped to 8-under, two shots behind the leaders. At the eighth hole Estes made a long putt to move into the lead at 11-under. Faldo soon caught him there.

I played the front nine at even par, bogeying one hole and making a birdie on another. As we made the turn at nine, I was three shots behind. I didn't panic, but I could feel the trophy slipping away. I was trying to be patient, yet I knew I had to do something soon. I was still hitting the ball well; I just couldn't get my putts to drop.

● ○ ●

Things got worse before they got better. On ten I hit a pretty putt from five or six feet. It had a great-looking roll, but it lipped out on the high side. As the ball curled around the cup, my knees buckled reflexively, and I dropped toward the turf, my spikes still firmly grabbing the green—so I looked as if I was suspended momentarily in midair. I dropped to the ground in disbelief that my putt had not gone in. Finally I got up and tapped it in for a bittersweet par. As I hurried off the green, I looked at Mark and shook my head. Mark understood. He knew that the putt should have been in the hole. We walked away from the green together, and then abruptly I left Mark standing there and literally ran through the crowd of people stretching against the ropes that formed a path up the hill to the next tee.

At eleven I hit an 8-iron to within ten or eleven feet of the hole. I took my time, carefully lined up the putt, and made what I thought was the perfect stroke. The ball rolled right to the edge of the cup, dipped about halfway into it, then lipped out again. I took off my visor and paced in a small circle on the edge of the green, in sheer frustration. Then I felt panic. I thought, *Oh, no! This thing is slipping away from me. It's not going to happen. I am going to miss another shot at winning a major!*

I was not going to give up easily. I calmed my nerves and went on to number twelve, talking to myself as I went: *Come on, Zinger! Get it together!*

The twelfth at Inverness is a short hole, 154 yards, par 3, so I took out a 9-iron and whipped the ball onto the green, pin high, about eighteen feet from the cup. Again I steadied my nerves and poured my putt right toward the center of the hole. This time the ball went in. Birdie!

The next hole was a "reachable" par 5, by which I mean that I thought I could reach the green on my second shot. My drive was fine, but I hit the second shot poorly. The ball landed to the left of the green in the upturned left-hand edge of the bunker—not a comfortable position. I had a decent lie, however, so I decided to risk a difficult shot. I wanted to slap the sand really hard with the club, hoping to get a lot of spin on the ball as it popped out of the trap. The ball had to be hit just right. If I misplayed it, I could easily hit it "fat" and leave the ball in the bunker, or I could "skull" the ball, catching it in the middle and sending it flying over the back of the green. That would cost me the championship for sure, not to mention some embarrassment in front of thousands of people in the gallery and millions more watching on television.

I slapped the sand with my club as hard as my nerves would allow, nipping the ball just right. Miraculously, it zinged out of the sand, plopped onto the green, and spun sideways. The ball rolled about fifteen feet past the hole. I was ecstatic!

The putt needed about a three-foot break—tricky up close and even more so at fifteen feet. I squatted down and eyed the angle. Then I got up and took a confident stroke with my putter. The ball rolled in a perfect banana-type break and landed in the hole. My second birdie in a row!

The tension was building inside me as I went to fourteen, but I took some deep breaths and prepared to tee off. My tee shot went right down the middle of the fairway. I was striding after it before the ball even stopped rolling. The pin on fourteen was placed directly in the center of the green, so I was in great position for my next shot.

The fourteenth green is a small, undulating target, so I pulled out an 8-iron. I flushed it right at the pin and came up beween twelve and fifteen feet short of the hole. I had a feeling I was going to make this putt, so I didn't take as much time lining it up. I approached the ball and, without a great deal of deliberation, poked it into the middle of the cup. I had made three birdies in a row, moving me to 11-under-par.

I suddenly realized I was tied for the lead in the last round of the last major of the year. That is when the tension nearly overwhelmed me. It was weird, because I had gone from being very patient on the front nine to being very aggressive on the back. In just three holes I had gone from wanting desperately to get into contention to suddenly being there, right where I wanted to be.

More significantly, I had gone from being calm and patient to being so nervous I could hardly stand it. I have lived with rapid mood swings most of my life, but the ups and downs I felt as I played those last three holes, taking perhaps twenty-five minutes, were more drastic than any I had known before.

Back in 1985, when I first led a top-flight tournament, I became so nervous I told my wife, "Toni, if I have to be this nervous to make a living, I think I'm going to give up golf and do something else!"

Afterward, I asked a veteran golfer, Bert Yancey, about those butterflies. Bert's reply was classic. He drawled, "Son, you want to welcome that chance to be nervous. You want to be so nervous you can't spit. Because if you aren't nervous, you are playing in the middle of the pack. And that's not where you want to be."

On that hot, August afternoon at Inverness, I was not only so nervous that I couldn't spit—I was so nervous I could barely breathe!

At the same time, I could sense that the momentum was now working for me rather than against me. The announcers in the television booth could feel it. People watching the tournament at home could feel it. And *I* could feel it. It was a crazy, intangible sensation, but it was real. The gallery on the golf course could feel it, too. The number of people following Bob Estes and me around the course grew larger.

Moving to fifteen, I was now in a four-way tie for the lead at 11-under, along with Nick Faldo, Vijay Singh, and Greg Norman.

The fifteenth hole at Inverness is the toughest par 4 on the back nine. The tee is set back between the trees, and I knew that if I didn't come straight out of the chute, I could be in big trouble. I tried to block out the mass of people swarmed all around the tee box. I hit an excellent tee shot, setting myself up perfectly in the middle of the fairway. Then I hit a 7-iron exactly where I was looking, about 180 yards away, right toward the middle of the green. I was playing it safe—maybe too safe, since I left myself a forty-foot right-to-left putt for birdie. It was a long shot, but if I could sink it, I would own the lead by myself.

I hit a great putt. As I watched it roll toward the cup, I thought for certain it would drop in. But right in front of the hole, it died and fell off slightly to the left. I dropped to one knee and grimaced. I was disappointed that I had not made birdie to move into sole possession of the lead, but I was thrilled that I had a "gimme"—a putt so short, I couldn't miss—for par. I still felt that good things were going to happen for me. As odd as it may sound to some people, I thought about God a lot during that last round of the PGA. Looking back on it now, I think I understand why.

On sixteen, I was able to hit an iron off the tee, which for some reason was something of a relief to me. The hole was playing short, so an iron club made better sense and gave me more control of the ball than a wood. The shot went right down the middle of the fairway.

As Mark and I strode toward the ball, I struggled to keep my nerves under control. My clothes were soaked with sweat in the heat and humidity. The crowd was greatly excited, and so was I. Attempting to calm down, I took deep breaths as we walked, inhaling for four counts, then slowly exhaling for four counts. These deep-breathing exercises were similar to those used by expectant mothers in labor to handle the pain.

I was trying to get a grip on my emotions and slow my pulse. My heart was beating like a bass drum—bam! Blam! Bam! BLAM! With every heartbeat I could feel and see a flash in my eyes. They were flashing like neon, in sync with my heart. Blam! Flash! Blam! Flash! Blam! Flash!

If anyone ever tells you, "Professional golfers are like machines—they don't really get nervous," let me set you straight. At least one golfer I know gets nervous. Real nervous!

I said to myself, *I've got to get this under control!*

Walking the sixteenth fairway, Mark and I had to go down one hill and up another. I looked over at him and said, "I'll tell you what, Mark. I am going on a cardiovascular program after this is over! I'm gasping for air out here."

Ever steady, Mark nodded. His emotions held steady. His mood never changed throughout the tournament. By staying on an even keel he helped to keep me focused on what I had to do. Mark's effect on me was a critical factor at the PGA.

Meanwhile, back on fifteen, Greg Norman had just gotten a huge break. His approach shot had landed in the rough to the left of the green, but the ball's spin caused it literally to hop through the rough and over the corner of the bunker beside the green. The ball dribbled onto the green. He still had an uphill, eighteen-foot putt for the lead, but even Greg had to chuckle as he walked up the fairway to take advantage of this incredible stroke of good luck. The huge gallery lining the fairway cheered him on.

Greg stroked the long putt to within one inch of the cup, where it stopped dead. He tapped the ball in, and we remained tied.

Ahead of me, Vijay Singh, playing with Tom Watson, fell back a stroke by three-putting the sixteenth green. Vijay finished the day at 70, putting him at 10-under-par for the tournament. Watson was out of the running at 8-under, along with my playing partner, Bob Estes, and Greg Norman's partner, Hale Irwin.

It appeared that the 1993 PGA champion was going to be Nick Faldo, Greg Norman, or me.

CHAPTER THREE
A TEST OF NERVES

I was in a perfect position on the right side of the sixteenth fairway, approximately 160 yards from the hole. The pin was cut to the left on Sunday. I wanted to land on the right side of the flag, which was the fat part of the green. I felt that any shot right of the flag would kick left, running me close to the hole. From the fairway Mark and I studied the shot as if waiting for the green to send me a message where to hit. It didn't. No problem; I already knew.

I tossed a few blades of grass into the air to check the wind. Nothing. Dead calm. I took two quick practice swings, yanked at my shirt sleeves as I always do just before a shot, then decided to check the wind again. The blades of grass again dropped straight down to the turf. I wiped the blade of my 9-iron with my glove, approached the ball, and made an aggressive swing.

The ball sailed toward the green and landed where I had hoped it would, about eighteen to twenty feet to the right of the pin. I was looking at a left-to-right putt with a downhill slope toward the green. I studied the break of that putt every way possible. I was battling my nerves and trying to steady myself. Hovering over the ball just before I swung my putter, I thought, *If I make this putt, I will take the lead in the tournament.*

I slowly pulled back my putter, brought it forward in a perfect pendulum motion, moving it gently toward the ball—and blasted the ball four feet past the hole.

Oh, no! The last thing I wanted to do on the sixteenth green was leave myself a nasty four-footer for par. A moment ago I was thinking about taking the lead; now I had to make this putt just to stay tied for the lead. I steeled my nerves again, went back to the ball, and stroked it straight into the hole.

The crowd erupted in cheers. As I walked from the green, the gallery spurred me on, "Come on, Zinger! You can do it!" Several people swatted me

29

on the back as I passed them on the roped-off path leading to the tee box at seventeen. I really appreciated their support, but I couldn't help thinking, *I sure hope nobody hits me on my shoulder!*

The seventeenth tee shot at Inverness is a tough one. It sets up as a "dog-leg" to the left, with a fairway bunker guarding the right side. There is also an elevation change toward the green. If I kept the ball on the fairway, it would run out far enough that I would be able to see the green on my second shot. If I didn't hit the ball far enough, or if I caught some rough, the green would be out of sight and I would have to guess at my approach shot.

I pulled out my 3-wood, addressed the ball, and ripped it. The ball shot off in a beautiful arc, sailing 280 yards, landing smack in the center of the fairway just left of the bend in the dogleg.

While I waited to hit my second shot at seventeen, I glanced behind me to sixteen, where Greg Norman was getting ready for his second shot. I had been keeping an eye on the leader board, so I knew where we stood. By now, Nick Faldo, who was a few groups in front of me, had finished at 11-under, which meant he, Greg, and I were tied for the lead at the moment. If Greg and I bogeyed any of our remaining holes, Nick would win.

When Greg hit his second shot, I knew there was no danger of his making a bogey. Quite the opposite. Using a pitching wedge, Greg nearly put the ball into the hole from about 130 yards away. His shot hit the green and rolled to within two feet of the pin. The roar of the crowd could be heard all over Inverness. Greg was left with a short, straight, uphill putt—the kind he rarely misses. He was a shoo-in for birdie. I had to put my approach shot to seventeen close to the hole, or else. . . .

I was 155 yards away, looking downhill at the green. I felt sure the hole would play like 140 because of a slight downwind and the downward slope. I jerked at my sleeves and stretched each arm high in the air as I addressed the ball. I swung with precise hip speed, the club met the ball perfectly. The ball dropped onto the green and stuck, dead solid perfect, five or six feet in front of the cup.

The roar from the gallery sounded like a stadium crowd cheering after a touchdown pass in the last thirty seconds of the Super Bowl. I struggled to maintain my composure, but I allowed myself a brief smile toward the gallery as I headed down the hill toward the green.

Over on sixteen, Greg could not ignore the noise that now enveloped me, but he did not let it get to him. He tapped in his putt for birdie and the lead at 12-under-par. Greg had said earlier in the week that he thought it would take a score of 12-under to win the Wanamaker this year. Now he had fulfilled his own prophecy.

Although I had just hit one of the most memorable shots of my career, I was still one stroke behind. I was looking at a five-or-six-foot putt, extremely makeable under ordinary conditions. But in the sauna that Inverness had become, I wasn't so sure. Worse still, after seventy holes of a major professional tournament, the greens were getting scuffed up badly. Three nasty-looking spike marks lay directly in the line of my putt. I also had to allow for some left-to-right break, so those spike marks loomed like cones in the middle of an automobile test course. I had only one choice—stroke the ball and hope for the best.

I hit the putt firmly and watched while the ball seemed to take forever to move the six feet to the hole. The ball hopped a bit as it rolled over the spike marks, veered slightly off course, edged toward the side of the cup—and dropped in. Twelve-under! Norman and I were tied again.

A wave of relief swept over me, and I gave a little fist pump, but I didn't want to show too much emotion. With the final hole coming up, I knew I needed to keep my emotions under control.

The crowd felt no such restraint. The noise was deafening.

I went to the tee box for eighteen. This signature hole at Inverness is 357 yards, par 4. It looks easy on the scorecard until you notice that the hole is made difficult by eight bunkers, with three of the deepest ones guarding the tiny green all the way around the front. *Time for another iron off the tee,* I thought.

As I addressed the ball and began my backswing, somebody in the gallery moved. I stopped in midswing and backed away from the ball. Slightly distracted, I approached my shot for the second time. I hit the ball solidly, but I pushed the shot off to the right. I hit it into some of the deepest rough on the course, on a hill no less. My heart sank.

Behind me, Norman was having troubles of his own. Greg's shot off the seventeenth tee did not hook at the bend of the dogleg as he had hoped. The ball landed in the bunker on the right side of the fairway. In the clubhouse Nick Faldo must have been smiling.

Greg's position in the bunker was not to be envied. The ball was sitting close to the front lip, but he had a fairly good lie. He was 187 yards away from the pin, normally 6-iron yardage. But Greg needed some extra loft to get the ball out of the bunker and over that lip, so he had to use a 7-iron. It was a risky shot, but Greg got all of it. He blasted the ball all the way to the front of the green.

Meanwhile, I was trudging up the hill to where my ball was lying in the rough above eighteen. I faced a tough decision. Should I simply try to pop the ball out of the rough in the general direction of the green and hope to stay even with Greg, or should I go for the pin? It was a gamble to go for it, because I did not have a lot of green with which to work.

Two factors influenced my decision. First, I had caught a fortunate lie in that the ball was not buried in the deep grass but instead was sitting up slightly, making it easier to get at. Second, the ball was located at my full sand wedge yardage. Like every pro golfer, I know my clubs and my particular strengths well enough to choose the right club for the exact distance I want the ball to fly—most of the time.

The ball was sitting 104 yards from the flag, a perfect sand wedge shot for me. I decided to go for it. I took a full swing and really crushed it. The ball streaked out of the rough and landed on the green about twenty feet from the cup. Again, the gallery roared.

Greg and I had been hitting at almost the exact same time. He heard the gallery over by me, but it didn't keep him from chipping off the fringe of the seventeenth green to within inches of the cup. Greg had just missed making another birdie!

Mark and I walked up to the green in silence. While I was elated to be on the green and putting for a birdie, I was just too nervous to talk. At the green Bob Estes, my partner, was willing to putt first out of respect for my position on the leader board—and perhaps out of self-preservation. He probably felt that if I sank that putt, the crowd would take forever to calm down before he could hit his.

I appreciated Bob's willingness to go first for that reason. I also thought that by watching him I might learn something about the way the green was playing. As Bob stroked the ball, I noticed that it definitely slowed down when it got within four or five feet of the hole. This was not going to be an easy putt for me.

Should I look at the leader board before I hit this putt? I wondered as I squatted to take a last look at my putting line. *I know this putt is either to win the championship or tie for it. But I have to give it the same effort regardless—so should I look or not?* Finally I gave in. *Yeah, I'd better look. I might hit this shot just a little bit differently if I can two-putt to win or force Greg to make birdie to tie.*

As inconspicuously as I could, given the fact that thousands of people in the gallery were watching my every move, along with millions of others on television, I looked over at the leader board. In a glance I saw that Greg had indeed parred the seventeenth, so we were still tied. That meant that if I sank this putt, I would finish 13-under and force Greg to make a birdie on eighteen—a feat accomplished by only eight golfers all day.

I felt pressure mounting. If I knocked the putt three feet past the hole, I would have a really difficult downhill putt coming back. I didn't want to fail in front of family and friends or the millions watching on television. Moreover, since I was still The Best Player in the World Never to Win a Major, I didn't want to choke off a putt that might relieve me of that title. If I missed this chance, I might never recover.

● ○ ●

I pulled back my putter and attempted to swing my arms in my usual pendulum motion. It was all I could do to hit that putt hard enough to make the uphill climb toward the hole. I watched the ball curve up the incline; it seemed to be rolling so slowly, I could read the Titleist logo as the ball turned over and over. I kept waiting for the ball to break toward the hole. Twelve inches away from the cup, the putt began losing speed drastically. I saw the ball hit a spike mark and wobble as it neared the edge of the cup, then it rolled on by, just kissing the left side. Had someone in the gallery sneezed just then, the air may have been enough to knock the ball in. Instead, it rolled four inches beyond the cup.

I tapped the ball in for a 68 for the day and finished at 12-under-par. I acknowledged the gallery's huge ovation, then slipped into the tour trailer to sign my card and to watch and wait.

In going to 12-under I dashed Nick Faldo's dreams of being the seventy-fifth PGA Champion. The best Nick could do was second place, but barring a major failure on Norman's part, Nick must be content with third. For both Nick and me, it all came down to Greg Norman.

From the eighteenth green Greg had watched me finish. He knew exactly what he needed to do to win—make a birdie. In the history of the PGA, only one man had ever won the Wanamaker Trophy by making a birdie on the last hole. His name was Bob Tway. Whom did he beat? Irony of ironies, Greg Norman.

Greg teed off with a 2-iron and dropped a perfect shot in the middle of the fairway. With ninety-eight yards to go to the green, he chose the longer of his two sand wedges and hit another incredible shot that landed on the green, spun backward, and stopped about twenty feet from the hole.

Inside the trailer I was watching the whole thing on television. I was too drained and numb to think of much, but I knew that my chances of hoisting that huge PGA trophy were getting slimmer with every sensational shot Greg made. He was now lying two on the green. I thought, *If Greg makes his next shot, it's over. He wins. If he misses the birdie putt and has to settle for par, we're tied. We will go into a sudden-death playoff—the first person to win a hole wins the tourney. If he three-putts and makes bogey, the championship is mine.*

Hale Irwin, Greg's playing partner, practically duplicated Greg's shots on the eighteenth hole. Both men still had tough putts back to the cup. Hale played his putt first and left it several inches short. Since Greg's ball was marked only inches from where Hale's shot had landed, by watching Hale's putt Greg knew the speed and break of the green. He also realized that his putt could break more than expected.

Greg eyed his putt from every angle, pacing around the green like a hungry lion stalking his prey. From where I was sitting, it seemed that Greg was taking forever to line up his shot. I was still in the trailer, and a television camera was trained on me. As Greg hit his putt, the viewing audience could watch my reaction in a corner inset on their screens. I was probably disappointing the network's producers—I was showing no emotion at all.

Finally Greg was ready. The gallery grew absolutely silent. Norman was putting to win.

It appeared to be a perfect putt. As soon as he hit it, Greg looked as though he knew it was in. The ball curved lazily left to right toward the hole. When it was eight feet from the cup, I was certain it would drop in. So were the TV commentators and most of the people in the gallery. As the crowd began to roar once more, someone yelled, "It's in the hole!"

But it wasn't.

Amazingly, the ball curled around the hole and lipped out.

Greg couldn't believe his eyes. He flipped his putter into the air and paced around the green in shocked disbelief. He couldn't sustain this reaction too long, however, because he now had to make an eighteen-inch putt to tie me. Still stunned, Greg stepped up to the ball and tapped it into the cup. He finished the day with a 69, leaving him 12-under-par for the tournament, like me.

I came out of the trailer, saw Toni, and gave her a quick kiss. It was no time to celebrate. We were going to a playoff.

CHAPTER FOUR
THE PGA PLAYOFF

Greg Norman's nickname is "the Shark." On Sunday during the PGA, Greg wore a multicolored shirt and a black hat, both emblazoned with a logo of a shark.

I grew up around water and learned quite a bit about sharks. A favorite pastime even today is to point my flatsboat out toward the sparkling waters of Tampa Bay to go sight-casting for sharks.

Shark sight-casting is different from normal bait-fishing or plug-casting—tossing a line with a lure. You don't simply toss out a line and hope a shark happens to notice. You hold your bait right at the boat, and when you see a shark, looking pitch black on the surface of the water, you cast to where you *think* he is going. When the shark glides over, takes the bait, and sucks the hook, it's time to hang on—you are in for the ride of your life.

Sharks have a "tough-guy" image. Thanks to Hollywood and a few highly publicized—but rare—reports of shark attacks upon swimmers, most people regard sharks as awesome predators that will eat anything in their path. The truth is, if you cast too close to a shark, he will "spook" and speed away, and you will never see him again.

From the very beginning of the last round of the '93 PGA, I had set my sights on "the Shark." Now, after eighteen holes of heart-pounding golf, in which I had come from three shots behind, making four clutch birdies over the final seven holes, I had finally caught up with him. I knew I was in for the ride of my life. And I knew that Greg Norman was one shark that would not spook.

Greg approached the PGA trailer to sign his scorecard. I shook his hand and said, "Great playing."

Greg was all business. Looking back granite-faced, he answered, "Yeah, bud. Great playing."

I was tired when I stepped out of the trailer to begin the sudden-death playoff. My back was sore, and my legs ached. Mostly, my fatigue stemmed from the stress and pressure that had built up over four days of riding an emotional roller coaster. My shoulder was sore, too, but the pain was minor compared with what I had felt a few weeks earlier at the New England Classic.

Despite my discomfort, I walked briskly to the television crew's cart that was to transport Greg and me back to the eighteenth tee, where the playoff was to begin. I climbed into the cart's passenger seat and sat with my body turned to the right. After signing his scorecard, Greg took the seat next to me, his body facing left. As the cart lurched into motion, we sat back-to-back in silence, but then I leaned over and said, "Man, I saw Faldo's name go up on the board, posting at 11-under . . ." I just shook my head.

With a twinkle in his eye, Greg leaned over and finished the sentence for me. "Yeah," he said, "I was thinking, *anybody* but him!" We both chuckled nervously, and I almost felt indebted to Nick Faldo for unwittingly providing some comic relief. Greg and I rode the rest of the way to the tee in absolute silence. This was no time for idle conversation.

When we arrived at the tee box, a PGA official held out lots for Greg and me to draw. I was not the only nervous person; the official was shaking like a leaf. Greg noticed, too, and teased him, "Look at you! You're shaking worse than we are."

I drew lot number one, which meant I was to tee off first. I decided to use a 3-iron. In regulation play on this same hole, I had hit a 1-iron that went into the rough on the right. This time I chose the shorter-distance club and drew the ball down the left side of the fairway. The ball trickled a few feet into the first cut of rough, but I knew the yardage was right, so I wasn't worried.

Greg virtually duplicated my shot off the tee, landing in the rough just ahead of me.

It was my turn again, and I used the longer of my two sand wedges to hit out of the rough. The ball shot straight toward the flag and dropped fifteen feet short of the hole in excellent position. I was on the green in two, leaving an uphill, slightly right-to-left putt.

Greg also hit a great wedge shot out of the rough. Incredibly, it landed only inches away from where he had played in regulation. He was left with the same eighteen-to-twenty-foot putt he had missed earlier that sent us into the playoff. Greg paced the green, lining up his putt for what seemed like an interminable amount of time. He knew this hole well. He knew the break he was reading, and he knew the speed of the green. But I couldn't blame him for taking his time. This shot could decide the championship.

Greg stroked the putt perfectly, and the ball rolled toward the hole. The closer it got, the more certain I was that it would fall in. Four feet, three feet, two feet—then, miraculously, the ball hit the edge of the cup, and—*sheew!* It power-lipped out! It was like watching an instant replay of Greg's eighteenth in regulation. As before, Greg flipped his putter in frustration.

I was thinking, *Man! I can't believe that putt missed the hole!* Then it hit me: *I am now putting to win my first major!* To say I was nervous would be like saying the Titanic took on a little water. I had not putted particularly well all day long. Although I hadn't three-putted on any hole, I was not rolling my putts the way I like to see them.

I carefully read the green, thinking the whole time, *This putt can win it for me.* When I felt I was ready, I stepped up and stroked the perfect putt— except for one thing. It didn't go in. The ball touched the top lip of the cup, then rolled on by, stopping eighteen inches past the hole. I tapped it in for par. Then Greg tapped in his. Walking off the green, I glanced up at the television broadcasters' booth, and Ken Venturi's eye caught mine. I shrugged my shoulders and mouthed the word *Wow!* Venturi nodded knowingly.

Greg and I headed for the tee on number ten, the second hole of sudden death. As we walked, I saw the huge gallery pouring across the fairways from number eighteen to number ten, to the dismay of the tournament officials, who were powerless to prevent the damage to the well-tended landscape. The scurrying crowd looked like the Israelites crossing the Red Sea.

On the way, Greg and I chatted about our putts. "Man, I thought you had it," I told Greg. I said I thought he had gotten the "paint job," referring to the old golfers' saying often used to explain a missed shot that should have gone in: The paint around the cup, or on the ball, was to blame for keeping the ball out.

Heat. Pressure. Sweat. The tension was so heavy on the number ten tee, I felt as if a thousand-pound weight were hanging from my shoulders. The stress was not lessened simply because number ten is a fairly easy hole. It is a short par 4, 361 yards long. The hole plays rather straightforwardly, although the fairway ends about 255 yards off the tee, making proper club selection critical. I chose to hit a 3-iron and put the ball along the left-hand edge of the fairway.

Greg hit his tee shot into the first cut of rough on the left side, which created a major problem for him because the pin was on the left side of the green. From the fairway it was downhill to the green, all the way to the cup, where the ground flattened out for a few feet and then sloped further downhill. This meant that from the rough, Greg was going to have to shoot straight at the pin and land his shot within a small three-or-four-foot circle if he hoped to get his ball close to the hole.

Greg went right for the pin. As soon I saw his ball in the air, I knew this shot was going to be long. It landed on the green, but about thirty-five feet beyond the cup.

I addressed my downhill approach shot. I was sitting on the fairway, 121 yards out. As usual, I checked the wind by holding up a few blades of grass. The wind was negligible, if there was any at all. Nevertheless, Mark Jimenez and I felt the hole was playing less than 115 yards because of the downhill grade. For me, that meant using a little pitching wedge. I thought for a moment that I might be able to crush a sand wedge shot, because the wind was calm and the ball was flying well. Then I reconsidered. *The way that green is sloped, if I hit a sand wedge and it hits the green pin-high, or even two or three feet short of the pin, it might backspin all the way down off the front of the green.* I decided to go with the pitching wedge and just take a little bit off the swing. I aimed for about five feet to the right of the pin.

I swung the club lightly and connected with the ball perfectly. The ball landed on the green and skipped toward the pin, stopping about ten feet away. That left me with a relatively easy, inside-right putt to the hole.

On the tenth green Greg took an unusually long time getting ready to hit. Later, someone suggested to me that Greg had done that on purpose, trying to "freeze" me. I doubt it, but that was the last thing on my mind. About that time, I was standing over by the green-side bunker trying to stretch the calves of my legs. I felt they could cramp up at any time. I wasn't worried about what Greg was doing; I was just thinking about what I had to do to sink my putt.

When Greg finally hit his putt, I was as surprised as anyone. After dropping in some incredible putts and missing others only by inches all day long, Greg left this potential "putt-of-a-lifetime" five feet short. The air pressure around the tenth green must have momentarily dropped as thousands of people in the gallery gasped in chorus.

As I saw where Greg's ball had stopped, I felt a surge of confidence. I knew he had a difficult second putt, because I had missed a putt from almost that exact spot earlier in the day. That missed putt had nearly put me out of contention.

So here I was again, on the tenth green, thinking as I approached my putt, *You have a ten-footer to win a major championship. You need to make this!*

I stood over the ball, swung my putter perfectly, and hit the ball precisely where I had been looking. I was so pleased when I hit that putt, I just stood and watched it, waiting for it to break toward the hole.

At that exact moment, while watching on television, Nick Price, the 1992 PGA Champion, turned and mentioned to his wife, Sue, "He will miss this putt on the right lip. I had this putt today, and it doesn't break."

Meanwhile, I kept watching my putt, thinking, *Break! BREAK! BREAK!*

It never broke. The ball caught the inside right of the cup, tipped tauntingly into the hole, spun two-thirds of the way in, and then lipped out, stopping six inches to the left. Another collective gasp went up from the gallery. I was barely breathing.

I slowly looked up and purposely attempted to control my emotions and my expression. I did not want anyone—especially Greg—to think that this missed putt was devastating to me. I walked over to my ball, lying a few inches from the hole, and tapped it in. I stepped to the back of the green, where I recognized a group of media people looking at me; I made a conscious effort to restrain my reaction. I stood at the edge of the green with my hands on my hips and stared at Greg, who was getting ready for his second putt. Greg had to make this putt to stay tied with me, and few people doubted he would sink it. Many of the younger members of the gallery were already running toward the tee at number eleven—the next hole designated for the playoff—in hopes of getting a good viewing spot. As far as I was concerned, I was ready to go to the next tee, too.

But Greg still had a nasty, curving, five-foot putt to negotiate. This was no "gimme." Greg hit it well, right on line, and we all held our breath waiting to see when and how far it would break. Unlike my putt, Greg's broke toward the hole. It caught the edge of the cup, dipped about one-third of the way in the hole, danced on the rim for what seemed like an eternity . . . and then squirted back out of the hole!

It was over. I had won it! Paul Azinger was the 1993 PGA Champion! More than that, I had won a *major!*

Greg and I approached each other on the green like two spent animals that had fought a heated turf battle and had decided, after nearly killing each other, that it was better to live in peace. When Greg got close enough to me, I grabbed his hand and squeezed it as I said, "I'm sorry." Greg knew what I meant. Of course, I wasn't sorry I had won. I was empathizing with him for missing that putt.

Greg gave me a little hug and replied, "It's all right. Good playing, bud. Congratulations."

That was all Greg said, but I believe it was from his heart. There wasn't time to say more, anyway, because suddenly, from everywhere, I was bombarded with congratulations.

Someone pointed me in the direction of CBS broadcaster Jim Nantz and PGA President Gary Schaal, who were waiting patiently along with a national television audience for the trophy presentation. Schaal began the brief ceremony, saying, "Congratulations! On behalf of the 23,000 golf professionals in our association, we are extremely proud of you, Zinger. It started with Jim Barnes, Byron Nelson, Ben Hogan, Nicklaus, and all the big guys, and you deserve to be there."

I was so physically and emotionally exhausted, I could barely speak, but I had looked forward to this moment throughout much of my career. I certainly was not going to allow it to pass without trying to say something positive about the One who had made it possible. "Thanks, Gary. I appreciate that. I just want to thank the Lord . . ." I knew that as soon as I mentioned the Lord, the people in the CBS booth would be upset, so I tried to think of something noncontroversial to say. "I just thank the Lord that he gave me the strength to be here today. I was pretty lucky on that last putt. I thought I hit a pretty good putt. I had the same putt Greg had earlier today—"

Jim Nantz broke into my sentence. "Paul? This is the moment you have been waiting for. How did you do it?"

I told Jim about the neon flashes going off in my eyes every time my heart beat, and then I got to the main thing I wanted to say. "Well, I thought about the Lord all day. I really had a peace . . . I was nervous, though, man; I really was . . . but some things are more important than golf . . . I'm at a loss for words right now." I was sincerely trying to get in a good word, but Jim interrupted me again, this time with the presentation of the Wanamaker Trophy.

"Well, take that Wanamaker Trophy and hoist it in the air, because you have won the PGA Championship!"

Gary Schaal handed me the huge prize. I grabbed the trophy by its handles and lifted it above my hips—where I had to stop to get a better grip on it. I had never picked up the Wanamaker Trophy, and I couldn't believe how heavy it was! I started to raise the trophy to my shoulder, where I was going to let it rest, as the photographers snapped their pictures and the gallery applauded. Toni and my two little girls, Sarah Jean and Josie Lynn, were standing in the background with Mark Jimenez. I waved them onto the green. It was one of the most triumphant moments of my life, and I wanted to share it with them. I gave Toni a big kiss while the girls hung onto her amid the crush of people.

Only one cloud darkened the celebration. When I lifted the Wanamaker, I felt a dull, throbbing pain in my right shoulder.

Later, in an interview on ESPN's *Sunday Conversation*, Jimmy Roberts asked me about my new goals, now that I was no longer The Best Player in the World Never to Win a Major. "Jimmy, my goal is longevity. I just want to stay healthy and have a long career."

● ○ ●

I did dozens of interviews for both the national and local media, and half the time I hardly knew whom I was talking to. I answered the same questions again and again, but I didn't really mind. I had proved to the golf world, and more importantly, to myself, that I was able to win "the big one."

Then I was whisked off to greet the special guests of the PGA. Still in my playing clothes, I stood in the sophisticated Inverness Clubhouse with the Wanamaker Trophy by my side. I shook hands and spoke with a line of well-wishers that traipsed by for more than an hour and a half. By the time I completed all my interviews, cleaned out my locker, and drove Toni and the kids back to our hotel, it was approaching eleven o'clock.

Elated but exhausted, we were just about ready to collapse into our beds when the telephone rang. It was Dr. Jobe.

The doctor was calling to congratulate me on the PGA victory. Better still, he said that we could put off the biopsy for a while. "Maybe the problem in your shoulder is simply some strange infection," he said. "Stay on your antibiotics, and we'll see what happens."

I thanked Dr. Jobe profusely for his call. Toni and I tumbled into bed and slept like babies. I was so tired, I barely noticed the nagging pain in my shoulder.

CHAPTER FIVE
THE 1993 RYDER CUP

The next morning Toni, the kids, and I flew home from Toledo. Several times during the flight I had to pinch myself to make sure I wasn't dreaming. Each time, I came up with the same answer: "I really have won my first major! Yes, I really am the 1993 PGA Champion."

Throughout my career prior to the '93 PGA, I had felt that I had nothing to prove to anyone but myself. I had been extremely successful in professional golf despite my never having won a major. Nevertheless, a subtle pressure was always there, like a taunting voice in the back of my mind: "You've never won a major!" Then came my win at the Memorial, and along with it came the extra burden of being known as the best player who had never won a big one.

Now I had done it. I had finally won a major. The burden had been lifted from my shoulders. As I closed my eyes and relaxed during the flight back home, a huge wave of satisfaction and contentment washed over me.

When we arrived at the Bradenton-Sarasota airport, we were met by some good friends, Bill and Sue Pleis, and their two sons, Scott and Steve; the Geigers, our neighbors from across the street; and, of course, my mom and dad, and some of our closest relatives. One of them bought a Bradenton newspaper and showed me the headlines: AZINGER BRINGS HOME A MAJOR!

Later that week my home club at River Wilderness held a huge celebration for me. About three hundred people crowded into the club dining room to hear me recount the inside story and a shot-by-shot description of the PGA. It was a great time. At the close of my talk I told the club members, "Now we have the 1993 Ryder Cup coming up, a tournament I am really looking forward to playing in."

Unquestionably, playing in a Ryder Cup is one of the greatest thrills a professional golfer can experience. Two Ryder Cup teams—one from Europe and one from the United States—are selected on a point basis every two years to compete against each other in a match-play format. (In match play, the team or player winning the most holes wins the match, whereas in stroke play—the format for most golf tournaments—the winner is the one with the lowest number of strokes.) In theory, members of these teams have been the "all-stars" of golf on both continents during the selection period. Besides being a great honor and a reward for outstanding play, Ryder Cup play is a team effort in a sport that exalts individual performance. For a few days, members of Ryder Cup teams enjoy a camaraderie that cannot be equaled anywhere else in the sport.

The event has become more international than it used to be. The Ryder Cup began in 1927 as a biannual golf match between the American players and the British and Irish. For years the American teams hammered the British teams. Most people in golf circles anticipated another Ryder Cup play with a colossal yawn: another boring victory for the Americans. Like the America's Cup in sailing, it was assumed the United States team would win—and it usually did.

In 1979, however, the British-Irish team expanded to become a truly European team. No longer is the competition between countries; now it is between continents. And no longer is an American victory a foregone conclusion. The Europeans won in 1985 and 1987. They played us to a draw in 1989.

Today the Ryder Cup is regarded as golf's most valued prize. Even including the four majors, the Ryder Cup competition is probably the most intense of any tournament in modern golf. A great deal of pride is on the line at a Ryder Cup match—personal pride, pride in one's team, and most of all, pride in one's country.

I don't mind saying that I love my country. If some people consider that old-fashioned or politically incorrect, that's their problem, not mine. My father was a career military man, so I lived on military bases until Dad retired when I was in my early teens. Dad was a navigator in the air force, a lieutenant colonel who flew missions in both Korea and Vietnam. He later worked with the Strategic Air Command. Needless to say, around our house we had great respect for the American flag.

I never served in the U.S. Armed Services—I went into professional golf right out of college—so I never had the privilege of wearing an American military uniform. But when I put on a Ryder Cup jacket with the Stars and Stripes, just wearing our American colors fills me with an overwhelming sense of patriotism. When I play on a Ryder Cup team, my chest swells with pride. I feel that I am representing not only the PGA, or even myself, as I stand on that tee, but also the United States of America.

● ○ ●

The '93 Ryder Cup was held at the Belfry, located in the picturesque English Midlands. The U.S. team consisted of Captain Tom Watson, Chip Beck, Corey Pavin, Lanny Wadkins, Fred Couples, Payne Stewart, Raymond Floyd, Jim Gallagher, Jr., Davis Love III, John Cook, Tom Kite, Lee Janzen, and me—not a bad lineup in any league. We were pitted against Europe's best: Seve Ballesteros, Nick Faldo, Ian Woosnam, Bernhard Langer, Jose Maria Olazabal, Colin Montgomerie, Mark James, Sam Torrance, and four first-time Ryder Cup players. It was truly a superstar card.

After two days of competition, both teams were playing nearly even. Before the final matches began, Tom Watson asked me if I minded playing last and anchoring our team. I said I didn't mind.

In Ryder Cup play, the last position is often the pressure spot. It may all come down to you. It wasn't exactly a coveted position, because we all had memories of Bernhard Langer in 1991, when, on the last day in the last group on the last hole, he carried the entire Ryder Cup match and the hopes of an entire continent on his shoulders as he stood over his final putt, a six-footer that would decide the outcome. Bernhard's putt missed by inches, and the U.S. team took home the cup. Of course, having such an enormous amount of pressure rest on one putt is unusual in Ryder Cup play, but it was enough to cause all of us to think twice before accepting the anchor position.

At our regular prematch meeting, I told my teammates, "Gentlemen, just do me a favor: Don't make my match count."

Nevertheless, I wasn't afraid of pulling the last position. I suspect my confidence confused some of the press corps covering the Ryder Cup. In an interview a month earlier, I was asked, "Would you like to be in the situation Bernhard Langer was in at the close of the 1991 matches?"

I answered emphatically, "No! And anybody who says they'd like that position is lying."

"Well, who would you *like* to see in that position?"

"Me," I answered without wavering.

To make my match even more interesting, I drew Nick Faldo in singles play on the last day of the '93 Ryder Cup. Nick was still smarting from his loss in the PGA, undoubtedly feeling not that I had beaten him, but that he had beaten himself.

The press played my match with Faldo to the hilt. According to them, this was the matchup everyone wanted to see. I was quoted as saying to Tom Watson that I "wanted" Nick Faldo. That was absolutely untrue. The whole idea was preposterous, since there was no way for me to know where the opposing team was going to place Nick in the playing order. The Ryder Cup matchups occur much the same way that baseball teams post their starting lineups before the national anthem is played. For the Ryder Cup, the European captain posts his twelve players in the order they will play, and the U.S. captain posts our twelve. No one knows who is playing whom until the lists are turned in to the officials.

The last day of the Ryder Cup matches was cold, damp, and windy. The blustery weather didn't help my aching shoulder one bit, but when the playing orders were announced, I was excited about the opportunity to take on Faldo head-to-head. As usual, I was nervous, so Nick and I didn't talk much. In the match, neither of us played particularly well. The lead shifted back and forth all day long. Nick would win a hole, then I'd win one, or we tied. Toward the end of the day, Nick and I were in fact tied, which would have been fine except that it looked as though the overall score was just as close. So the cup might come down to how I fared here after all. By all indications, I might now be in the one situation we had all hoped to avoid: the pressure spot.

On the thirteenth green I had about a thirty-inch putt, and Nick had about a two-footer with some break in it. Since we were tied anyway, I said, "Good, good?" which is the traditional way of saying, "I'll give you your putt if you will give me mine"—the traditional "gimme."

He answered in his icy English accent, "Yours is a bit longer than mine."

I said, "Come on, man!"

Sounding almost indifferent, Nick spat out, "Aw, pick it up."

On fourteen Nick made a hole in one to go one up on me. When he holed that shot, the crowd noise was thunderous. I merely walked to the next tee and didn't even go up to the green to watch Nick celebrate by kissing his ball.

I birdied the next hole and tied the match again.

When we got to the sixteenth green, Nick had about a five-footer, and my putt was about two feet. Recalling that I had offered "gimmes" on thirteen, Nick posed, "Good, good?"

I answered sardonically, "I don't think so."

"Come on, you've already won!" Nick chided.

"What do you mean?" I had been concentrating so much on my match, I had not noticed how my teammates were doing. So now I turned and asked the referee, "Is that true?"

"Yes, you have retained the cup," the official replied.

I looked back at Nick, and in a tone of voice similar to that which he had used at the thirteenth hole, I snapped, "Pick it up!" I gave him the putt.

As I stepped up to the next tee, I was thrilled that my match was no longer the deciding factor in the outcome of this year's Ryder Cup. Not concentrating, I popped up my drive about 180 yards out and was totally embarrassed by this poor shot. Cup or no cup, I should not have been so careless.

Davis Love III came running up to me, calling out, "Hey, Zinger! Settle down! We haven't won this thing yet—we have only tied!"

"Whaaat? You're kidding me!" I shouted.

I quickly reviewed mentally what the referee had said on the sixteenth green: "Yes, you have retained the cup." In Ryder Cup play, if the teams tie, the team that last held the cup retains it. The U.S. had won the cup in 1991; therefore, the referee had not lied to me. We had assured a tie—but we had not won.

Nick whacked his next drive up the fairway perfectly.

My next shot was a horrible 5-iron that landed short of the creek. Then I hit a 6-iron fat that ended up short of the bunker. I finally recovered my poise, but by then it was too late. Meanwhile, Nick laid his shot in perfect position, on the other side of the creek. Then he hit a sand wedge shot that landed an inch from the hole. He tapped in, making birdie, to go 1-up in the match.

Fortunately, Raymond Floyd, playing in front of me, grabbed a point by besting Jose Olazabal on the eighteenth. We had won, after all, regardless of how I finished.

Even so, I wasn't taking any more chances. At eighteen I buckled down. Both Nick and I hit good drives straight down the fairway. Neither of us flinching, we both hit great approach shots right at the flag. Nick's shot landed about fifteen feet away, and mine was about ten feet out. Then Nick missed his putt.

At that point I was still 1-down, and I was putting to tie our match. I looked over at Nick, expecting the "gimme." Although I don't make a habit of looking for freebies, I thought that since our match no longer had any impact on the outcome of the competition, Nick might give me the putt. That would have been a gracious gesture on Nick's part. We would have earned a half point for each team and walked away feeling good about battling each other to a tie. But Nick declined, and he stood off to the side while I labored over what should have been a meaningless putt. That made me mad.

Nevertheless, I sank the putt, giving me the satisfaction of tying our match.

More important, America retained the Ryder Cup.

● ○ ●

With our triumph at the Belfry, the most intense, competitive part of my '93 golf season came to a close. By no means, however, was I planning to slow down. There were still several exciting, enjoyable, and big-purse tournaments in which to play before the end of the year. As the new PGA Champion, I was looking forward to playing in the Grand Slam of Golf, a tournament featuring the winners of the year's four majors. Then there was Greg Norman's Shark Shoot-Out, to which I was already committed, as well as the Skins Game, another fun event for big money, this year featuring Arnold Palmer, Fred Couples, Payne Stewart, and me.

I also planned to play in the Tour Championship, the final PGA-sponsored event of 1993, which is basically a tournament for the top thirty money winners of the year. There I would have a chance to win "Player of the Year" honors as well as the Arnold Palmer Trophy, which is awarded to the leading money winner of the year. Then, to close out the season I was looking forward to joining the best golfers from around the world at the Johnny Walker World Championship of Golf in Jamaica during the week before Christmas.

All in all, I had a busy schedule in front of me. I was just wishing my shoulder felt better.

CHAPTER SIX

THE SLAM, THE SHOOT-OUT, THE SKINS, AND THE SCAN

T hroughout October and early November, the pain in my shoulder intensified. The shoulder area seemed to be growing hotter to the touch, and the slightest pressure on or near that area sent me reeling in pain. As Dr. Jobe had advised, I continued to take my antibiotics and anti-inflammatories such as Motrin or Advil. Nothing seemed to help.

I was examined by my doctors in Florida, and they did a bone scan of my right shoulder, especially the bone out on the end called the acromion. The bone scan revealed a dark spot on the shoulder, but the doctors assured me it didn't look serious. This was the same area in which Dr. Jobe had performed arthroscopic surgery in 1991, so the doctors in Florida thought that perhaps the shoulder had developed some sort of inflammation that could be treated with anti-inflammatories. They even minimized the possibility of an infection, saying I had a one-tenth of one percent chance of that. The chances of its being anything more serious were far less than that. It was probably tendinitis due to overuse, they said.

Nevertheless, Toni encouraged me to be examined by Dr. Jobe. Although I remembered Dr. Jobe's insistent phone call at the PGA Championship and his urgent plea to have a biopsy done, I kept trying to put it off. "I'll be out in California for several tournaments in November, Toni. I'll check in with Dr. Jobe then."

Toni knew I was procrastinating, but she dutifully scheduled an appointment for me with Dr. Jobe after Thanksgiving, the week following the Skins Game.

My plan was to play in three "made-for-TV" events in California: the Grand Slam of Golf, Greg Norman's Shark Shoot-Out, and the Skins Game. I could stop by to see Dr. Jobe, then get back home as quickly as possible.

It didn't work that way.

● ○ ●

My parents flew out to Palm Springs with me to attend the Grand Slam. It was a great tournament, featuring the winners of the four majors: Bernhard Langer, who had won the Masters; Lee Janzen, the winner of the U.S. Open; Greg Norman, the British Open champion; and me, winner of the PGA. The sponsors probably could have convinced us to play for nothing more than pride, but instead they made it a "can't-lose" situation. With only four players, the winner was to receive $400,000; the loser would walk away with no less than $150,000.

As it turned out, Greg Norman won the big prize, beating me by two strokes. I placed second with a score of 147 for the two days, earning $250,000. Bernhard and Lee were right on my heels, tied at 148 and each earning $175,000.

After the Grand Slam, my parents stayed in California for the Shark Shoot-Out, after which they planned to return to Florida. Toni, seven-year-old Sarah Jean, and four-year-old Josie were to join me at the Skins Game, since the kids had off from school for the Thanksgiving vacation. Our good friends, Payne and Tracey Stewart were flying in from Morocco so Payne could play along with me in the Shoot-Out and the Skins Game. We all planned to spend Thanksgiving together in Palm Springs.

On Thursday I played in Greg Norman's Pro-Am. My shoulder was killing me, and to make matters worse, I was experiencing back problems. The middle of my back felt as though someone had wrapped a belt around me and was pulling it tighter and tighter with every shot. Finally, on the seventh hole I asked Mark Jimenez to "crack" my back, hoping that with a little luck, my caddie-turned-amateur-chiropractor could snap it into place.

"Here, let me show you how to do it," I told Mark. I stepped behind Mark, put my arms around him, and pulled him an inch or two off the ground, as though I were performing the Heimlich maneuver. Mark weighs in at about 210 pounds; I barely tip the scales to 175 pounds soaking wet. As I pulled on Mark, a spasm shot through my back like a spring coming unwound. Instantly I dropped Mark back to the ground. I knew I was in trouble, and so did Mark.

Spasms of pain were ripping through my torso. I could hardly move, and I had no torso rotation whatsoever.

"I'm okay, Mark. Let's just finish this thing."

I struggled through the next two holes, finishing the front nine. At the turn, instead of heading to the tenth tee, I withdrew from the tournament. I could barely swing a club. I was done.

I hoped that with a few days of rest my back would feel better, but the problem persisted. I managed to crawl out of bed with a great deal of difficulty. Once on my feet, however, I could only walk around like a bad Boris Karloff imitation. I called Dr. Wadkins, who works with Dr. Jobe, and arranged to see him on Monday about my back. We arranged to move my appointment with Dr. Jobe to the same day.

On Monday I drove from the Shark Shoot-Out to Centinela Hospital in Los Angeles where both doctors had their offices. The docs immediately ordered an MRI—magnetic resonance image—to isolate my shoulder and get a good look inside me. They also did a bone scan from head to toe, hoping to discover what was causing my back problems. When the doctors looked at the results of the scans, my back problems were the least of their concerns. Their full attention was riveted to the dark spot on the spine of the scapula.

They showed me the X-ray-type photos, and even with my limited medical knowledge, I knew the scan did not look good. The scan revealed all the bones of my body. It was like looking at one of those skeletons some people hang on their doors at Halloween. My bones were outlined in a white translucent glow—except for one bone in my right shoulder area. It was pitch black.

"What does it mean?" I asked Dr. Jobe.

"It means there are no ifs, ands, or buts about it," Dr. Jobe replied calmly but emphatically. "We are doing a biopsy on Tuesday after the Skins Game."

The doctors gave me a copy of the bone scan, and I pointed my rental car back toward Palm Springs, wondering every mile of the way what next Tuesday's biopsy would uncover.

● ○ ●

During the week of Thanksgiving I rested as much as possible, hoping my back would be in shape for the Skins Game. The Skins Game is a special four-player, invitation-only tournament, with each hole worth a fortune. The winner of an early hole—the winner being the one who "skins" his fellow players—can make $20,000. If a hole is tied and there is no winner, the money is carried over to the next hole, which would then be worth $40,000 to the winner. The last few holes are played for $30,000 per hole, all in front of a national television audience. Besides having a good payoff, the Skins Game has come to be regarded as a status symbol in professional golf. The popular perception of the event, though it is not necessarily true, is that only the best players are invited to play.

My back was still out of whack, so each day during the week preceding the Skins Game I received a massage and back treatments. During my massage on Friday, the therapist worked in too closely to the hot spot on my shoulder, and it flared up. Around 4:30 A.M. on the Saturday I was to play, I woke up in excruciating pain. I could hardly roll out of bed. When I tried to get dressed for the tournament, my shoulder hurt so bad I couldn't put my right hand in my hip pocket.

At 6:00 A.M. I called Chuck Gerber, who was running the tournament. "Chuck, I'm in terrible pain," I said. "I don't think I can play." Chuck knew that I had been having trouble with my back for more than a week, and now my shoulder was acting up, too. "What can we do, Chuck?"

"I don't know, Zinger. Let me check. I'll call you back."

When Chuck called back a half-hour later, he left me with few options. The Seniors Tour had been in town that week, and I had been hoping that Chi Chi Rodriguez or one of the other Senior guys might be available to replace me in the tournament. The Skins people didn't want to do that. The best Chuck could do was to delay the start of the tournament by an hour. In my condition, I knew that would not help much.

I took a muscle relaxant and a couple of pain pills. Right before I teed off I gobbled down six or eight Advil tablets. If I'd have won any Skins and the tournament officials had ordered a urinalysis, I would have had to give my money back. But I didn't win any Skins; in fact, I played terribly.

I don't know what I expected of myself. I didn't really have much of a chance. I was in pretty bad shape. Not only did I have the stress of knowing I was playing in a major television event, with a severely strained back and an extremely sore shoulder, but I also knew I was facing a biopsy on Tuesday. Nevertheless, I played the entire two days. What should have been an enjoyable event was more like an endurance contest. By Sunday evening I was hurting badly.

● ○ ●

The Stewarts were traveling on to Australia after the Skins Game, so they had chartered a King Air flight to Los Angeles on Sunday evening. Payne knew I needed to return to L.A., so he invited my family and me to fly back on his plane. I was glad for every mile I didn't have to drive and every minute that would let me crawl into bed sooner, so we accepted Payne's offer.

Toni, Sarah Jean, Josie, and I met Payne, Tracey, and Mike Hicks, Payne's caddie, at the airport. The adults and kids clamored aboard, then waited for me as I carefully eased myself into a seat and tried to sit back for the short, twenty-minute flight from Palm Springs to L.A. Payne and Tracey knew I was going there to have the biopsy, so I pulled out the picture of my MRI.

Trying to sound nonchalant, I quipped, "Hey, check out my bone-scan pictures," and handed the images to Payne.

Payne held the scans up to the window of the small plane, where the California sunset provided enough light to see the outlines of my bones. Payne immediately noticed the dark area on the spine of the scapula. "Well, what's this?" he asked, pointing to it.

I didn't quite know how to respond. For months now, I had been trying to convince myself that all I had was tendinitis. Deep inside, I guess I knew the problem was probably bone-related, but I didn't want to believe that. Besides, my doctors in Florida had said as late as last month that the odds of my having anything serious were minuscule. I was desperately hanging onto their words.

I answered Payne quietly, "I don't really know yet. That's the problem, right there."

By now, Mike Hicks was stretching over my seat and peering at the bone-scan images. "Wow!" he blurted. "You've gotta be kidding! That looks bad!" Mike was deeply concerned.

At the airport we all said our good-byes and wished each other well. Mike carefully touched my arm and said, "Man, I just hope you're all right."

"Thanks, Mike; I'll be fine."

The California sunshine had disappeared over the horizon, and a chilly breeze whipped at us in the darkness as Toni, the kids, and I headed for the terminal to rent a car and drive to our hotel. I was tired and sore, and I couldn't wait to crawl into bed. I wanted to get a good night's rest. Tomorrow we'd be seeing Dr. Jobe.

CHAPTER SEVEN
THREE WORDS THAT CHANGED MY LIFE

On Monday Dr. Jobe performed an exploratory examination, probing the shoulder area. It hurt—it really hurt. I showed him the spot where the pain was most severe, which was red hot to the touch. Gently Dr. Jobe took an ink pen and drew a line right across that spot.

"I'm going to make an incision in this direction right here," he explained as he softly ran his finger over the shoulder. He smiled. "Don't shower that line off tomorrow morning." Then he gave me instructions to help me to prepare for the operation on Tuesday.

Mildred Henderson, a wonderful Christian woman who had been our baby-sitter at the Skins Game, came to Los Angeles from San Diego to stay with Sarah Jean and Josie at the hotel. On Tuesday morning I kissed our daughters, told them I loved them, and said good-bye. It felt strange, leaving our children at a hotel with a sitter while I went off to surgery, but we really had no choice.

Toni and I drove to Centinela Hospital, where I registered and then was taken to a small room to strip for surgery. An orderly escorted me to a waiting room, where I sat for what seemed like hours dressed only in a backless, white hospital gown. I thought the orderly would inject me with a muscle-relaxant drug, but he didn't.

Eventually a nurse brought a wheelchair and took me to the elevator. Toni kissed me, then watched and waved as the elevator doors closed behind the nurse and me.

The preoperative area was a busy place. Doctors, nurses, and other hospital personnel bustled about the room. Numerous patients were lying on gurneys, awaiting surgery. Many of them were already groggy from anesthesia. I was one of the few patients sitting up in a wheelchair, and as far as I could tell, I was the only patient who was completely alert. I wondered if my doctors had forgotten to prescribe an anesthetic.

At last Dr. Jobe arrived and rescued me from the surreal atmosphere of the pre-op room. "Are you ready?" he asked calmly.

I took a deep breath. "I'm ready."

An orderly wheeled me down the corridor, past several operating rooms that were already in use. Someone had just entered one room, and the door was slow to close, so I caught a glimpse inside. I saw a large bag of blood hanging above a gurney surrounded by doctors and nurses. If my stomach wasn't queasy before, it was now.

The orderly took me to a smaller room on the left side of the hallway. He wheeled me inside and helped me get onto an operating table. I was still wide awake. The room was freezing cold in contrast to its bright, pristine appearance, and I was nervous lying on that table. As another orderly began laying out the knives the doctor was going to use, I felt as though I were watching a grade-B horror movie.

Much to my relief, an anesthesiologist finally arrived and injected my left arm. As he pulled out the needle, he said, "You're going to be out of it here in a few minutes."

I thought, *Ha! I'm not going to let this stuff affect me.*

The next thing I knew I was waking up, shivering in a recovery room. I heard voices: "You're in the recovery room, Paul. You're waking up." I recalled immediately where I was, but I couldn't remember anything about the surgery. Had it not been for the intravenous lines running to my arm, I might have tried to get up.

Toni and the kids came in to see me, and Sarah Jean and Josie started crying because their daddy was looking so ratty. I was still weak and groggy, and my hair was matted to my head, but other than that, I was feeling fine.

That evening, Dr. Jobe and several of his assistants came by. Dr. Jobe explained what he had done inside my shoulder. He had scraped all around the outside of the bone. Then he cut out a little window and scraped material from inside the bone itself. It sounded to me as if he had done a lot of scratching inside me.

Dr. Jobe said he had removed about a soda-cap full of material for the biopsy. He was very thorough. He knew exactly where each little piece of bone matter came from.

As he explained all this, Dr. Jobe seemed upbeat. He said he and the other doctors were extremely pleased at the results of the surgery. From what they could tell at this point, it didn't look as though there was any malignancy. Nevertheless, it would be seven to ten days before they knew the results of the biopsy.

I spent two nights in the hospital and was discharged Thursday morning. We returned to our hotel. We were scheduled to fly back to Florida on Saturday, but I told Toni, "Dr. Jobe said it looked pretty good to him, that it didn't look like any kind of tumor or malignancy or anything. You know we're scheduled to fly home and then get the results. I feel pretty good. Let's stay and relax for a few days."

Late Thursday afternoon I received a telephone call at the hotel from Dr. Jobe's secretary. Dr. Jobe wanted to see me in his office at one o'clock Friday afternoon.

"Something's not right," I told Toni. "They said it would be seven to ten days before we heard anything about the test results."

I didn't eat anything the rest of the night, nor did I eat on Friday before we left for Dr. Jobe's office. I sensed something was wrong, and it was turning my insides upside down.

● ○ ●

The sky was blue and the sun was shining as Toni, the kids, and I pulled into the parking lot at the Kerlan-Jobe Sports Medicine Clinic, across the street from Centinela Hospital. Mildred, our baby-sitter had already returned home, so we had to take the children with us to the clinic. The kids were happily chattering away, just as usual, but my mood was somber. I quickly herded the family through the large double doors, passing the pharmacy on the left and the physical therapy center on the right. We rode up two floors to Dr. Jobe's suite of offices and precisely at one o'clock stepped out of the elevator into Dr. Jobe's large waiting area. The room was crowded with patients waiting to see Dr. Jobe or one of his assistants.

I knew Dr. Jobe would be waiting for me, so we passed right on through the waiting area toward a side door. We burst through the door with me leading the way like General Custer leading his troops into battle. Toni and the girls were almost running to keep up with me as we virtually galloped down a thirty-foot-long, narrow corridor to Dr. Jobe's secretaries' workstations.

I greeted the secretaries by name, Carol and Arlene, as I made the right-hand turn past a chest-high partition around their desks and headed down the final hallway toward Dr. Jobe's office. The secretaries seemed not at all surprised to see me hightailing it through their work area. If they knew anything about my condition, they did not let on; they maintained a friendly but very professional manner.

Dr. Jobe must have heard my voice, because I had no sooner rounded the turn than he came out of a corner office.

I blurted out, "How am I?" I didn't say "Hello," or "Hi, Dr. Jobe, how are you?" Not a word of greeting.

Dr. Jobe was equally direct. He shook his head and said, "It's not good," as he pointed the way into his office.

I took a side step directly into the room. Tightly holding onto Sarah Jean and Josie's hands, Toni caught up and followed me.

Dr. Jobe's office could easily pass for a room in a sports hall of fame. The room is relatively small, considering what a noted surgeon he is, and the walls are covered with photos of famous athletes who have been his clients—major league pitchers Orel Hershiser and Ken Dayley, NBA basketball stars, all kinds of athletes from all around the world. My picture was not on the wall.

The doctor waited until the whole family had entered, then he closed the door. He circled around to his desk and sat down in his large leather chair. Toni and I sat down in two chairs facing the doctor's desk; the children took two chairs against the wall right behind us. Toni reached over, and I clasped her hand and held onto it tightly.

Without a word of warning, Dr. Jobe looked me straight in the eye and in an even tone of voice said, "You have cancer."

● ○ ●

Whooom! The room exploded around me. It was as though someone had dropped an atomic bomb into my heart and mind.

Cancer!

I have cancer!

Toni squeezed my hand tighter as we sat in stunned silence.

Dr. Jobe's next words were encouraging. "You're lucky," he said. "It's the most curable kind."

I wasn't feeling lucky at the moment. I was in shock. I had thought that Dr. Jobe would tell me they had discovered some form of weird infection in my shoulder or possibly even a stress fracture. The one thing I never expected to hear him say was *cancer*.

"How do you treat it?" I managed to ask.

"With chemotherapy and radiation," the doctor responded. He didn't try to cheer me up. Nor did he try to make it sound as though I was dying. All he said was that this form of cancer is very treatable.

Toni and I made lots of eye contact, but neither of us could say a word. Dr. Jobe said nothing more. We all sat in absolute silence, just looking at each other, for perhaps fifteen seconds, twenty seconds . . . what seemed like an eternity.

Silence. Deafening silence.

Finally I turned to Dr. Jobe and asked, "Well, what do we do next?"

"We're going to go see if it has spread."

See if it has spread! I hadn't even considered that the cancer might have spread. My thoughts started racing. When Dr. Jobe had operated on my shoulder in 1991, I had a biopsy on the acromion then also, but the pathologists' report had come back negative. Now Dr. Jobe was saying we have to see if the cancer has spread! My first thought was, *The doctors missed it in 1991. They misdiagnosed the problem. For the past two years I have been living on anti-inflammatory medicines. By now, that cancer could be all through my body!*

That's when it really hit me. This is a *big deal.* This is *cancer* we're talking about! People *die* from cancer. *I* might die from cancer!

I was rocking back and forth in my chair, shaking my head up and down, when suddenly something like a blood rush overwhelmed me. I said, "I need to go to the bathroom."

I jumped up, quickly ran out the door, and raced down the same hallway we had come in. I took a left into the bathroom and threw up.

I was scared to death. Bent over in that tiny bathroom, I put my head in my hands and cried. I thought about the cancer that might be riddling my body. I thought about my family—my wonderful wife, Toni, and my children, Sarah Jean, almost eight, and Josie, who was four. I thought about golf, and it occurred to me that I may never be able to play the game again.

Most of all, I thought about God. I knew I was not ready to meet my Maker. I cried out to God to save me. Whether it was to save my life or save my soul, I wasn't really sure. I just knew I needed him, now more than ever.

CHAPTER EIGHT
AN AIR FORCE BRAT WITH A FISHING POLE

Perhaps it goes without saying that few of us encounter the kind of traumatic experiences in childhood that might fully prepare us to confront a life-threatening situation later on. I know I didn't. Yet I could draw on two strong resources as I faced the reality that I had cancer. I was greatly blessed to grow up in a secure family environment, and I had early on developed an intense competitive spirit through sports that equipped me to face even unknown adversaries.

My family had a rocky start. Jean Stratton, one of eight children of Irish immigrants, married Richard Gaudino, an air force pilot. They were living in Europe and had two baby boys—Jeff, twenty-two months, and Joe, three months old—when Richard was killed in an airplane crash during routine training maneuvers. Ten other men died in the crash.

To stay busy and to help keep her mind off the tragedy, Jean began to play golf. She soon discovered that she was fairly good at it. She never took any lessons; the game just came naturally to her.

Jean liked the security of the military lifestyle, so it was not surprising when nearly four years later, in March 1959, she married another air force officer, Ralph Azinger. Ralph was also from immigrant stock, his grandparents having come from Sweden and Germany.

Ralph was a golfer, too. He probably took the game more seriously, but Jean had more fun at it and achieved more success with it. Jean won numerous state and regional tournaments, and when she was seven months pregnant with me, she played an exhibition match with Patty Berg, one of the great women's professional champions. Jean chipped in three times that day. To this day, some people claim I inherited my golfing talent from her through osmosis.

Although she would rather have been golfing, Mom did take enough time away from her game to give birth to me. I didn't make it easy for her.

Mom had endured fifty-four hours of labor when she gave birth to my older brother, Joe, in an English hospital. She was not about to endure anything like that when it came time for me to be born. She and Dad were living near the military base in Chicopee Falls, Massachusetts. She put off going to the hospital as long as possible. Even after her water broke one evening, she did not go into labor. When her contractions had still not begun by the next morning, Dad decided to take her to the hospital anyway. It's a good thing he did.

Despite the doctor's inducing labor at 8:00 A.M., Mom still did not begin to have contractions until nearly 6:00 P.M. At last, on January 6, 1960, at 8:20 P.M.—more than twenty-five hours after Mom's water had broken and over twelve hours after labor had been induced—I finally arrived. They named me Paul William Azinger.

When I was only six weeks old, Mom and Dad thought they might lose me. I started running an extremely high fever, couldn't keep anything in my stomach, and began to become dehydrated. It took three days in the hospital, hooked to an intravenous line, before I finally began to put on weight. Once I started to eat, my appetite became voracious. By the time I was two, I had become a chubby little pudge-ball.

We moved to Homestead Air Force Base in Florida in 1962. My brother, Jed, was born there when I was two. The base had a golf course, so Mom and Dad could walk out their back door, through our neighbors' yard, and be ready to play. By my third birthday, Dad was taking me along with him, riding atop a golf club pull-cart. Mom and Dad played golf together often, and rather than leaving their boys with baby-sitters, they took us along. I never really had any formal golf lessons as I was learning how to play. The closest I came were a few instructions at age eight from the course "pro," Major Bill Eichstedt. Mostly, I simply fell in love with the game by watching Mom and Dad and playing with them.

I was introduced to another of my great loves while we lived at Homestead—fishing. Since we were living near the water, Dad bought a small fishing boat even though he had never done much fishing or boating. Mom, however, enjoyed the challenge of pulling in a big one. Except for golf, she enjoyed nothing more than to pack a picnic lunch, take a tackle box and her boys, and spend the day fishing off the banks of the Intercoastal Waterway.

We moved from Homestead in 1967, taking with us many great memories. Besides the fun times, we had survived two major hurricanes while living there. Sadly, the base that spawned my two greatest sporting loves was obliterated by Hurricane Andrew in 1992.

Dad's new assignment was at McGuire Air Force Base in New Jersey. The Vietnam War was on, and we knew there was a possibility of Dad's having to go to 'Nam at any time. Because of that, perhaps, Dad spent extra time with each of his boys. Jed and I were in the Little League, and Dad was our best coach and biggest fan.

I loved baseball as a boy. By the time I was eight, my pudginess was gone, and I was a lean and agile player. I had an especially strong right arm, so I was a pitcher in the Little League. All three years we lived in New Jersey, the teams I played for won the championship. I threw several no-hitters. Because I threw the ball so hard, many hitters were afraid I might bean them, so they kept their distance from the plate.

After my dad was reassigned again, I played my last year of Little League in Sarasota, Florida. My coach there wanted me to throw a curve ball, but Dad would not allow it. He said I might hurt my arm or my shoulder by throwing curves at such a young age. Dad was right. The coach, however, wasn't worried about my arm; he wanted to win. When I refused to throw a curve ball, he refused to let me pitch. He played me at shortstop, but I wanted to be on the mound, where the action was! I wanted the pressure of being in control of my own destiny. Playing short just wasn't as much fun. Our team won the championship that year, but it was my last year to play organized baseball, although I remain a big fan of the game to this day.

When I wasn't playing baseball, I was playing pool or throwing darts. There was always a pool table in our home. It was a great family focal point, besides being a lot of fun. And I played to win. I hated to lose at anything, so anyone who played me—Mom, Dad, brothers, or friends—knew that I would be going for broke.

We also always had a dartboard. As I got a little older, I spent every day after school throwing darts. I wasn't content to hit the bull's-eye. My goal was to first put a dart in the bull's-eye, then put another dart in the one that was already stuck. On more than a few occasions I was able to do it.

● ○ ●

Even though we expected it, Dad's call to prepare for service in Vietnam threw our family into another unsettling move, this time to the Armed Forces Staff College in Norfolk, Virginia. When Dad reported for duty in Vietnam, it was tough to watch him go. Even at our young ages, my brothers and I knew he was heading into the heat of the war. While Dad was overseas, Mom and we boys lived in Tampa so we could be closer to relatives who were living across the bay in Clearwater.

Mom did her best to maintain a sense of normalcy in our family while Dad was away. That wasn't easy, with daily body counts being reported in the news media. Mom took extra measures to shield us from the worst reports. Once, however, we heard that Dad's air base in Vietnam had been bombed. The chapel had been totally destroyed, and we knew from Dad's letters that his barracks were right next to the chapel. We were scared to death that Dad might have been hit.

Then the telephone rang. It was Dad!

He was calling us from an airplane on which he was the navigator. As an airborne command center, the plane had a short-wave radio on board. After completing a sentence, we always had to say, "Over." If we forgot to end our portion of conversation with "Over," we sat there in silence. It was a strange conversation.

"Dad! How are you? Over."

"I'm fine, son. Don't worry. Over."

"Are you sure you are okay, Dad? Over."

"Give the phone to your mother, son. Over."

My brothers and I didn't realize at the time how close we had come to losing Dad. He was in the barracks when the attack occurred and dived under a bed to avoid falling debris. We had little idea of the day-to-day dangers of the war or the atrocities our father was witnessing. We just had absolute confidence that he would come back to us safely. We had a very joyful reunion when he finally came home from Vietnam.

Dad was reassigned to Mount Holly, New Jersey, near Philadelphia. We weren't thrilled about living in Jersey again after having lived in Florida, but at least we got to see the Phillies play big league baseball. That almost made it worth the move.

In 1971, Dad retired from the air force with the rank of lieutenant colonel. We packed and moved back to Sarasota, where Dad had gained part ownership of a marina business.

It was also about that time that Mom and Dad began to notice my golfing ability. In New Jersey they had belonged to three golf courses, so we played a lot. Mom allowed me to use a set of her clubs, including some MacGregor irons with black club faces. At age ten I started out-driving Mom. A year later, with our move back to Florida, where we could play year-round, I was hitting my drives farther than Dad.

Mom and Dad bought me my own golf clubs—a set of Ben Hogan Producers with the Ben Hogan woods—when I was in eighth or ninth grade. I used those same clubs through the remainder of junior high, throughout high school, and into college. When I first qualified for the professional tour, I was still using those same clubs.

● ○ ●

I never got in any real trouble as a kid. My friends and I weren't bad boys—merely mischievous. For instance, when I was about thirteen, the thing we liked to do most was play out in a cow pasture and harass the cows. Use your imagination! A close second was taking our BB guns into the pasture to shoot down tweetie birds. Every now and then we would see a bobcat or a Florida panther. It was incredibly exciting, and I grew up with a love for the outdoors. Whenever Mom and Dad ever needed to discipline me, all they had to do was confine me to the indoors. I was born to be outside.

By the time I was in my mid-teens I was working part-time at Dad's marina. The marina was on the Intercoastal Waterway that leads to the Gulf of Mexico. The gulf waters we could see just a half-mile to the west were deep enough to have a gorgeous color of green in that area, yet there were shallow flats interspersed throughout the Sarasota Bay, creating a kaleidoscope of shimmering turquoises and greens. It was a fantastic view.

The marina itself had a long, rusty steel and aluminum roof sheltering dozens and dozens of boats that were on dollies or big Styrofoam buoys. We housed several hundred boats, most of them owned by local residents. At any given time we also had a small number of boats for sale out front.

One of the first boats the family owned was a sixteen-foot Boston Whaler. My brothers and I loved that boat. It was next to impossible to sink that tub, so when we got old enough to handle it ourselves, we liked to chase the biggest boats we could find and jump our boat across their wakes. It was an exhilarating feeling to hit the water and fly through the air, barely touching the water before we hit another huge wake rolling off the boat in front of us.

Since Dad was president and part owner of the Gulfwind Marina when I was young, I worked there on weekends, pumping gas at the dock. When I got a little older, my job was scraping smelly barnacles off boat bottoms in the Florida heat. It was only part-time work, but Dad paid me to do it. He was teaching me not only a work ethic, but also the responsibility of managing money.

I always took my job seriously and tried to keep all the customers happy. I prided myself in giving quick, efficient service so the boaters could get their fuel and get back out on the bay. Occasionally something would throw me off track and then I'd have to work like crazy to catch up.

For instance, one weekend, when we had no mechanics on duty, four guys pulled their boat up to the dock and one of them asked if I had a screwdriver. I went back into the service department to find one, but the tool boxes were locked up for the weekend. All our mechanics had their own tools, and they always locked the boxes when they were not around. I looked all over the place and finally managed to find one sitting on a workbench. By the time I got back out to the pumps, boats were lined up all the way down the dock and out of the marina. The traffic was an absolute mess.

The guy who had asked for the screwdriver was standing in his boat, so I handed the tool to him. He pulled a beer out of a cooler and punched a hole in the bottom of the can with the screwdriver. He raised the can to his mouth, popped the lid, and the pressure caused the beer to blast down his throat. I was angry. I couldn't believe he had wasted my time just so he could "shotgun" his beer. It took me more than forty minutes to catch up on my work.

Despite the occasional kook, I enjoyed working the gas pumps at the marina. Everyone had to gas up sooner or later, so I got a chance to meet many of the Sarasota boaters—especially the pretty girls. Two girls stand out in my memory. Their parents were regular customers, and the girls usually showed up at the dock every weekend. One day when they came to buy gas, I was trying to dock their boat while the tide was ripping and the wind was blowing. I reached out and put one foot on the boat and the other one on the dock. Just then, the boat drifted away from the dock, and I did an embarrassing "banana split" right into the water. Why couldn't it be any boat but that one! I never got to date either of those girls. To them, I was a buffoon.

Actually, I didn't date much in high school. Sure, I had the usual teenage crushes, but I never got too serious with any girl for long. I was always too busy with my buddies, golf, or fishing.

● ○ ●

I didn't have much time for church, either. Although we were raised to believe in God, I didn't think much about him while growing up. Whether it was because of the military lifestyle or because of Mom and Dad's upbringing, religion was just not a big part of our lives.

I had my first exposure to church when Dad was preparing to go to Vietnam. Mom and Dad decided to send us boys to Sunday school at the base chapel. They did not ordinarily attend chapel with us, but they made sure Jeff, Joe, Paul, and Jed were up and dressed in our finest every Sunday morning. I hated it. I found Sunday school boring. I wanted to be out playing baseball or fishing or doing just about anything besides listening to a bunch of ancient stories that had no apparent relevance to my life.

By adolescence I was thoroughly schooled in evolution and secular humanism and didn't even know there was an alternative way of looking at things. Once, at a friend's house, I opened up a Bible and started reading the Creation account on the first page of Genesis. I thought, *Whew! No way! Who could ever believe this stuff?*

Another time, I attended a youth function with some kids my age at a church in Sarasota. As the program concluded, some guy started telling me

I was a sinner and that I should ask God for forgiveness. The fellow was right on both counts, but I felt he was going about it all wrong if he hoped to reach me. Nevertheless, I got down on my knees with him at the front of the church and "prayed." Well, actually, not knowing what to pray, I didn't say anything, so the guy prayed for me, and I repeated his words after him.

No doubt, he went home and chalked me up in the group of kids who had gotten "saved" that night. I was a notch in his spiritual six-gun. But the prayer had not meant a thing to me. In fact, I left that night more spiritually jaded rather than closer to God. While I appreciate that young man's good intentions, one important thing I have learned in recent years about a relationship with the Lord is that it has to be real, from the heart, or it doesn't work at all.

● ○ ●

Dad called the shots around our house. He was an extremely opinionated, staunch, conservative Republican. Many people who knew the Azinger family thought we were rich because Dad was president and co-owner of the marina and we lived on a golf course. We were never close to being wealthy, but Dad was always a conscientious, family man who took great care of us. He was also incredibly stubborn.

Right across the road from the marina office, for example, was a restaurant run by a couple named Pat and T.J. One day Dad ordered something to eat, and he waited and waited, but still his order didn't come. He had to go back to work, so he asked Pat to hurry it up. Pat got belligerent with Dad and insulted him.

Dad walked out of that restaurant vowing never to return. And he never did, even though he worked at the marina for eleven years and could have found his way to the restaurant blindfolded.

The same stubbornness was often manifested as amazing willpower. Dad habitually smoked two to three packs of cigarettes a day. When I was born, Dad quit smoking "cold turkey." He said, "I'm never smoking again." He tossed his cigarettes into the garbage and never smoked again. He is a man of his word and cannot relate to anyone who is not.

In more than a few ways, I see my father in me. At the B.C. Open in 1984 (a tournament named after the comic strip *B.C.*), I had a few beers at dinner to celebrate shooting a 67 for the day. The following day, I was still among the top ten on the leader board and fighting to stay in contention. At dinner that night, as I was about to order my usual beverage, I wondered about the impact the alcohol might be having on me. I had no social or religious convictions about the consumption of alcohol, but I thought, *This is a variable I can eliminate from my game.* I decided to quit drinking and have not had a beer since that moment—and I haven't missed it.

If Dad provided a strong, quiet sense of security around our house, Mom provided the day-to-day discipline. My brothers and I loved each other, but we also loved to fight with each other. We still do. Back then, though, we competed in more rowdy ways, like boys. One of Mom's favorite tools of discipline—and most readily accessible—was a rolled-up newspaper. The older we got, however, the less afraid we became of the paper. But not wanting Mom to know that we were no longer intimidated by her whacks, we pretended to cower in fear every time she reached for the paper.

Our ruse was exposed one night when Jed was about ten and I was twelve. We were due for some discipline, and Jed whispered, "As soon as she hits you with the paper the first time, start crying, and she will stop." The only problem was, I was trying so hard to cry that I burst out laughing. Soon Jed was laughing hysterically. Mom realized that she had been taken, and she cracked up in laughter, too. The good news is that this was the last time she ever punished us by whacking us with a newspaper. The bad news is that from then on, her favorite tactic was to pull our hair.

● ○ ●

I continued to play golf throughout my teens. I made the golf team at school, but I didn't take it too seriously. I played golf in junior high and high school mostly for the fun of it. In ninth grade I scored consistently around 39 for nine holes. By the time I was a senior in high school I was averaging around 42. That's what happens when you get a driver's license.

I was never a golf fanatic. My only golf hero during that time was Don January and that was only because my birthday is in January. I really had no aspirations to make it to the pro tour. I enjoyed the game, but I was just having a good time.

I did not get motivated about golf until I realized that if I didn't go to college, I was going to have to get a full-time job. My high school grades were good, but no one was going to offer me an academic scholarship. On the contrary, golf might provide one way to get into college. College golf was sounding better and better.

CHAPTER NINE

BREVARD AND BAY HILL

Anyone who knew me in high school is probably astounded that I now make my living as a professional golfer. Those who might be most surprised are my teammates on the Sarasota High School golf team. I just wasn't much of a player back then.

I started out well, however. At Macintosh Junior High, one my first coaches, Ryan Friemeyer, was a great encouragement to me. He was a strict disciplinarian who emphasized the fundamentals of golf. For instance, one of our drills was chipping over a golf bag to the green. Coach Friemeyer would not allow us to play a round in practice until we had chipped five shots into the hole. Some days, several of us never made it to the course! The drills really helped me, and I played in the high 30s to low 40s through much of junior high.

When I moved up to the varsity team as a sophomore at Sarasota High, I was expecting to be welcomed with open arms as a budding young star. Uh-uh! My high school team was incredible! There were at least seventeen guys who could shoot par any day of the week. Our team was undefeated that year, and I never got to play in a match against another school.

After that, I seemed to lose my enthusiasm for the game. Or perhaps it's more accurate to say I was goofing off too much with my friends to be concerned about golf. I had never been good about practicing, and after my sophomore year I rarely practiced at all. Even so, I made the team as a regular during my junior and senior years. We lost only three matches during those two seasons. We won the district championship my last year and were touted as the team to beat in state competition. Unfortunately, we never got there.

Sarasota High had a class attendance policy that allowed for seven unexcused absences. Eight of them mandated an automatic failure in that class.

The star player on the golf team was taking a snap course called Tennis Assistance Class. Ostensibly he was supposed to be learning how to be a tennis coach or a tennis coach's assistant; actually the class was like a study hall. A lot of us skipped classes occasionally, but the star skipped Tennis Assistance once too often.

Ironically, the teacher was the wife of the golf coach of our biggest rival, Riverview High. Riverview had finished second to us in district competition. We were preparing to go to State and had even played a practice round when we read on the local sports page: SARASOTA HIGH GOLF TEAM DISQUALIFIED; RIVERVIEW GOING TO STATE.

We were devastated!

Apparently someone had reported that the star had failed "Tennis Assisting," which meant we had an ineligible player on our team. That was grounds for disqualification. It was purely a political play that allowed Riverview to go to State that year instead of us. It seemed unfair to punish the team members who had not violated any rules for the sake of one player's misconduct. But as I observed repeatedly in golf in years to come, the rules do not bend.

● ○ ●

When I graduated high school, I realized I was going to have to get a "real job" to replace my weekend work at the marina. It was either that or go to college.

At the time, Floyd Horrigan, the golf coach at Brevard Junior College in Cocoa, Florida, was heavily recruiting one of my friends and teammates, Rick Stallings, one of the top high school golfers in the state. Although Brevard has a reputation as a premier training ground for future professional golfers, Coach Horrigan assumed that he could not get Rick to commit to Brevard unless he got me there as well. Horrigan's assumption was wrong, but it worked to my advantage. Horrigan invited me to come to Brevard even though he could not offer me a scholarship, as he was willing to do for Rick.

I had to think about that one. Scraping barnacles, or playing golf at junior college? It took me about ten seconds to make up my mind to attend Brevard. I was impressed with Horrigan as a coach. He had all sorts of fancy video equipment and other interesting teaching tools. I figured, *What do I have to lose?*

What I nearly lost was my career in golf. Floyd Horrigan did not think I had a chance to make his golf team; he would never have given me a second look had it not been for Rick. By the time Rick and I arrived at Brevard that fall, Horrigan had moved on to another school. He never gave advance notice that he was leaving, which would have enabled the players he recruited to reconsider Brevard. So we were stuck. Over the years I have been asked what

Floyd Horrigan taught me about the game of golf; the main lesson was not to be so naive.

Nevertheless, Horrigan's abrupt departure from Brevard opened the door for me to meet two of the greatest influences on my golfing career, Jim Suttie and John Redman.

Suttie replaced Horrigan as coach at Brevard. Suttie didn't care whether I was the number one guy on the team or number twenty; he was willing to spend time working with me as long as I was willing to work. Many times, long after the other players had gone home, he was still on the practice tees with me, watching and instructing me as I hit balls until dark.

The first time Coach Suttie filmed my golf swing, I was really excited. I thought my form looked terrific. "Looks pretty good, huh, Coach?" I offered hopefully as we viewed the video together.

Suttie was anything but subtle in his answer. "Well, you are across the line, you are way past parallel, you are on your left side at the top, your club face is dead shut, and you have no leg action."

In other words, I was a golf teacher's worst nightmare.

"Oh, really?" I replied, my ego totally deflated. "Where do we start?"

We started by working on my leg action, but we probably could have started anywhere. Suttie revamped my entire swing, not necessarily according to established golf norms, but according to what worked for me. About the only thing he didn't change was my grip. I have always held my clubs with my left hand riding on top of the shaft as I swing, so my knuckles face up toward the sky as I make contact with the ball. In golf terms, the unorthodox way I hold the club is known as an extremely "strong" grip. Suttie must have decided either that my grip was beyond repair, or that since it was working well for me, he shouldn't mess with it.

When I entered college, I was rarely able to score below 80 for eighteen holes on two consecutive days. During my first year at Brevard, I played only a couple of tournaments. I was the number-three man on the "B" team. Under Suttie's tutelage I felt myself starting to improve, and the better I played, the better I wanted to play.

Suttie gave me several drills that improved my game. For instance, he put a golf ball under my left heel while I was addressing the tee ball and made me hit balls that way. The ball under my heel forced me to let my left knee go behind the ball when I started my swing, which helped me turn my hips and gave me more power when I brought my club back down through the swing.

Another exercise was to grip the club, then have someone wrap my wrist to the club with an Ace bandage. It was a great way to make my hands work properly. It forced me to cock my wrists in a cupped position rather than an arched position. In addition, the wrap around my wrists made me raise my arms to the top of my swing in one motion.

One of the simplest but most helpful drills devised by Suttie had me tuck a towel under my right arm while I was swinging so that my right elbow would stay close to my side. That drill alone proved worth the price of my education at Brevard when, a few years later, I began to experience pain in my right shoulder. Because Suttie had taught me to keep my elbow close to my body, my arm never entered the area of "arc pain" that was to become so troublesome. Consequently, I was able to swing a golf club when I could barely put my scorecard in my back pocket.

● ○ ●

Besides believing in Paul Azinger when few people apart from my parents did, one of the best things Jim Suttie did was to introduce me to John Redman. Redman was a golf instructor who operated a driving range not far from Brevard. We were short on practice space at the college, and Suttie knew that Redman had worked with some Brevard teams in the past. So Suttie asked Redman if he could bring the team over to his range. Redman replied, "Sure, bring them on over. They can hit all the balls they want, on one condition."

"What's that?" Suttie asked.

"When they are done hitting balls, they have to pick them up," Redman answered.

One afternoon Jim Suttie took our entire team to Redman's range during John's "slow" time. John watched all of us hit balls, but he took a special interest in me. John later said he liked me because I was friendly and was willing to listen to him tell lies about the good old days.

When I first met John, I was a gangling, six-foot-two, 155-pound, mediocre player with a long, "loose" backswing. I swung with all my might and hit the ball a long way, but not always in the direction in which I was aiming. Redman teases me to this day that one of the reasons he consented to help me was self-defense.

"The range was very large," John explained, "with an airport on one side and a highway on the other, and you were having a hard time keeping the ball on the range. Between the two—the planes landing at the airport and the cars on the road—I was afraid you were going to hit something! I didn't have enough money to raise my insurance coverage, so I figured it was cheaper to help you."

Redman fixed my backswing immediately. John is a "hands-on" instructor, so he grabbed my hips and turned them to where he wanted them; then he grabbed my hands and brought my arms up to where the club should be at the top of the backswing. As he was showing me how he wanted me to swing, he'd say, "I don't want you here. I want you *here!*" Redman had a knack for knowing where my most natural positions were, so when I followed his instructions, I could actually feel the club moving into the correct position.

When John first spied my unusual grip, I expected him to chew me out. But he didn't. He surprised me by saying, "If you ever change that grip, I won't work with you anymore." Redman said that my grip was natural for me. So let it alone.

Doing what comes naturally with a golf club is one of the secrets of John Redman's teaching success. He insisted that I keep my swing simple, with no fancy stuff to remember. The swing John taught me—the swing I still use today—is simply a level turn to the right, as though I were standing waist-high in a barrel. As a result, I am extremely lower-body conscious when I swing a golf club. Just as my club "sets" at the top of my swing, I begin turning my hips to the left. Still level, I turn my hips back toward the target, keeping my hands and arms very relaxed as I bring the club through the hitting area. When my club strikes the ball, the knuckles on my left hand are facing up. This causes me to hold the "attack" angle a little longer than most players.

For me, this is a perfectly natural grip and swing. It is a simple, powerful, accurate, and most important of all, repeatable way to hit a golf ball. It is important to have a swing you can repeat under pressure because when you get nervous, your heart rate changes, your hands sweat, your eyes squint, and all sorts of other things can throw off your form. To play golf well, you must have a swing you can depend on regardless of what other people say about your style. The truth is, the best golf style in the world is the method that works best for you. I can live fairly well with mine, thanks largely to Jim Suttie and John Redman.

● ○ ●

During the summer after my first year at Brevard, I took a job at Bay Hill Golf Course in Orlando, working as a counselor for the Arnold Palmer Golf Academy. Actually, the title "counselor" may be a bit grandiose. Students attending the two-week academy ranged in age from twelve to seventeen. We transported them to and from Orlando International Airport and did bed checks and all—like camp counselors, except that in this case the campers and counselors were staying at the beautiful Bay Hill Hotel next to the golf course.

The academy employed eight pros as golf teachers along with us eight counselors. Besides keeping the students from destroying the hotel, the counselors helped the pros on the course and at the range. We were paid eighty dollars a week and had playing privileges when we were off duty. Far more valuable than my wages were the valuable insights about the game that I gained by watching and listening to the pros as they taught the campers. It was almost like getting paid to go to golf school.

I seized every opportunity I had to play at Bay Hill. I played at least one round of golf every day and hit an average of five hundred balls per day off the range—some of this as part of my counseling duties. I didn't think of it as practice or work; to me, it was fun.

One task for counselors was to drive the range-picker, the machine that picks up all the balls hit off the driving range. The counselor driving the machine sat in a screened-in driver's seat to protect him from errant shots hit off the practice tees. The driver was perfectly safe, but a well-placed golf ball hitting the side of that screen could scare the daylights out of a person. One of my favorite stunts at Bay Hill was to aim my shots off the practice tee at the guy driving the range-picker.

If a driver was quick, he could swerve the machine to avoid the ball, so I started zinging my shots in at a low, hard-to-see angle. I'd hammer him plenty of times. I got really good at hitting the "knock-down" shot. Nowadays when reporters ask me how I developed my famous "Zinger knock-down" game, I just have to smile as I think of the guy in the range-picker trying to dodge my shots.

● ○ ●

After a year of working with Jim Suttie and John Redman, I was a different golfer. When I started college, I wasn't good enough to make the "A" team. But after that summer at Bay Hill, I qualified as Brevard's number one man. Many weekends I would drive home simply because I couldn't wait to show Mom and Dad what I was learning from my coaches. In 1980 I broke 70 for eighteen holes for the very first time.

I continued to improve throughout my sophomore year. Although I wasn't breaking any records, someone at Florida State University noticed me and offered a scholarship of tuition, books, and meals. It wasn't a "full ride," but it was enough to keep me excited about being in school.

Don Veller was the golf coach at FSU, and he must have been at least seventy-five years old. During the summer before I enrolled, I visited the Tallahassee area several times to look for an apartment or some other place to live. Whenever I visited the campus, I stopped to talk with Veller in his office. He assured me that he was delighted to have me coming to Florida State.

But when the first day of school rolled around and I reported to Coach Veller, he barely remembered my name. And I was there on a golf scholarship!

At our first golf meeting, twenty-five players showed up, hoping to make the team. Veller announced that he had four players returning who had gone to NCAA competition the previous year. Those four guys, he said, were automatically on the team. The rest of us were going to have a twelve-round tournament, and the winner would qualify for the final spot on the five-man team.

After eight rounds I had a five-shot lead over the rest of the pack. With four rounds to go, the coach came out to watch me for the first time. When he saw my strong grip, Coach Veller was concerned. Perhaps he didn't think it would hold up under the pressure of a bigtime college tournament. Shortly after that practice round, Coach Veller called a team meeting. He said, "Here's what we are going to do. We are going to take the top ten players, and we will have a three-round qualifier. Everybody starts over."

"Coach!" I protested. "I have a five-shot lead!"

Veller was adamant. "That's what we're doing," he said.

I went out again, my eight-round lead having been rubbed out, and played poorly. With only nine holes to go in the three-round tournament, I was seven shots behind.

The last half of that final qualifying round of golf turned out to be one of those pivotal points in my life that can only be explained by saying, "It was meant to be." The fellow leading the tournament shot a surprisingly high 43 on the last nine holes. At the same time, I shot a 35 to win by one stroke. There was no other qualifier for the five-man team that entire year. Had I not made the team that day, my golf career might have stalled right there.

I believe I was destined to play at Florida State that year. After all, there was a pretty little woman in Tallahassee that Someone up there apparently wanted me to meet.

CHAPTER TEN

TONI

Oooh! You have great veins. I'd like to stick those veins!"

I knew right away that this was not a normal "college pickup" line. Toni Houston, the pretty, perky daughter of a southern judge from Blackshear, Georgia, just north of Waycross, was working her way through Florida State as a phlebotomist. Her part-time job included drawing blood from people in the "plasma center." She was accustomed to looking at people's veins, and apparently she saw something in mine that interested her. We struck up a conversation in the noisy, college hangout that night, and we have been needling each other ever since.

For our first date we went to see the horror movie *The Shining*, based on the Stephen King novel. Toni was holding my hand immediately! From that night on, neither of us dated anyone else.

I knew I was in love. Only true love could get me up at six o'clock in the morning to drive ten miles across Tallahassee, from my apartment to Toni's, just so I could go jogging with her. Then I would ride back home and go back to sleep. It was worth the effort; I just wanted to be with this woman every chance I had. I even consented to go to church with her, just to be near her. Toni attended a Methodist church near the Florida State campus, so I suddenly acquired a fondness for John Wesley's style of worship. For someone who was as spiritually indifferent as I had been most of my life, I spent an extraordinary amount of time with Toni in church.

Within three months from the day we met, we were engaged to be married.

I wanted to ask Toni's dad for her hand in marriage before I "officially" proposed to her, but I was a bit uneasy about it. I didn't have a lot of security to offer the judge's daughter. I had not yet graduated from college, I didn't have a real job, I didn't have much money in a savings account, and I had not qualified for the professional golfer's tour yet. Nor did I have any guarantee that I ever would make the Tour. But Toni believed in me, and that was all the incentive I needed.

On the night I finally worked up enough courage to approach Toni's father, I found him fast asleep in his favorite easy chair in the television den. I had been to Blackshear with Toni often enough to know better than to interrupt a southern gentleman's nap. While he was snoring, I mustered my composure and planned my speech so I would be ready when he awakened.

Finally, in between snoozes I had his attention long enough to say, "Mr. Houston, I love your daughter, and I want to know if I can marry her?"

That woke him up in a hurry!

Judge Houston rubbed his chin thoughtfully, looked me right in the eyes, and replied in his deep Georgian drawl, "Well, are you sure you love her?"

"Yes, sir. I love her."

"And will you take good care of her?"

"Yes, sir. I will take good care of her." I wasn't quite sure how I was going to make a living, but I knew I would take good care of Toni.

"Well, all right, then," Judge Houston answered. He shut his eyes and, like a bear that had been momentarily disturbed from hibernation, went back to sleep.

● ○ ●

Throughout 1981, while Toni and I were engaged, I was busy playing in amateur tournaments as I waited for my opportunity to qualify for the professional golf tour. We had already decided that I had gone as far as I could go in the Florida State University golf program. So Toni continued on in her studies, but I left college to set out for the big time.

The first thing I needed was a "tour card." This is sort of a PGA membership card. It shows that you have earned the right to compete on the PGA Tour for that year. Tour cards cannot be purchased; they must be earned by going to "tour school."

Golfer John Daly once described tour school as the "fifth major." Aptly said. Tour school involves some of the most intense pressure most golfers will ever feel. It is not an academic program or a vocational institute. Actually, there is no schooling associated with the program at all, although it is definitely a time of learning. Basically, tour school is a once-a-year qualifying tournament for golfers hoping to play on the PGA Tour.

Anyone who pays the entry fee can attend tour school, so there is usually quite a variety of competitors in the field. Some are young kids, fresh out of college golf programs. Others are old dreamers who have always wanted a shot at the big time. Some are bona fide local golf pros and instructors who have something to prove to themselves or their students. Many are weekend players—good local golfers who started believing the compliments bestowed on them by their clubhouse buddies: "Hey, Bob, you ought to try out for the Tour. You're as good as Nicklaus, Palmer, or any of those other guys I've seen on TV."

"Graduating" tour school depends on what the cut-off score is for that particular tournament. The top forty tour school players are "in"; they have earned the right to play the PGA Tour.

A tour card did not guarantee a spot in a tournament; it merely allowed you the privilege of trying to qualify for a particular tournament. During my rookie year the PGA Tour still used the "Monday qualifying" system, irreverently referred to as the "rabbit system." Every Monday at a tournament site was qualifying day, when nonexempt golfers could pay an entry fee, play a round of golf, and hope to make the cut and be allowed to compete in the money tournament later in the week. The top sixty players on the money list along with those who had won tournaments during the year were exempt from having to qualify. The nonexempt aspirants were known as "rabbits" because they had to "hop" from tournament to tournament in their efforts to make a cut, nibbling at the leftover spots not scooped up by the exempt players.

Once a golfer survived tour school and earned his card, he had to maintain it each year by winning at least the minimum amount of money required by the Tour. When I first qualified in 1981, the minimum was $23,000.

Despite its pitfalls, the Monday qualifying system had its good points. It was relatively fair. If a player did well and made the cut, he was rewarded by not having to qualify at the next week's tournament. By contrast, if a player missed a cut or decided to pass up a tournament, he had to requalify on the Monday preceding the next tournament he wanted to enter. On the current PGA Tour, the previous year's top 125 money winners are exempt as well as those who have won tournaments in the preceding two years.

● ○ ●

I qualified on my first try, which was in the fall of 1981. I called Toni from Texas, where I was competing, and said, "Toni, I made the tour! I've earned my card. Let's get married!"

Toni and I tied the knot on January 3, 1982. I had been nervous at golf tournaments, but that couldn't compare with the butterflies I felt in my stomach the morning of our wedding. To ease the tension, before we headed for the church I took a 3-iron out into the parking lot of the motel where my family was staying. Dressed in a rented tuxedo, with cuffs that were too short, I ripped a shot off the pavement and over the roof of the motel. It relieved a bit of my stress, but I don't think it did much for the motel owner's.

At the wedding reception, Toni's Uncle Clyde, Uncle Johnny, and Uncle Charles were worried about us already. Uncle Johnny just shook his head and in a deep southern drawl lamented, "Poor Toni! She married a golfer."

Clyde and Charles shook their heads in agreement.

Johnny continued woefully. "Yeah, Clyde. That poor girl ain't never gonna eat good!"

Her uncles were almost correct. We spent our first night as a married couple in Jacksonville, then drove to St. Petersburg to a time-share resort hotel that a friend of our family was allowing us to use as a wedding present. The desk clerk could not find our reservation and would not give us our room. After more than an hour of heated negotiations, the clerk finally realized his mistake and gave us a beautiful room on the seventh floor that overlooked the swimming pool.

In the middle of the night we were awakened by voices below our window. I opened the sliding glass doors, looked down, and saw two guys sitting around the swimming pool. I've always been a bit of a prankster, so honeymoon or not, I couldn't resist.

I went to the sink and poured a few glasses of water.

"Paul, what are you doing?" Toni called groggily from bed.

"Shhhhh! I'm just going to teach some guys to be quiet at night," I answered, carefully carrying the cups of water across the room.

I opened the glass doors just far enough to get my arm through, waited until I heard the voices below, and then let it rip. I tossed the water over the side and splattered the guys below.

"Hey!" they bellowed. "Who's up there? Cut that out!"

I waited until they calmed down, then I doused them again. I scored a direct hit this time. Toni and I were rolling on the floor laughing.

The third time I prepared to attack, I must have gotten careless, because the guys below looked up and saw me just as I tossed the water.

"Hey! We see you up there! You're gonna get it!"

Toni and I were still in hysterics. We dove back into bed and pulled the covers over our heads so the noise of our laughter couldn't be heard.

Suddenly we heard BANG! BANG! BANG! at our door. Toni jumped out of bed and opened the door. Standing there was the same desk clerk who had given us such a hard time when we had checked in. He had that "Oh, no! It's you!" look on his face.

"Er . . . excuse me, ma'am, but a couple of fellows said somebody is throwing water from this room."

Toni pretended to be indignant. "What?" she said. "I don't know what you are talking about. Don't you know? We're on our honeymoon!"

What a woman! It was one of the many times in our marriage that Toni covered for me. She probably saved my career, because if those soaking-wet guys below our window had gotten hold of me, I would probably have ended up with a few broken bones.

Right after the honeymoon, Toni and I reluctantly kissed good-bye. She had to finish her last semester of college, and I had to go on tour. Worse yet, I took most of our money—which wasn't much anyway—with me. Toni had to call her dad to borrow some money to buy groceries. It's a wonder the judge didn't send the posse out looking for his renegade son-in-law! Meanwhile, I had talked a high school friend into going along to caddie for me, and I was off to make my mark as a pro golfer.

CHAPTER ELEVEN
THE CAMPER TOUR

T echnically I turned pro at the end of 1981 when I qualified at tour school. But having a card that says you are a professional golfer and making a living as a pro are two radically different realities. I didn't exactly set the course on fire when I first went out on tour.

During my rookie year of 1982 I earned a grand total of $10,665. I lost my tour card because I didn't stay in the top 125 on the money list. Nevertheless, Toni and I were not discouraged. Looking at it positively, we made over $10,000 our first year out. It had only been two years since I had first shot below 70. I qualified for the Tour the next year. And now, in 1982, here I was on the professional golf tour with the big boys, and I had made ten grand! To us that was incredible progress, not failure.

During my first year on the Tour, Dad had arranged for eight individuals to sponsor me. Each person put up $3,000, providing Toni and me with enough money on which to live while I tried to get established as a golfer. Most of our early supporters were family members or close family friends. I had to approach them for another $1,000 one time after their initial loan. A few years later, when I started earning enough money for Toni and me to survive on our own, I paid back all my benefactors.

Their support during the early stages of my career was critical. It allowed me to play golf and not worry about getting a supplementary job to pay the bills. Early on, Dad had driven into my head, "Don't play golf for the money. Play for the game." Dad assured me that if I concentrated on playing good golf, the money would come eventually. He was right.

I can honestly say that Toni and I have never worried much about money. Like most people, we enjoy what money can do for us, but we have never been in love with it, and we refuse to allow it to alter our attitudes about what is most important in life. Maybe because it wasn't the focus of our goals or the center of our relationship back in the early years of my career, we can now enjoy having money without its "having" us.

That's not to say we didn't have some tight times, especially when I lost my card in 1982. Since I had not earned enough money to maintain my professional status, I had to requalify by attending tour school again. On top of that, I "flunked" tour school that year, missing the cut. This meant I was ineligible to play on the PGA Tour the following year.

● ○ ●

Rather than sitting around and sulking, Toni and I decided we may as well make the best of it. We drove straight south for the Florida Keys. We weren't flat broke, but we weren't far from it. Did I say that money didn't matter much?

On the way I stopped to call Dad, and he mentioned a friend of his who worked as a guide in the Keys. "He would love to take you fishing," Dad suggested.

Upon arriving in the Keys we called Dad's friend, introduced ourselves, and asked if he was available to take us bonefishing.

"Yes, of course! I would love to take you bonefishing!" he answered.

Toni and I had heard a lot of exciting stories about bonefishing, but neither of us had done it. Bonefish are a shallow-water game fish—inedible because of their inordinate number of bones, but strong and fast and fun to catch. They are not, however, easy to catch. An eight-pound bonefish can run 150 yards of line off a fishing reel in a matter of seconds, and they frighten easily. It takes patience. You may sit in a boat for hours and not see one, yet you must be extremely quiet and still. Obviously, bonefishing is only for die-hard fishermen . . . like me!

It is not for newlywed wives . . . like Toni.

We spent eight hours out on the water in relative silence with our guide and never saw a single bonefish. Toni remembers it as the most boring day of her life! Every time she wanted to talk, I hushed her. After all, we might scare the fish. We couldn't *see* any fish—but there might be one nearby!

After we were done "fishing," Dad's friend invited us to his apartment for a soft drink. We sat around talking for a while, and it seemed as though he was waiting for something. Suddenly it struck me: *Maybe he is expecting us to pay him for his guide services.* Toni and I hadn't considered the possibility that he might charge us. We thought the fellow was just being nice to us as a favor to my dad. We had even told him all about losing my tour card, so I was temporarily "unemployed." As the time wore on and the conversation grew thinner, I figured I'd take a chance.

I stood up, indicating to Toni that it was time to go, and said boldly, "What do we owe you?"—hoping against hope that Dad's friend would say something like, "Oh, nothing, son. It's been my pleasure to spend the day with you kids. Any friend of your father. . . ."

He didn't say anything like that.

"One hundred seventy-five dollars," he replied in a businesslike tone.

Toni's and my eyes popped wide open as we looked at each other with expressions of shock and sheer panic on our faces. *One hundred seventy-five dollars. That's almost more money than we have!*

I wrote the man a check. We were barely out the guy's door, when Toni screeched, "That's a rip-off! We're never doing that again. Real good friend of your dad's, huh?"

● ○ ●

What could have been devastating—losing my tour card in 1982—turned out to be one of the greatest times of our lives for us. It was unquestionably a pivotal point in my career.

Since I was ineligible to play on the PGA Tour, I was relegated to playing all of 1983 on the "Mini-tour." The Mini-tour in golf is comparable to the minor leagues of professional baseball. It comprises struggling, young wannabees and slightly over-the-hill has-beens. You won't find the big money players on the Mini-tour, but you will find players with some of the most intense passion for the game and the biggest hearts in professional golf.

When I first joined the Mini-tour, I didn't know enough about the sport to realize that many of the players there are excellent golfers. Because I had been on the PGA Tour for a year, I naively thought I would be the "big kid on the block" on the Mini-tour. I didn't realize that I would be competing against many guys with much more Tour experience than mine. Other soon-to-be-great players were there, too; they just hadn't made it to the big show yet.

People say that golf is a mental game, and they are right. Because I thought I could do well on the Mini-tour, I was less intimidated than I had been on the PGA Tour. Consequently I played extremely well. The golf courses were not significantly different; the quality of play was not markedly different. The change was within me. The key was how I felt about myself. When I naively didn't know any better and believed I was going to clean up, my confidence soared and my scores came way down. Because I *thought* I was better, I played better.

In my first tournament on the Mini-tour I shot rounds of 67 and 68, finished second, and earned $4,000, which was more money than I had earned in any event on the PGA Tour. I thought, *I'm going to make a fortune playing on this tour!*

Playing on the Mini-tour was fun, but also chaotic. Toni and I were constantly on the road, and despite the fact that I was now earning some money, we were still paying more for travel, food, and lodging than I was making. We had no car or house of our own. We had been married for more than a year and still did not have a place to call home. All we owned were our clothes, a set of golf clubs, and Cleo, a Persian cat we acquired in Binghamton, New York, at the B.C. Open during the '82 season.

Recognizing that we needed more than mere transportation, late in 1982 my parents used their Cadillac as a down payment on a Vogue motor home for us. We loved that little camper. It had only 14,000 miles on it; more important, it was a self-contained home on wheels. The Vogue had a stove, refrigerator, shower, pull-out bed, and enough storage space to stow my clubs and fishing gear, with a little bit of room left over for clothing. What more could any couple want?

It took a while, though, to get used to driving the motor home. Soon after we got it, I pulled into the parking lot at the New England Classic. The registration trailer was on the top tier of the parking lot, so special electric lines had been strung from there down the hill to the clubhouse.

I had always wondered why the department of transportation puts those clearance signs on overpasses. I soon found out.

Without even considering how high our motor home was, I drove right under the temporary electric lines and on past the registration trailer. As I did, I heard a noise, something like *Eeerrreee . . . snap!* I stopped the motor home and jumped out just in time to see the wires swinging back and forth as if someone were using them as a giant jump rope. The entire luggage rack atop the motor home was bent straight up in the air.

I had wanted to create some sparks on the tour, but not like this.

● ○ ●

Toni and I lived in the camper for three years—some of the most carefree years of our lives. We would roll down the interstate highways, traveling from tournament to tournament, often not even taking time to stop to switch drivers. When it was Toni's turn to drive, I'd simply hit the "cruise" button and jump out of the driver's seat while holding onto the wheel as Toni scooted under my arm into the driver's seat. We got to the point where we could switch drivers in about two seconds. At night we would park in the golf course parking lot and sleep right in the camper.

At times we would park on the side of a bridge spanning one of Florida's many waterways, or even under an old bridge or overpass. Back then, we felt safe to do something like that because I always carried a gun in the motor home. On one occasion that gun caused more trouble than it was worth.

Between tournaments, Toni and I were en route to one of our favorite vacations spots, Islamorada, in the Florida Keys. Toni's thirteen-year-old sister, Becky, was traveling with us. One night, instead of staying in the motor home we decided to "upgrade" a little and stay in a fine motel. We didn't have much money, but we found a place that looked as if it might fit our budget. It was called the "Malibou Motel," located just off the main road, right across from "Robbie's Bait Shop and Boat Rental." The sign out front read, BEAUTIFUL SALTWATER POOL.

The rates were cheap, so we checked in, then went out back to look at the pool. The tide was out, and the "beautiful saltwater pool" was nothing more than a ditch with about two feet of scummy water lying in it. Algae was floating on the water, and a huge crab was clinging to the wall. It looked like a cesspool. Something told us we were in for a long night.

Because the air was hot and humid, we opened the windows to our non-air-conditioned room before going to bed. About midnight we heard something that sounded like thunder outside our windows. There we saw more than a dozen members of a motorcycle gang revving their engines and riding up and down in front of the motel. Others were unpacking their bikes and looking as though they were going to be staying the night. They were a rough and scruffy-looking bunch. Even the women in the gang had tattoos covering their arms, legs, and faces.

Becky was scared. Never known for talking quietly, I said loudly, "Don't worry, Becky! I have a gun. If anyone messes with us, I'll get my gun and shoot them!"

The walls of the motel were thin anyhow, but with the open windows, the sound of my voice pierced the darkness like a foghorn. One of the women outside heard me and yelled, "Watch out! Somebody in that room said they were going to shoot us!"

Instantly the cyclists turned the place into the shoot-out at the Not-So-OK Corral. Gang members huffed and puffed, "Ugh! Ain't nobody gonna shoot me!" as they stomped around, looking for a fight.

Nearly frightened to death, Toni, Becky, and I put on some street clothes and wondered what we should do next. With all the bravery I could manage in my frail, 155-pound frame, I knew I was no match for that bunch of raunchy bikers. I weighed our options carefully, then made a recommendation to my fellow travelers:

"Run!"

All three of us bolted for the camper, leaving our clothes and suitcases in the motel room. We flew into the motor home, and I had it rolling past the cycles and out of the parking lot before Toni and Becky could even sit down. We careened around the corner, utensils in the camper flying everywhere, and onto the main road. I drove as fast as I could, watching in my rearview mirror for motorcycle lights. None followed us, but we played it safe. We spent the night in the camper parked in a church parking lot.

The next day I returned to the motel and complained about all the noise. I told the woman behind the registration desk, "We were just minding our own business last night when this motorcycle gang tried to harass us. I want my fifteen bucks back!" She gave me half of it and allowed us to get our clothes out of the room. Under the circumstances I thought that was a pretty good deal.

● ○ ●

We didn't put nearly as many miles on the camper in 1983 as we did later on, because many of my Mini-tour events took place in central Florida, near Orlando. That turned out to be a big advantage of playing the Mini-tour—it gave me another chance to work with John Redman.

I had not seen much of John during my years at Florida State or my first year on the Tour, but I felt that John could help me move my game to the next level. I had improved greatly while I was on the Tour, picking up pointers wherever I could from other pros, but I was concerned about one thing: my grip.

When I started working with John again in '83, I said, "John, I'll have to change my grip. Everybody on the Tour tells me that if I ever want to really make it, I should change it. One famous pro even told me that I'll never be any good until I do change my grip."

John was unimpressed. He simply said, "If you ever change your grip, don't ever come to see me for help again." He reminded me that the grip I use is natural for me, no matter what anyone else says. I decided John was right. I stopped being self-conscious about my grip and haven't changed it to this day.

I spent hours at John's driving range in 1983. Anytime I was not playing on the Mini-tour, I pulled our motor home into John's place and hit balls until dark. John's help, coupled with the experience I had gathered on the Tour and the competitive confidence I was developing on the Mini-tour, was transforming me into a contender.

● ○ ●

I met another person that year who had a profound influence on my life without even knowing it. Like me, Marc Arnette was an up-and-coming player on the Mini-tour. We were paired together in my first Mini-tour event at Errol Estates, and we hit it off right away. I liked the way Marc played the game, but more than that, I liked him. He was positive about life and, more significantly, seemed to possess a peace of mind that I knew I did not have. That intrigued me. Here was a fellow who played the game with passion and intensity, yet seemed to have a deeper purpose in life than merely winning golf tournaments.

Marc's wife, Patti, and Toni became good friends as well. We visited them often in their home in Jacksonville. Marc and Patti, we soon discovered, were sincere Christians. They believed the Bible from cover to cover, and there was no doubt in their minds that God is who he said he is. They seemed to have a strong, vital faith that permeated every part of their lives.

Although Toni and I had attended church early in our dating days, we really didn't have much of a clue about Christianity. I had never even read the Bible, let alone believed it. Toni had more of an understanding than I did because she had gone to church as a little girl. But neither of us had established a real relationship with the Lord.

With Marc and Patti, we saw Christianity not merely in a book, but in their lives. They never preached at us or tried to ram the Bible down our throats. They never pressured us about committing our lives to Christ or even going to church with them. They simply lived in a way that made us hungry for what they had. Marc stopped touring after a few years to become a teaching pro, and I have not seen much of him since, but I will be eternally grateful for the influence he and Patti had on Toni and me during that time in our lives.

● ○ ●

I was the leading money winner on the Mini-tour in 1983, earning $53,000. I probably could have continued playing the Mini-tour and made a comfortable living, but by the end of the year I was ready to get back out on the course with the big guys. I went back to tour school for the third time, and this time I qualified.

When I returned to the PGA Tour, it was with renewed confidence. But it didn't take me long to become intimidated once again. Feelings of inferiority haunted me, and the fear of failure in the big time was constant. I just didn't like the pressure of constantly having to put myself in a position to fail in front of huge crowds of people. Before long, my scores started to climb again.

Despite my sluggish golf game, Toni and I were having a good time going from one tournament to another in the camper. We would pack up after a round of golf, travel to the next course, and park at the nearest campground, preferably one with a good fishing lake. I would roll out the camper's awning, pull out my fishing gear, and try to catch a few fish for dinner while Toni fired up the hibachi, in the faith that I would bring home our supper. At some tournaments we stayed in the golf course parking lot, and occasionally I would fish the course lakes for some bass. After a while we realized that eating those fish might not be the most healthful idea, given the amount of chemicals used on courses nowadays. I didn't mind driving a few extra miles to a campground to avoid contaminated golf-course fish.

In the summer of '84, the motor home started giving us trouble. We had driven the vehicle all over the country, so it shouldn't have surprised us when our home on wheels began demanding some attention. The camper finally got to the point where it could no longer reach the highway speed limit. When I tried to exceed 45 miles per hour, the engine started expressing some strange golf terms: "Ka-two-putt . . . two-putt . . . putt."

Returning from Blackshear to Sarasota—a five-to-six-hour drive under normal conditions—the camper began coughing, spitting, and sputtering every time I got it past 45.

Not far from Gainesville, I was going uphill on an overpass and I could barely nudge the motor home past 38 miles per hour. A line of traffic was following me. I finally reached the crest of the overpass, working the pedal like a champ, and then started picking up speed on our downhill roll. We made it up to a breezy 45, then to 50. It felt great! I had been topping out at 48 for the past three hours, and now we were edging up toward 55. Come on, baby! Just a little farther to go. We made it—55 m.p.h. And then I saw the red lights flashing in our mirror.

I wasn't about to take a ticket without an argument. At first I tried tact, explaining to the officer that our vehicle was mechanically unable to exceed the speed limit. He just looked at me as if to say, "Sure, bud! You and everybody else," as he kept writing.

"Jump in and I'll give you a ride!" I offered to prove my point to the trooper. In retrospect, I realize that may not have been the wisest thing to say to the policeman.

"You were speeding, son," he said as he wrote up the costliest ticket I ever got.

● ○ ●

Later in '84 I missed the cut at Doral by one stroke after playing poorly on the last few holes. I was angry with myself, so I just threw my clubs and shoes into the camper and said to Toni, "You drive. I'm going to lie down."

I was fast asleep on the couch when I suddenly heard a loud, screeching noise that sounded like a giant running his fingernails across a huge chalkboard. The camper jolted to a stop, sending Cleo the cat screaming through the air just past my nose. I jumped to my feet and looked out the window. Toni was hysterical in the driver's seat.

Toni had driven the motor home into an overhang while attempting to get through a toll booth that was meant for smaller vehicles. Now the camper was wedged between the walls. When we backed out of the toll booth, the whole awning tore off the camper. I looked at Toni.

She shrugged her shoulders. "It looked like it would fit!"

I lost my playing privileges again in 1984, earning only $27,000 and ending the season 144th on the PGA money list. Since I had not finished in the top 125,on the money list, it was back to tour school again. This time I did it right. I was the medalist at the 1984 Qualifying Tournament, winning myself an exemption from having to qualify on the PGA Tour throughout 1985. That was the last time I would ever have to go through tour school.

Much of my success then and yet today can be attributed to a guy who didn't know how to hold a golf club.

CHAPTER TWELVE

How "Crazy Mac" Changed My Game

T oni's mother died when Toni was only five years old. An older couple, long-time friends of the family, took a special interest in Toni. Mac and Juanita McKee were almost like another set of grandparents for Toni. She often spent after-school hours at their home.

Mac was a rugged, rough-and-tumble, gruff sort of guy. For most of his life he made a living by training boxers. Mac had learned his craft well. He used to travel with a carnival, and at every county fair where they performed, he would take on all comers who wanted to test their mettle in the ring. People called him "Crazy Mac."

Juanita was just the opposite—soft-spoken and sensible. She offered a good balance to Mac and probably kept him out of trouble.

When I first met Mac, I didn't like him at all. Toni had told me about her special friends before my first trip to Blackshear. So while I wasn't quite sure what to expect, whatever it was, Mac wasn't it. Mac was a big man, with silver-gray hair, a silver beard and mustache, who looked a lot like Santa Claus, except that Mac was in incredible physical condition. He had maintained a disciplined, regimented exercise routine throughout his life, and although he was now aged sixty-five and semiretired, he worked in a lumberyard.

I was impressed with Mac's physical stature, but I wasn't prepared for his brusque attitude. When Toni told him I was a professional golfer, Mac huffed, "Hmmph! Golfers aren't athletes. That Ben Hogan was so uncoordinated, he couldn't catch a ball."

I didn't say much at the time, but when Toni and I were alone later that evening, I told her, "Well, he doesn't know me very well. I can sure catch a ball!" I have always had good hand-eye coordination, and I was insulted that this old guy could not appreciate the skill involved in hitting a golf ball well.

93

●○●

Whenever Toni and I went back to Blackshear during the first few years of our marriage, I avoided visiting Mac and Juanita if possible. But gradually, as I got to know and understand him better, I began almost to like Mac. Then before long, I found myself actually liking him. Beneath Mac's harsh exterior beat a soft heart.

One day in the summer of 1984, as we were talking about how I made my living, Mac said, "I don't know anything about golf, but I know I can make you the best golfer that you can possibly be."

Mac had my attention. "Oh, yeah? How are you going to do that?" I challenged him.

"By teaching you to concentrate," he replied.

"I do concentrate, Mac. Otherwise I would never be able to hit a ball."

"No, I mean really concentrate. I don't know how good you can be because I don't know much about your game, but I know I can help you be the best you can be." Mac explained that he had done a lot of study on why the Germans were so good in sports and why the Japanese were so strong in gymnastics and that sort of thing. It all came down to concentration, Mac believed.

I was struggling with my game at the time, just missing the cuts at tournament after tournament, so I agreed to let Mac teach me to concentrate. I was a skeptical student, but by the time I returned to tour school, Mac's instruction was paying off in a big way.

What Mac taught me was simple yet so profound. First, he taught me Lamaze-type deep-breathing exercises. When I get nervous or excited, he said, I should inhale for four counts, very slowly, then exhale for four counts, slowly blowing the air out my mouth. Mac calculated that I would have a tough time concentrating if my emotions were sending my heart rate too high. Golf is not like football, where an extra boost of adrenaline can actually help a player. In golf, the calmer you can remain, the better your chances of hitting a good shot.

Second, Mac emphasized that I must picture each shot in my mind before I hit the ball. I learned not only to picture swinging the club, but to see myself hitting the ball exactly where I wanted it to go. Instead of my concentrating on what I didn't want to happen—hitting the ball into a hazard—Mac taught me to picture myself hitting a perfect shot.

Great performers in every field have made use of this "secret" for years. Athletes, astronauts, public speakers, airplane pilots, and a variety of other professionals have long recognized the value of mental rehearsal. Recent research at Stanford University has substantiated that the subconscious mind cannot tell the difference between a real experience and a mental experience, one that is vividly imagined. Subconscious experiences may be more influential in controlling our performance than conscious experiences.

The key, of course, is to picture yourself doing things correctly. That is how I was able to combine all the work I had done with Jim Suttie at Brevard and John Redman on his driving range with the concentration techniques Mac taught me. Rather than simply stepping up to the ball and swinging, I have disciplined myself to take a few deep breaths and try to see in my mind the trajectory over which I want the ball to go. Do I always concentrate the way I should? Obviously not. You can see the difference on my scorecard.

Third, Mac helped me to realize that concentration is a learned behavior. It doesn't happen automatically. Therefore it is helpful to establish some easily repeatable routines you can depend on under pressure. You may have noticed that most pros have a routine that they go through before almost every shot. If you watch me carefully, you will find that once I get ready to hit, the amount of time I take and the things I do before my actual address, swing, and follow-through vary only by a few seconds from shot to shot. That is not an accident. That is learned behavior, and it helps me to concentrate.

● ○ ●

Mac wouldn't think of accepting money for helping me, which was fortunate, because at that point Toni and I didn't have much extra cash. But Mac did allow me to give him a new bicycle. He was an avid cyclist, so I bought him a beautiful Richard Sax racer. Even at his age he would ride twenty-five to thirty-five miles a day.

Although he wouldn't know a sand wedge from a driver, Mac McKee changed the way I play golf. Working with Mac was a major stepping-stone in my career. When I won at tour school in '84, I never looked back. But that's not to say that I didn't still have a lot to learn.

CHAPTER THIRTEEN
UNDER PRESSURE

Winning the tour school in 1984 did more than give me an exemption from having to four-spot qualify for tournaments during 1985. It also brought me an invitation to some key tournaments, namely, Arnold Palmer's Bay Hill Classic and the MCI Heritage Classic on Hilton Head Island.

At Bay Hill I led a PGA Tour event for the first time. It was also my first experience dealing with the press. I was leading at the end of the second round, but in the next day's press I was given virtually no chance to win the tournament. The reports made me more angry and less nervous than I might have been otherwise during the third round.

The press was partially right. I did not win, but I tied for fifth place and earned $18,000. Not bad money for someone given no chance.

The next time I was in the pressure cooker was at Hilton Head. Working on my concentration with Mac in late '84 had dramatically improved my game. But at Hilton Head I allowed the circumstances to overwhelm me and dictate how I played.

For instance, I was not used to teeing off so late. On the PGA Tour, because of television coverage, tournament leaders tee off around midday. I was accustomed to starting earlier in the day. I liked that, because I have always been an early riser.

On the third day at Hilton Head, however, I was to play with Bernhard Langer and Bobby Watkins, and our tee time was scheduled for close to noon. I got up early and by nine o'clock was going stir-crazy. I was not used to sitting around and waiting. By the time I teed off, I was like a puppy that had been cooped up too long. On the course my concentration, not to mention my game, just came undone. I finished eleventh, winning a nice check—$10,000—which, when added to my Bay Hill earnings, was a huge improvement over the previous season.

● ○ ●

I knew exactly what had gone wrong. The best explanation for my unhinging at Hilton Head was that I was not prepared to deal with the pressure of playing well enough to win. Ironically, after fighting and clawing my way to get there, once I was perched atop a PGA leader board I wasn't sure I wanted to have to deal with that sort of pressure and the fear of failure before the public week after week. It was after blowing the lead at Hilton Head that I told Toni, "If I have to be this nervous to make a living, I might quit and do something else."

A few weeks later, my brief but game-changing conversation with Bert Yancey took place. When I asked the famed pro about being nervous, Bert replied in his inimitable style, "Son, you want to be so nervous you can't even spit." From that day on, I changed my goal. Rather than attempting to avoid pressure spots, I purposely plotted to get myself into a position to be nervous. I wanted to thrive on the tension that came with the territory near the top of the leader board. I made up my mind: I was not content merely to play in the middle of the pack; I wanted to contend for a championship.

As a result of my successful perforamnces at Bay Hill and Hilton Head, I was invited to play in the Memorial Tournament. At the Memorial I shot a 67 on the last day, passing fifty-three other players to finish twelfth and earning another $12,600. That was enough to put me into the top 125 players on the money list and guarantee my exemption from qualifying for 1986. It was a great feeling. I was on a roll!

● ○ ●

Through the latter part of 1984 I had become difficult to live with, and Toni was starting to let me know it. We were still madly in love with each other, but lately I had fallen into the habit of harping on every little thing Toni did. Nothing she said or did seemed to be good enough for me; it was never quite right. Little did I realize that my headstrong ideas were pushing her toward a precipice. No one else knew it, either.

Young and in love, carefree, living the life of golf nomads, traveling the country in our motor home—we seemed to have it all together. After all, we were having fun. But inside the camper there was a tenseness that had never existed before in our relationship. Worse yet, we didn't know what to do about it or where to turn for help. It was a very trying time for both of us.

For my part, I was experiencing occasional drastic mood swings, and this emotional upheaval led me to take things out on Toni. Often I spoke harshly or made especially sarcastic comments. I wasn't trying to hurt Toni; I was just lashing out at life, and she loved me enough to listen. Still, my words stung, and after a while she naturally recoiled from them. Before long, we were at each other over silly, trivial issues that threatened to destroy us.

One night Toni couldn't take it anymore. She stormed out of the motor home, slamming the door behind her. For a while I sat there fuming, then slowly, almost imperceptibly, I began to feel guilty. I knew our relationship wasn't where it should be, and I blamed myself. Toni's unconditional love was the best thing that had ever happened to me, yet I was on the verge of driving her away. I didn't want to lose Toni, but I didn't know how to deal with the pressures we were facing.

I sensed that somehow or other, the answers to our problems were spiritually based, but I had an extremely shallow spiritual reservoir from which to draw. I had never really prayed with any confidence that God was there or that he cared about me. Now, in desperation I called out to him. I knew I needed help, and I wanted to change. Yet I also recognized my inability to change myself—not the real me, anyway, the Paul Azinger on the inside whom nobody else knew.

As I prayed with all sincerity that night, probably for the first time in my life, I sensed that God heard my prayer. No lightning bolts lit up the sky; nor were there any Cecil B. DeMille-type special effects that signified his presence. But he was there with me in the motor home.

When Toni came home—she had only gone as far as the grocery store—I apologized to her. I told her that I wanted to change and that I had asked God to help me. Toni's spiritual well didn't go much deeper than mine, but she agreed that God was the answer we were looking for. As uninformed as children we began reading the Bible and praying together and occasionally going to church when I wasn't playing on Sunday. Slowly but surely our faith grew. And our relationship with each other improved immensely.

We still faced many of the same problems. The pressures were still the same. A relationship with God did not improve my putting. But in a real way we now had a Resource, someone to whom we could turn for inner strength, for forgiveness of our sins, for power to face whatever situations life held for us.

I was aware that a number of the guys on the Tour met regularly for Bible studies, conducted by Larry Moody's organization, Search Ministries. As with the Baseball Chapel in the major leagues, the Tour Bible studies are not affiliated with any particular church, and they are open to any players and their families who want to attend. I decided to go to the Bible studies whenever I could fit them into my schedule.

● ○ ●

As 1985 progressed, my game picked up. I was playing better and better. In fact, Lee Trevino was in the television broadcasting booth that year, and he made comments such as, "This is the guy. This is the next great superstar in the making. Keep an eye on this kid." Lee and I had played together a few times, and he liked my action. I think he saw a little bit of himself in my stance and swing.

● ○ ●

For Toni and me, our hearts were knit much closer by our newfound faith and our love for each other was growing deeper. Consequently, Toni and I were not surprised to discover in late March that she was pregnant. That was good news and bad news. We were ecstatic about having a child, but we were still living in a camper. When we were not on the road, we stayed at Toni's parents' home or my parents' home. But with a child on the way, I had to start thinking about putting down some roots.

The only drawback to Toni's being pregnant was that we had to get rid of our beautiful, red-orange Persian cat, Cleo. Cleo had been a part of our lives since we were first married, but Toni's doctor was adamant that cat litter and pregnant women should not be in close proximity. Because we were both so attached to Cleo, it became my responsibility to do away with her.

"Hmm, hmm, good! I am really amazed that cats taste so much like chicken!" I told my friends who I knew were animal rights activists. They looked at me in horror, not quite sure whether to take me seriously or not. Actually we gave Cleo away to some good friends.

Around the sixth month of the pregnancy, I received what Toni and I considered to be an incredible offer. Gary Geiger, a club pro in Bradenton, contacted us about a new golf community that was being developed just outside of town. He invited me to play the new golf course. He showed us pictures and drawings of beautiful homes and villas being built all around the course. The complex, complete with gates and security guards, was known as River Wilderness. Gary introduced me to the property developer, who asked if I would be willing to wear a visor with the River Wilderness logo every time I played in a Tour event for the next five years, in exchange for a villa worth approximately $150,000.

We could hardly believe it! With not much money in the bank, nowhere to live but a motor home, and Toni's being six months pregnant, I responded, "Where do I sign?"

I didn't have an agent in those days, and this deal seemed too good to be true. Furthermore, I was so naive about professional golf, I didn't realize that top players often got paid huge sums of money, frequently in annual amounts reaching the high six figures, in exchange for wearing and displaying logos of certain products or places they played.

Nevertheless, I wore the River Wilderness visor for nearly six years. As such, I provided the developer a "billboard" for national exposure for only about $25,000 per year. Toni and I will be forever grateful for our first home that wasn't on wheels, but my lack of business prowess in regard to this endorsement was merely a preview of things to come.

But who knew, then, what was going to happen in my career within the next eighteen months?

CHAPTER FOURTEEN
AZINGERS DIDN'T USED TO HAVE LITTLE GIRLS

From the time I first considered turning professional, I thought that winning a golf tournament would be the ultimate high I could experience. I was wrong. Winning the largest purse on earth could not compare with the sheer exhilaration and joy I experienced at the birth of my children. During the last few weeks of Toni's first pregnancy, however, I was beginning to have my doubts.

I was scheduled to play in a tournament in the Bahamas the first week in January, right around the time the baby was due to arrive. The tournament guaranteed a sizable amount of money, even for last place, so with the new baby coming, I felt it would be silly to pass up the chance to play. After all, what did I know about birthing babies? That was Toni's area.

Besides, we had taken the Lamaze classes. The deep breathing exercises they wanted Toni to do were similar to what Mac had taught me, so I figured, *We've got this baby delivery thing down pat.* We felt fairly confident right up to the end of the classes, when they showed a film of an actual birth. When I saw that movie, I came unglued. Even Toni said, "I don't think I can do this!"

"Too late to think about that now, Tone."

● ○ ●

Toni had received most of her prenatal care from her doctor in Waycross, a short distance from her parents' home. Because her due date was approaching, we went to Blackshear right before Christmas.

The weather was dismal, gray, and cold with a temperature of about twenty-five degrees outside, but Toni's body was burning up. At night, she insisted on opening every window in the bedroom, and she was still too warm. We were accustomed to sleeping close together—our camper bed didn't allow for any other options—but every time I tried to snuggle next to Toni during those last few days before she delivered, she howled, "Get your leg off me; it's making me sweat! Get those covers off me! It's too hot in here!" Meanwhile, I was freezing.

Early on December 27 I drove over to the golf course at Okefenokee Country Club. I was a nervous wreck as I sat in the pro shop, my face covered with acne from the stress of worrying about being in the delivery room with Toni. I knew Toni could handle everything well; I wasn't sure about me. I had heard horror stories about big, tough guys who had fainted and keeled over at the first sight of blood during the delivery. I could envision the orderlies picking me up off the floor as my wife was giving birth.

Just then, the phone rang in the pro shop. It was Toni. It was time. I mean, it was TIME!

I jumped into the car and bolted to the house. When I got there, Toni had already begun her labor. Immediately I turned into "super-dad" as I did my best to time Toni's contractions.

"Those were ten minutes apart ... eight minutes ... twelve minutes ... six minutes ... fourteen minutes." I couldn't discern any pattern to her contractions. Around four o'clock in the afternoon we called the doctor, and he instructed us to come in to the hospital. We spent several hours there, and finally the doctor sent us back home. Toni wasn't quite ready yet, he said.

"Easy for him to say," Toni sniffed.

Back home it was more of the same. We collapsed on the bed, and I tried to time Toni's contractions, comfort her, and encourage her, just as our Lamaze instructor had taught us.

"Eight minutes, Toni. Remember to breathe...."

"Shut up!" my ordinarily soft-spoken, sweet, demure wife bellowed.

All the windows were open in the bedroom, so I was freezing. Toni was sweating, writhing in back labor, and shouting, "Aaarrrrrgghh!" I pulled the covers over me and tried to get some sleep.

By one o'clock in the morning I had slipped into a sound sleep. Suddenly I felt as though I had been hit by a speeding baseball right in the center of my back. Toni had belted me with her palm with all her might.

"Are you going to do anything to help me, or what?" she shrieked.

I bounded to my feet, called the hospital, and shouted into the phone, "I'm bringing her down, no matter what!"

● ○ ●

Toni suffered through twenty-eight hours of painful labor before the doctor finally decided he needed to take the baby by a Caesarian section. I felt so sorry for Toni. Because the operating room was too small, I was not allowed to accompany her.

"Sheew!" I wiped perspiration from my forehead, feeling as though I had dodged a bullet. I wasn't going to complain about not being present in that operating room.

Once in the waiting room, however, as jittery as I may have been, I started wishing I could be with Toni. I had to wait downstairs while my wife entered the shadow of death in order to bring forth a new life.

At last a nurse brought a newborn baby into the nursery and placed the child under the heat lamps. I peered through the windows, my nose pressed to the glass. "Is that an Azinger baby?" I asked the nurse.

"Yes, it is."

"That's a little boy, isn't it?"

"No, it's a little girl."

"A little girl?" Azingers didn't have little girls.

The nurse gave me a sterile gown to put on and invited me to come into the nursery. "Daddy, do you want to hold your little girl?"

"Can I?"

Our tiny baby girl was screaming at the top of her lungs as the nurse helped me hold her for the very first time. Throughout the pregnancy I had talked to the baby in the womb. Often I had placed my hand on Toni's stomach and had spoken in my best baby-talk voice, "Hey! You'd better recognize my voice when you come out of there."

Now the bright lights were shining on her beautiful little face, her eyes were shut, and our little girl was screaming so loudly she could barely catch her breath. I looked down at her and said, "Hey, do you recognize my voice?"

Instantly our daughter stopped crying. Her little eyes opened slightly . . . and I started crying. I loved that baby right there; an immediate bond was forged between us at that moment. No trophy, no amount of fame or fortune, could possibly rival the tremendous love that overwhelmed me as I looked into the face of our baby. We named her Sarah Jean—Sarah, which means "princess" in Hebrew, and Jean, after my mom.

● ○ ●

I spent the night in Toni's hospital room. Every few hours a nurse would come in, flip on the fluorescent lights, hand Sarah Jean to Toni for a feeding, and get Toni up to walk. I was on the couch, trying to sleep, without much success.

The next morning I told Toni, "I'm going home! I'm going to bed. I never slept a wink all night!"

Just call me Mr. Compassionate.

A few days later, with mother and baby still in the hospital, I kissed Toni good-bye and took off for the Bahamas to play in the golf tournament. Toni hasn't let me forget that to this day!

I closed out the '85 season finishing ninety-third on the money list. I earned more than $80,000, which is not an astronomical amount in golfing circles. But compared with my first few years, Toni and I thought it was a fortune.

Besides, what more could we ask for? We had a newfound faith in God, a renewed love in our marriage, and a new baby, and in a few weeks we would move into our brand-new home. The only thing missing was a tournament trophy.

And that was about to change.

CHAPTER FIFTEEN
RISING WITH THE PHOENIX

In 1986 I earned more than three times the amount I had won the previous year, and people on the Tour started taking me seriously. Although I still had not won a PGA Tour event, I played some great golf in '86, finishing twenty-ninth on the money list and leading the Tour in "sand saves." The top thirty players on the PGA Tour are automatically exempt for all four majors, so I was really looking forward to playing the 1987 season.

During the off-season near the end of 1986, however, I began to notice a strange sensation in my right shoulder. I had played many games of tennis and Ping-Pong with my friends and family over the holidays, so I thought I may have stretched for a shot and pulled my shoulder out of place. Or maybe I had just overdone it.

Besides that, I went fishing nearly every day during the off-season. I used a bait-casting rod with a "pistol grip" on it, which is much different from casting with a spinning rod. It placed a constant strain on my arm and shoulder, especially since I did a lot of sidearm casting and overhand casting. Perhaps I had pulled a muscle, I thought.

I also did extensive dove hunting and shotgun shooting during that time. I thought that the constant recoiling of the shotgun kicking against my shoulder may have bruised the area somehow. Whatever the cause, right before the start of the 1987 season the pain was so bad that I couldn't raise my arm.

I saw a doctor, and he diagnosed me as having tendinitis. He prescribed some stretching and strengthening exercises and suggested that I take some Motrin to ease the discomfort while the shoulder was healing.

● ○ ●

The Bob Hope Classic was to be my first tournament of the year, but I had to withdraw. The pain in my shoulder was too severe for me to play.

The following week I entered the Phoenix Open, which was played on a tough Tournament Players Club (TPC) course in Scottsdale. I played the entire Phoenix Open with intense shoulder pain.

I hit the ball extremely well coming down the final stretch at Phoenix, when the pressure was on. Toward the end it appeared that the battle would be between Hal Sutton and me. I was playing with Corey Pavin and Doug Tewell on that last day. Corey had just won the Bob Hope Classic the week before, so he was really hot; but at Phoenix he began to fade toward the end and fell out of contention for the top spot. Doug wasn't having that great a day, either.

I hit a super shot on the fifteenth hole and just missed an eagle putt, settling for a birdie. We went to sixteen, which is a tricky little par 3 with the pin on the left side of the green and a huge pothole bunker guarding the pin. I hit a beautiful 8-iron right at the flag, but it came up a yard short and rolled down into the pothole.

Oh, no! I thought. *There's no way to get it up and down out of that.*

As I walked off the tee, heading toward the bunker, Doug Tewell said to me three times, "Just get it up and down. Just get it up and down. Just get it up and down."

That was all he said, but Doug was right. Instead of worrying about the ball and where I hit in that bunker, Doug immediately put my focus on all that mattered at the moment—getting it up out of the bunker and down near the pin. All of my work with Mac—learning to concentrate and focus on where I wanted the ball to go rather than where I did not want to hit it—was on the line.

My ball was touching Corey Pavin's ball, which had also found the bunker. Corey marked his ball so I could I hit from the lie that I had. I went into the bunker and focused on what I had to do. I swung confidently and blasted it out about fifteen feet, a great shot!

Corey was able to rake the bunker and place his ball, and he still couldn't get it inside mine—that's how well my bunker shot came out. I made the putt for par.

I parred the seventeenth hole as well. On eighteen Hal Sutton had to putt through his shadow, which is always difficult to do, but especially when putting for the lead on the last hole of a tournament. Hal missed the putt for par. I now had a one-shot lead. I hit an excellent drive off the last tee. It could easily have been an iron hole, but there was water to my left, and I didn't want to take any chances. For my second shot I hit a 7-iron and smoked it right at the pin. It was a rather risky shot when I think about it now, but at the time I was confident and could almost taste my first victory. Again I focused on where I wanted the ball to go, not where I was afraid it might end up. The ball landed on the green, leaving me a relatively easy two-putt.

I had finally done it! I had won my first PGA Tour tournament!

● ○ ●

An incredible feeling of satisfaction swept over me. Not only had I been competing against the course and the other players, but I had also been battling myself all week long—trying to defeat the anxiety that comes with playing to win. It's something every player has to conquer when trying to win a tournament. The question keeps coming back: Are you going to let yourself do it?

When you know that you have a shot at winning, the mental pressure is relentless. You think about it constantly through the day. You're nervous in the morning before you get started. Until you hit your first drive, the feeling doesn't go away. Once you get off the tee, you can relax for a while and do what you do best, but if you are in contention, the pressure builds as the day progresses. You are putting yourself in a position to make a mistake in front of the world, willingly putting yourself in a compromising situation in which you can fail in front of everybody.

And when I have failed, people have always felt me approachable enough to comment about it. "Hey, Zinger! What happened during that third round? Did you choke, or what? Better luck next time!"

"Thanks, I think."

● ○ ●

After that win at the Phoenix Open, I saw another doctor to get a second opinion on my shoulder. This doctor put me on a regimented program of weight training to rebuild my shoulder muscles. For a while the program seemed to be working. As I faithfully followed the prescribed regimen, the discomfort would go away for a few weeks. If I slacked off on my exercises, the pain always returned.

Despite the pain, I was playing really well throughout 1987. I was growing more confident with each tournament, feeling as though I really did belong on the Tour now. I had no more worries about losing my card or having to find some other way to make a living for at least two years. I was a PGA tournament winner.

Over the next several months I came close to winning on a few occasions, but I couldn't put it all together again until midway through the season at the Panasonic Las Vegas Invitational, which was played on three separate courses.

The last round was played at Las Vegas Country Club, which was lined with houses on both sides of each fairway. That meant both sides of the fairways were out of bounds. Low, knee-high stone walls with wrought-iron fences along the top protected the homes from errant shots. I decided that I would purposely hit every drive as low as I could because the desert fairways were so fast and those walls were so low. I told Billy Poore, my caddie at that time, "If my ball goes out of bounds today, it will be because it took a bad hop!" I was determined not to hit anything high enough to fly over those walls.

One day of the tournament was rained out, so the event was shortened from five days to four. I got off to a mediocre start, hitting the ball well but being unable to make anything exciting happen during the first two rounds. In the next-to-last round, with thirty-three holes to play, I was twelve shots behind. Then suddenly my game caught fire. I holed a 5-iron from a fairway bunker on number eight for an eagle. I birdied holes nine and ten and shot a 67 for the day. In the clubhouse afterward, I told my mom, who had made the trip along with Toni and me, that I thought I would probably be eight shots behind by the time everyone else finished later that day.

Meanwhile, the leader, Kenny Perry, stumbled. The wind kicked up that afternoon and caused Kenny to miss shots he might otherwise have made. Later that evening, when I walked outside our hotel, adjacent to the course, I looked up at the leader board. I was shocked to see that I was only two shots behind!

On Sunday, before the final round, I had a weird sense that I was going to putt well that day. While hitting putts with David Frost on the putting green prior to my tee time, I told David, "Man, I am making everything today!"

I played unbelievably well all day. I made a bunch of birdies, and by the time we got to the eighteenth hole, I was 6-under for the day and tied for the lead with Curtis Strange and Hal Sutton.

At the eighteenth tee I wanted to hit a low fade around a fairway bunker. The hole was 550 yards, par 5, with the green reachable in two if you hit a good drive. The second shot was over water. I was using an old wooden driver, and instead of the low fade I wanted, I hit a push hook, off the toe of the club. The ball went straight up and out, and I thought, *That is out of bounds, to the right.*

Just then the ball started hooking back. It carried the bunker. As it finally came down, it hit a small slope on the rock-hard fairway and then simply took off. When my tee shot stopped rolling, I had only 167 yards to go to the pin. In the desert atmosphere, that meant I was looking at an 8-iron shot. But not just any 8-iron shot—it was over water, and I was shooting for the lead in a tournament that offered a first-place prize of $225,000, the largest purse in the history of the Tour at that time.

I could feel the pressure enveloping me. As I took my practice swing on the eighteenth fairway, my arms were so hot, my fingertips throbbed in rhythm with my racing heartbeat. I took several deep breaths, went through my usual preshot routine, and put a beautiful 8-iron straight at the pin and about twenty-five feet short of it.

Curtis hit his second shot into the bunker and didn't get it up and down. He would be unable to make birdie.

From twenty-five feet away, I was putting for eagle. I hit my putt firmly, and it raced across the dry green and slammed into the back of the hole for an eagle. I could hardly believe it. I jumped up and down in unrestrained glee.

Hal was playing behind me, and he hit a great shot about fifteen feet from the pin. Knowing I had just eagled the hole, he felt extra pressure as he lined up his putt. The best he could do was tie and force us into a playoff. Hal stroked his putt well. It rolled right on line—and then lipped out.

I had come from twelve shots behind to win my second tournament of the year.

And what a great win it was! By winning this single tournament, I took home almost as much money as I had made in all of 1986.

● ○ ●

The Phoenix Open will always be special to me because it was my first tournament win; Vegas was great because I won there on that long putt for a huge purse. But by far, my most meaningful win of the '87 season came at the Greater Hartford Open in Connecticut.

My mom and dad were originally from Manchester, not far from Hartford, and of course, I was born in Holyoke, a little ways north across the Massachusetts state line. When I committed to play in the Canon-Sammy Davis Jr. Greater Hartford Open, it was like signing up to attend the Azinger family reunion. Although Dad could not attend, Mom did, as did every friend and family member within driving distance.

I hit the ball well throughout the tournament. On the last day I was paired with Bernhard Langer, a tremendous competitor and a sincere Christian. Bernhard was playing superbly all week, until the third hole on the last day. From the fairway he blasted a shot that sailed far over the green, landed, and bounced about thirty feet into the air.

I said to Billy Poore, "Man, I didn't know there was a cart path back there."

"Neither did I," Billy answered in amazement.

When we got up to the green, we noticed a crowd of people around a woman who was sitting in a chair beyond the green, directly behind the pin.

A lump was rising on the woman's head that cast a shadow about three inches long across her face. Langer's long ball had hit her squarely in the forehead! Bernhard was deeply upset and concerned for the woman. He wasn't the same the rest of the day; his concentration was completely shot.

Late in the day I had a one-shot lead over Dan Forsman. On eighteen I hit a good tee shot. For my second shot I hit an 8-iron onto the left fringe about twenty feet from the hole.

Ken Venturi, in the broadcasting booth, was saying, "He's just going to tap this putt down there. I'll be surprised if this gets past the hole." Thanks for the vote of confidence, Ken, but we both know it isn't that easy.

The greens were fast, and I underestimated the speed my ball would have coming off the fringe. I hit it too hard. As soon as I hit it, I rose up onto the balls of my feet, and my left knee literally shook as I watched the Titleist logo turn over and over . . . and over and over. The ball went on the low side of the hole and then skidded past by at least eight feet. I left myself with a right-to-left break coming back.

I studied that putt from every conceivable angle. I didn't want to three-putt myself into a playoff. I thought, *If ever you were going to make one, make this one!* I stroked it perfectly and won my third tournament of the year.

● ○ ●

The crowd, filled with Azinger relatives and hometown friends, went wild. I was so excited, I threw my arms high into the air as I backpedaled off the green. Just then, my caddie, Billy Poore, met me on the green, my arms still raised above my head. I thought Billy was going to slap me a "high five," but he was so pumped up, he grabbed my right hand with his. As he did, our fingers interlocked, and Billy held on, pressing my arm back past my head. A familiar pain seared through the back of my shoulder.

Two days later, the tendinitis came back so severely, I could not lift my arm. I was scheduled to play the following week at the Canadian Open with a living legend, Jack Nicklaus. It was the first time I had been paired with the Golden Bear, and I wasn't going to miss that for anything, no matter how much my shoulder hurt.

I went to the tournament and took two tablets of Motrin before I teed off. I played well in spite of the shoulder pain. I didn't win, but it didn't matter. Just to be able to play side-by-side with Jack was a thrill. Besides, the British Open was coming up soon. Now *that* was a tournament I wanted to win.

CHAPTER SIXTEEN
DISASTER ON THE SCOTTISH COAST

I almost didn't go to the 1987 British Open. As it turned out, it was one of those tournaments I would love to have had a chance to replay at a later date.

The week before the tournament, I was laid up with the flu, so I reluctantly resigned myself to not playing in the British Open. But at the last minute I decided I couldn't pass it up. After all, I had won three tournaments this year; I was considered one of the top American players on the '87 PGA Tour. I recalled a statement Bert Yancey had made to me earlier in the year: "Son, you can win all the Phoenix Opens you want, but you can't make history unless you win a major. And if you don't play the British Open, you have cut yourself out of 25 percent of the major championships."

I had never competed in the British Open, so I didn't really know what to expect. This year the tournament was being played at Muirfield, Scotland, one of the world's most picturesque courses, rich in golf tradition. Toni and I booked a flight on the Concorde, turning what would otherwise be an all-day trip into a three-hour evening jaunt. The next morning we awakened to a beautiful, sun-drenched day—a rarity, our greeters told us, for British Open weather. Toni and I immediately fell in love with the Scottish atmosphere, including the kilt-clad bagpipers whose music serenaded our arrival at the golf course. Except for my coughing, wheezing, and still trying to get rid of the remnants of the flu, our first day at Muirfield was like a fairy tale. Everything about the course is a golfer's delight.

The golf course lies close to Scotland's southeastern seashore. The Scottish coastline is infamous for its crags, crooks, and crannies, which have proven disastrous for many naive or foolish fishermen and seafarers, both in legend and in real life. The golf course at Muirfield harbors a similar reputation. Many a golfer has been devastated by Muirfield in merely attempting to negotiate it, much less conquer it.

True to form, by the time we teed off for the first round the skies over Muirfield had turned dark, dank, and dreary. Gray clouds came sweeping in from the sea, hovering over the course as if on guard duty and periodically pelting the players with a cold, blowing rain—perfect weather for recovering from the flu.

Despite the climate, I hit the ball fantastically well. I shot a 68 the first round, which was good enough to share second place on the leader board with Nick Price and some fellow I had never heard of: Nick Faldo. Faldo had won at Hilton Head a few years previously and had finished in the top ten at four of the past five British Opens. But since I had not really followed professional golf closely before becoming involved in it, I did not know Nick's record, nor was I aware that he was being touted as England's next great golfing hope.

After my first round, I was ecstatic. I told the media, "I had a great first round and I feel great. This is my best first round ever in a major. I can't wait to see what tomorrow brings!"

Rodger Davis laid sole claim to first place on the first-round leader board by posting an incredible 64. Rodger self-destructed during the second round, however, shooting nine strokes above that. Both days' play was hampered by storms and squalls. Nick Price dropped three strokes the second day, and Nick Faldo dropped one. In the meantime, I shot another 68, grabbing the lead in a major for the first time in my life.

Rather than allowing the pressure to get to me, I decided to turn the tables. I told the press, "This is great! I have never been in contention in a major before. I am really looking forward to seeing how nervous I am going to be!"

I was paired with Faldo on Saturday, and Nick never said a word to me all day long. It was just as well. I probably would not have been able to hear him anyway. The weather was horrible! The wind and rain were howling so badly, the third round could have been postponed and nobody would have questioned the decision. Residents of the British Isles, however, are a hearty stock who take blustery storms in stride; the tournament went on. But the weather took its toll. Twelve players shot scores of 80 or above that day, including Jack Nicklaus, who was playing in his twenty-sixth British Open, and the U.S. Open champion, Scott Simpson.

When, at the end of three rounds, I was 6-under-par and still ahead of Faldo by one stroke, I told the media, "I'm really looking forward to seeing how I am going to respond tomorrow." I was purposely challenging my own nerves.

● ○ ●

At the start of the fog-shrouded final day, the contenders nipping at my one-shot lead were Nick Faldo and David Frost at 5-under and Payne Stewart, Tom Watson, and Craig Stadler at 4-under. Ordinarily I would have been extremely nervous, but for some reason I wasn't. Reminiscent of my Bay Hill days, before the round I was knocking 1-iron, 2-iron, and 3-iron shots off the range-picker. I was having a great time warming up. I felt really loose.

My body must have been running on sheer adrenaline. I was still trying to kick the flu I had brought with me. I had that queasy feeling, similar to a stomach virus, all week long, and for once it was due to something besides nerves.

Beyond that, I was having trouble eating; nothing really tasted that good all week. I lost close to ten pounds in the two weeks ending with the British Open. I attributed my fatigue to stress and the flu. Little did I know that, for other physiological reasons, I was literally running out of energy.

The weather conditions remained severe for most of Sunday: damp and cold with unpredictable wind gusts. With nine holes to go, I had stretched my lead to three shots. But then I bogeyed holes ten and eleven, three-putting both. Faldo was making par on every hole, so my miscues gave him the chance he was hoping for. I still led by a stroke, however, as we came down to the last two holes.

The seventeenth at Muirfield is par 5, with bunkers on the left side of the fairway. Because of the distance and the wind, I pulled out my driver. I know now that I should have hit an iron off the tee, but at the time the driver seemed to be the right choice. I conferred with my caddie, but as always, the choice of club was mine.

I had an excellent caddie for the British Open, but I missed my regular caddie, Billy Poore, who did not make the trip to Scotland. Billy had worked with me long enough that he felt free to offer his opinion if he thought I was about to try something unwise. Had Billy been at Muirfield, he may have encouraged me to hit an iron. But he was thousands of miles away across the Atlantic, and I decided to go with the driver.

As soon as my club contacted the ball, I groaned aloud, "If that's enough club to reach those bunkers, then that's the wrong club." I was right about that much, anyway. My shot faced dead into the wind and landed in one of the fairway bunkers. I hit a sand wedge out sideways back to the fairway, and I made a bogey.

I hit another bad second shot on eighteen, my 5-iron finding the left green-side bunker. When I saw the way the ball was lying in the bunker, my spirits sank. There was hardly enough room to take a decent stance. I did the best I could to blast it out of there with my sand wedge, but the shot fell way short. I two-putted for another bogey, virtually handing the victory to Nick Faldo, who had parred every hole during the final round.

● ○ ●

I was devastated. I quickly walked off the green toward the trailer to sign my scorecard. Once behind the trailer's closed doors, as hard as I tried, I could not hold back a trickle of tears. I signed the card and attempted to dry my eyes and pull myself together before going out to face the inevitable interviews. When I walked out the door, Al Trautwig of ABC Sports was right there to ask me some questions. I answered his queries, but for the life of me I do not remember what I said. I was in a daze.

The worst, however, was yet to come. Rodger Davis and I had tied for second place, so according to tradition, we both had to join Nick Faldo on the eighteenth green for the trophy presentation. It was humiliating. Rodger and I stood there with blank expressions on our faces while Faldo planted a big smooch on the trophy and waved to his fans. The crowd ate it up. They were going wild for Faldo, and he in turn was savoring every moment of his first British Open victory celebration.

Nick finally made his way over to me, extended his hand, and said simply, "Sorry about that." That was all he said. I couldn't believe it! I had led the entire week, and I confess that it hurt a little that he wasn't more consoling.

After the trophy presentation, it was off to the press tent for more interviews. Reporters jockeyed for position around me and called out the expected questions: "What happened? How do you feel? Will this affect your game?" I did my best to respond, but it was difficult under the circumstances. Trying to put the best face on defeat, I told one group of reporters, "Don't anybody feel sorry for me." They didn't have to; I was feeling bad enough for all of us! Then I went on, "I've proven I can play with anybody, anywhere, and I'll be a better player for this."

What else could I say? I was a twenty-seven-year-old guy who had just blown a shot to win his first major. I had been telling the press all week long that I wanted to know how it felt to be in contention in a major. Now I knew.

When I finished fielding questions, John Redman, Toni, and I walked back toward the clubhouse. To get to our car we had to pass in front of an immense bay window overlooking the eighteenth green. My head was hanging down, and my eyes were on the ground. As we passed the window, the Muirfield members who had huddled inside to escape the foul weather stood to their feet and gave me a standing ovation. I was so overwhelmed with disappointment, I didn't even notice my well-wishers. Redman nudged me and pointed to the left. I raised my head long enough to acknowledge the crowd and tipped my visor toward them.

We were staying at the Marine Hotel at Muirfield, and the ride from the golf course to the hotel was one of the longest of my life. As we got into the car, John said to me, "I'm really proud of you, bud." John, Toni, and I sat in silence for most of the trip. There was nothing to say.

The next evening, Toni and I flew back to the States. At one point Toni got up to move around, and Larry Mize came and sat down next to me for a few minutes. Larry had won the Masters in 1987. He knew what it meant to come close in a major. Larry is also a committed Christian, with a quiet but consistent walk with the Lord. Larry simply put his arm around my shoulder and tried to console me. He probably never gave his gesture a second thought. It was just Larry being Larry. But I really appreciated Larry's thoughtfulness.

● ○ ●

Toni and I went straight from Muirfield to the Buick Open in Michigan. I didn't get much sleep due to the time change, plus my every thought was consumed with mental replays of the British Open. Upon arriving in Michigan, I didn't even want to go to the golf course to play a practice round. I didn't want to see all the players who had not been at Muirfield but who had watched my demise on television. I didn't want to have to hear everyone say, "Nice try." Frankly, I didn't want to see anyone.

I forced myself to go to the putting green before the opening round. As I was trying to regain my composure, I heard a familiar voice say, "Hey." I looked up from my ball and saw a veteran player calling from across the putting green.

"Nice playing."

"Thanks," I said appreciatively. I didn't have to ask him what he was talking about.

"That's really too bad."

"Well, I learned a lot, I guess...."

"Yeah, you may never get that chance again."

Whap! Why didn't he just hit me in the stomach with a baseball bat? I didn't know how to respond to his comment, so I said nothing.

Perhaps realizing the insensitivity of his remark, the old pro shrugged his shoulders and said prophetically, "Eh, you might."

● ○ ●

I missed the cut at the Buick, so Toni and I just packed up and went home. That week, still smarting from my defeat at Muirfield, I did the interview that sparked the ruckus between Greg Norman and me. Poor Greg. He hadn't even been in contention at the British Open, finishing at 7-over, but I was in no mood to talk about the foreign players as "better ball strikers."

For months, everywhere I went, people asked me if I had choked at the British Open. I didn't choke. Nor did I lose the tournament because of nerves. John Redman is convinced that I lost the Open because I "lost my legs" during that last round. Maybe so, but to my mind, the answer is more basic: I lost the British Open due to poor course management. I chose the wrong clubs, and I hit some poor shots. That's it. Nothing more profound than that.

Nevertheless, for the next several years, in nearly every article written about me or broadcast in which my name was mentioned, I was constantly referred to as "Paul Azinger, who finished bogey-bogey at the 1987 British Open."

Over the years since then, I've had at least a hundred people come up to me and tell me they were on that tee at Muirfield. They say sincerely, "I was standing there on seventeen, and I was thinking, 'I hope he doesn't hit a driver here.'" Actually, the gallery on the tee that day comprised perhaps as many as thirty-five rain-drenched people. I guess it's only natural for people to want to imagine themselves a part of history, even if they are not.

● ○ ●

Back out on Tour, I felt rather angry the rest of the year because of the way I had finished the British Open. It definitely affected my attitude. Moreover, I had an opportunity to win "PGA Player of the Year" honors, and the loss at Muirfield worked against me. The Player of the Year is chosen on a point system. For example, thirty points are awarded for winning a major, ten for a regular Tour event, and zero for finishing second. Twenty points were given to the top money winner and also to the player with the best scoring average. The honor was based strictly on achievement; it was not a popularity contest among players or fans.

Eventually, however, I realized that this was not a once-in-a-lifetime occasion. If I stayed healthy, I could have many opportunities to make my mark in golf history. By changing my attitude, I was able to relax a little bit the last week.

In the final regular tournament of the year, the Nabisco Championship in San Antonio, Texas, I played poorly the first day and shot 73. After that I changed putters and shot 67, 67, and 66. As John Redman is fond of saying, "A change is as good as a rest."

Going into that final tournament of 1987, Curtis Strange and I were contending for both the money title and Player of the Year. Curtis finished dead last in San Antonio, and I finished third, so I did become the PGA Player of the Year. It was a great feeling; it didn't take the sting out of the British Open, but it brought a great boost to my morale. In less than five years I had gone from qualifying at tour school to the top player on the PGA Tour.

The only negative about winning the Player of the Year title was that I had to give a speech in front of six hundred people at a gala banquet and award ceremony. I was shaking all over as I got up to speak in front of all those people. About that time I was wishing I had taken that speech course in college.

● ○ ●

Curtis won the 1987 money title. That year the top thirty players on a points list were invited to the Nabisco Championship. Unlike the Player of the Year, which had a clearly defined point system and player goals, the point system for the Nabisco invitations was confusing and, in the eyes of many, unfair. One player, John Cook, finished twenty-fifth on the money list but did not qualify for the Nabisco because he didn't have enough points.

Actually, I would have won the money title in '87 had there not been a points list. I won more "official" money—money earned in PGA tournaments—than anyone else in golf that year, more than $800,000. But because some tournaments were allocated more points than others, Curtis was the top point-getter, which included a bonus award of $175,000 of official money. (At third on the points list, I received $68,000.) That bonus was enough to garner for Curtis the Arnold Palmer Trophy as the top money winner of the year.

Ironically, I had suggested abolishing the point system for the Nabisco tournament, at the first players' meeting I ever attended. Rick Fehr and I argued that the points list shouldn't be official money. It was just bonus money at the end of the year. Our suggestion to change that part of the system was soundly defeated.

The PGA Tour eliminated the point system shortly thereafter. But should I complain? It took Arnold Palmer thirteen years to earn a million dollars on the Tour. I almost equaled that amount in twelve months. But some things are more important than money and trophies, and I was about to be reminded of that.

CHAPTER SEVENTEEN
IS ZINGER A FLUKE?

I couldn't believe it when I saw the title to the article in a major golf publication, but there it was in bold letters: IS PAUL AZINGER A FLUKE?

Back in 1985 and 1986, numerous members of the media had picked up on Lee Trevino's comments that I was an up-and-coming player to watch. In 1987 I had validated Lee's predictions by winning three tournaments and achieving the honor of PGA Player of the Year. Now, however, those same writers and broadcasters were asking, "Is Azinger for real?"

At the beginning of 1988, recent multiple winners were having trouble pulling off wins of any kind. Tom Watson, for example, won three times in 1984, but did not win again until 1987. Curtis Strange had won three times in 1985, but had only won twice since then. Bob Tway won four times in 1986 and not at all the next year. Perhaps dry spells like these can be explained in part by the pressure placed on players to meet other people's expectations.

Certainly, analysis and prognostications come with the territory when anyone wins in any sport. We see this all the time when a team wins the World Series or the Stanley Cup or the Super Bowl. The question on everyone's mind as the next season gets under way is "Will they be able to repeat?" or "Can they do it again?"

In individual sports like golf or tennis, the probing becomes more personal. Obviously, if Paul Azinger is going to be in the winner's circle again, I have to do it myself; there are no substitutes, pinch-hitters, or back-up quarterbacks to take my place.

I was surprised, however, how quickly people's expectations could be disappointed. As usual, my season started on the West Coast; I didn't necessarily contend, but I didn't play badly, either. I played six times and earned $75,000 out west, an average of a little more than $12,000 a week. I was in the top twenty on the money list, so I surely wasn't complaining.

But now, just four months after being named Player of the Year, I had to answer the question whether I was a fluke. It didn't make sense. My game had not changed, I was not hitting the ball any differently, nor had I become lackadaisical or complacent. It wasn't as if winning was as easy as falling off a log.

I was learning a valuable lesson, though, about the fickleness of celebrity and the fleeting contentment it brings. It reinforced my belief that I had nothing to prove to anyone but me; if I allowed myself to worry about living up to other people's expectations, I would always be miserable. I began to understand that as long as I did my best, that is all that really matters.

● ○ ●

Upon finishing the swing on the West Coast, I returned to Florida to play in Arnold Palmer's Bay Hill Classic in Orlando. I had many fond memories of Bay Hill going back to when I was a counselor at Arnie's summer golf academy in my college days. I had also led at Bay Hill in '85 when I was just starting out on the Tour. Now I was returning as Player of the Year. Many of my friends and family came out to watch me in that tournament, and in the first two rounds they had plenty of reasons to cheer. I shot 66 both days to capture a four-shot lead.

I woke up at four o'clock Saturday morning, and when I sat up in bed, I could tell right away that something was wrong. I had terrible dizziness. I fell back to sleep until about 7:30, but when I awoke, the problem was still there. I slept another half-hour, but still the whirling in my head didn't stop.

I had to do something, because my tee time was 1:30. I took a hot shower, bracing myself against the walls as the water poured over my body. The hot shower didn't help. Perhaps a cold shower would clear my head. That proved no better. Whatever this was, I couldn't shake it.

Toni called a friend of mine, Dr. Doug Morrow, and I went back to bed. I slept until about 11:30. When I awoke, the doctor was in the room and told me that I had vertigo as a result of an inner-ear infection. Doug recommended that I take some Dramamine. That didn't dispel all the dizziness, but enough that I was able to go to the course and get ready to play. The weird sensations stayed with me all day.

I got off to a good start, and at one point I had a seven-shot lead. But by the end of the day, thanks to a late charge by Tom Kite and some late bogeys in my play, I managed to finish the eighteenth hole with only a one-shot lead. I shot 73 for the round.

That evening I began to feel a lot better. When I awoke Sunday morning, the vertigo had gone completely. I went out and played a great heads-up match with Kite. Tom and I made some birdies early in the round, and we quickly distanced ourselves from the field, turning the tournament into a two-man battle. The lead seesawed, but after nine holes I was one shot ahead. After eleven, that became two.

At fourteen, a tough par 3, things began to turn my way. Tom hit into a green-side bunker. I hit a good 3-iron shot that landed just behind the green. Tom hit out of the bunker to within ten feet of the pin. I chipped from about twenty-five feet, and it went in! Tom missed his par putt, so now I had a four-shot lead.

After making par on fifteen and sixteen, I confronted seventeen, an extremely difficult hole. The tees there were up near the front of the tee box, and the pin was cut to the back right on the green. As a special attraction for the tournament, seventeen had been declared a "million-dollar hole." Any player who made a hole in one there would receive one million dollars, half of which would go to charity. That was the last thing on my mind. I hit a beautiful fade with a 5-iron and put the ball about six feet from the cup. I didn't win the million, but I was in good putting position. Tom hit in the bunker again and made another bogey. I made my putt for birdie.

I was on the eighteenth tee with a six-shot lead. I felt pretty comfortable coming down the stretch, and it was gratifying to play so well in front of friends and family. Numerous members of the club that I represented near Bradenton were at Bay Hill, and the support was incredible. The crowd noise was definitely in my favor that day.

Before Bay Hill, people were wondering about my golf game. But nobody asked, "Is Paul Azinger a fluke?" when Arnold Palmer put the winner's jacket on me.

I won some good money that day along with the jacket, but Don Pooley upstaged me. Don became the only golfer in history to win a million dollars with one shot. He made a hole in one on that fabled seventeenth, winning more money with one stroke than he had won up to that point during his entire career on the Tour.

● ○ ●

Although I didn't win another tournament in the rest of 1988, I was relatively happy with my game. I came close to winning the PGA Championship at Oak Tree; I led most of the way and played well enough to win. But Jeff Sluman scorched the course by shooting 65 on the final day to notch his first win.

I did have one of the greatest thrills of my career at that PGA. I had hurt my back during a tournament the previous week and had had to withdraw. Upon arriving at Oak Tree for the PGA, I was able to play only one practice round. As I drove around in a cart to check out the course, one hole terrified me the instant I saw it. It was all water, all carry, to a green that was not very wide and fairly deep. The green itself was perched atop a wall of railroad ties.

It cut in a bit on the left side, but there was no bail-out. The hole required either a great shot or a steep price.

On Saturday, a picture-perfect, blue-sky day, the pin was sort of in front of the green, up about thirteen steps. From the tee I had 174 yards to carry the water and another 13 yards to the hole. It was slightly downwind, so it was a very tough shot. I chose a 6-iron, but I knew I would have to catch it full. I was leading the tournament at this point, and a mistake here would mean double bogey.

I swung hard, and the ball went up nice and high—a little higher than usual, but with a good, straight trajectory. It seemed to take forever to clear the water—and I did carry it over by three or four yards—then finally I saw it hit the green. It bounced three times and started to roll. It was rolling on a straight line with the pin . . . rolling . . . rolling . . . *Come on, baby! Just a little more!* . . . and it was in! A hole in one! On the hole that scared me the most! While leading a major!

The roar that went up from the crowd could be heard all over the golf course. Instinctively my arms flew up in the air; I ripped off my visor at the same time and whipped it underhanded straight up. I threw it so hard, the visor landed in a tree and stuck there. With the crowd still cheering and my arms still aloft, all I could think was, *I sure hope my visor comes down.* Fortunately, it started dropping from branch to branch and finally tumbled to the ground.

I must have let my emotions get the better of me. On the next hole my tee shot went up against a sapling that was no bigger around than my wrist. I had to hack my ball out and away from it, and it cost me a chance to reach the green in regulation. I finally knocked my ball onto the green and two-putted for a double bogey.

That deflating experience taught me a lesson: I can't get too emotional in my play, whether something good happens or something bad, because the course is the great equalizer. I have become much more reserved in expressing myself after a shot.

My second-place finish for the tournament was a big disappointment. I had now lost two majors that I had come within a hairbreadth of winning. I was discovering that it took more than playing well to win a major. And I didn't feel nearly as bad about losing the '88 PGA as I did the '87 British Open. In fact, I didn't feel so much that I had lost the PGA as that Jeff Sluman had won it.

I ended 1988 at number eleven on the money list, earning close to $600,000—a fine performance in anyone's book. Little did I know that that would be the worst I would finish on the money list for the next five years.

● ○ ●

In 1989, for example, my game was hot. I did not win until nearly midyear, but I had fifteen top-ten finishes.

It was a busy year, to say the least. Toni and I were still living in the villa that was part of my endorsement deal. We were expecting our second baby, so we decided to build a larger home. We didn't make it in time. Josie Lynn was born on April 21. The house was not completed until later in the year.

Compared with the tension surrounding Sarah Jean's birth, our pregnancy with Josie was a snap . . . well, at least it was for me. Toni and I enjoyed sharing the excitement and anticipation of the new baby with three-year-old Sarah Jean. We kept telling her that she was going to have a little baby brother or sister. "Which would you rather have—a brother or a sister?" we would ask her.

"A puppy," she would reply.

"And what should we name this baby?"

"Lipstick or Crouton," she would answer almost every time.

Sarah Jean especially enjoyed talking to the baby in Toni's tummy. By the time Josie was born, she and Sarah Jean were best friends for life.

I was present in the delivery room for Josie's birth. I marveled at the miracle of a new human being, our baby, taking her first breaths outside the womb.

God must have known that Toni and I would need that reminder of the gift of life, because a few months later, our good friend Mac McKee died.

Toni and I were at the U.S. Open at Oak Hill when she got the news of Mac's death. When I came off the course after playing the second round and got back to the house where we were staying that week, I saw that Toni was visibly shaken. I couldn't believe what had happened. I had just talked with Mac by telephone the night before, and he had sounded great. The next day he was going to take a long bike ride; he was averaging nearly forty miles per ride at that time. Just as he was about to mount his bike—the bicycle that Toni and I had bought for him—he fell over with a heart attack.

I was heartbroken. Toni and I both shed many tears for Mac. We would miss him dearly. I managed to complete the U.S. Open, finishing ninth— which, considering how distraught I was over Mac's death, may have been the best tribute I could have given him.

● ○ ●

Mac died in June 1989. Although I had won a lot of money during the year, I had not yet won a tournament. Again the questions started coming, "What's wrong with Paul Azinger?" And again my answer was, "Nothing is wrong. I'm doing just fine." By the time I arrived at the Canon Greater Hartford Open, I was due for a win.

I had won at Hartford in '87, and because of that and because of our many friends and relatives in the area, I was sort of the local favorite coming down the home stretch. On the final day I was paired with Billy Britton, and I played like Jekyll and Hyde. On the front nine I shot 6-under to get myself into the lead. But on the back nine I had to hole a bunch of three- and four-footers for pars.

When Billy and I got to eighteen, we were warmly greeted by the huge gallery surrounding the green. The gallery there was one of the largest in golf, numbering close to 65,000 people, more than any other tournament in which I have participated. I was tied for the lead with Wayne Levi, but things were not looking good. I had hit a bad drive, which landed in the right-hand rough. My second shot was no better. I put the ball up on the hill above the green, and it kicked down to the left and into the short rough.

Now, as I neared the green, I could see that even though I was in the rough, my chip shot looked to be fairly straightforward. Nevertheless, I knew I did not want to leave myself with another three- or four-putt. I had gone to the well to save par so many times that afternoon that another stressful putt to win or tie was more than I could take.

I hit a nice, soft pitch, lofting the ball beautifully onto the green. The ball hit the grass and took a perfectly straight bounce toward the hole. Instinctively I pointed my club at the hole, as if the club would somehow help the ball along its path. It must have done some good. That ball rolled right into the center of the cup! The crowd went wild. I tossed my visor thirty feet into the air. Birdie! I finished with a four-round score of 267, 17-under-par, to beat Wayne and win the Hartford by one stroke.

The Hartford Open presented me with a check for $180,000 and a gorgeous lead trophy. The win also guaranteed me enough points to earn a spot on the 1989 Ryder Cup team. Yet the satisfaction I received by winning in front of my parents' hometown crowd in such a dramatic fashion far exceeded any other prizes. Toni was there for the trophy presentation, holding one of our most precious "trophies," two-month-old Josie in one hand and a lovely bouquet of roses presented to her by the Open in the other. My mother, Sarah Jean, and her "Garfield" stuffed animal were there, too. It was an unforgettable family victory.

I finished 1989 in third place on the money list, earning more than $950,000. But the highlight of my life on the golf course that year had little to do with money. It had to do with pride and patriotism.

CHAPTER EIGHTEEN
KING OF THE RYDER CUP

Throughout the 1980s Seve Ballesteros of Spain was the premier player on the international golf scene. No player has done more than he to raise the level of the Ryder Cup competition.

Seve has been winning major golf tournaments for more than fifteen years. He won his first major, the British Open, at the age of twenty-two. He won the Masters the next year, becoming the youngest player ever to win the green jacket. Three years later, Seve won the Masters again. He won the British Open again in 1984 and in 1988.

My first opportunity to be paired with Seve was at the 1987 PGA Championship, the next major following my loss at the British Open. I played horribly all week, coming in with scores such as 83 and 78. I don't remember hitting a single great shot in that tournament, and I missed several that I am accustomed to making. Seve knew I was still brooding about the British Open, and my lackluster performance at the PGA only exacerbated the pain I was feeling.

As we went to eighteen, he said to me in his somewhat broken English, "You no worry about this. You are a very good player. You have many more chances."

I thanked Seve, and thought, *Wow! That was mighty nice of him to say that.*

The following year, during the last round of the U.S. Open, Seve and I were playing together once again. On the first hole, he duck-hooked the ball out of bounds and made a double bogey. He was out of contention for the remainder of the day.

In the meantime, after a dismal Saturday in which I three-putted three greens and even four-putted one, my game on Sunday took a decisive change for the better. I shot 6-under on the front nine to tie a record for the lowest nine-hole score ever shot in a major. Suddenly I had a chance to win.

I was only a few shots back as we made the turn after nine. The leaders were just teeing off. Seve noticed where I was on the leader board, and although he was playing poorly himself, he started encouraging me.

On fifteen I hit a 1-iron off the tee, planning to hit a 7-iron to the green on my second shot. Seve was puzzled. "How come you hit 1-iron off this tee? You hit driver, you only need pitching wedge to the green."

"Seve, right now I am swinging so well, I feel I can hit a 7-iron as close as I can hit a wedge," I answered.

"Then it's okay," Seve replied. "You need to make one more birdie, you win the tournament."

Again, I was struck by Seve's enthusiasm and support for me. It was like having a personal cheerleader with me on the course. That kind of encouragement comes often from fans, but it's even better when it comes from a great golfer like Seve.

I put my 7-iron shot onto the green, but the ball landed about fifteen feet from the pin, and I missed the putt for birdie.

Seve was undaunted. "It's okay," he reassured me. "You just need to make one more birdie."

On sixteen I put a 7-iron shot to within one foot of the hole. I tapped it in for birdie. I was right on the number as far as Seve was concerned.

At seventeen my approach shot landed ten feet behind the hole. It would have been a tough putt in any case, but this green was extremely fast and had a downhill slope. I stroked my putt as easily as I could, just barely tapping the ball, but it suddenly caught the slope and zoomed about thirty feet past the cup. I missed the long putt coming back, so I bogeyed the hole.

Seve was still confident I could win. "It's okay," he said. "You no worry about this. This is over. You need to birdie this hole."

No wonder all the European Ryder Cup players like to play alongside Seve. Even if he is not playing well, he is still a major factor on the course because of his encouraging attitude.

I parred the last hole by sinking a long putt. Seve could not have been more gracious. Although I did not win the tournament—I finished three strokes off the lead, behind Nick Faldo and the winner, Curtis Strange—I came away from the U.S. Open with tremendous respect and appreciation for Seve Ballesteros.

But then we went to the 1989 Ryder Cup at the Belfry.

"The Zinger Swing." My grip and swing have been analyzed and criticized by a wide variety of teachers, writers, commentators, and other golfers.

Frank Christian, Augusta, Georgia

My mom says this was my first golf swing. (Opposite page, top inset) I get teased about my image every once in a while, but I really was a scout at eight. (Opposite page, top)

The Brothers. Jed, Jeff, Paul, and Joe at Homestead Air Force Base in 1967. (Opposite page, bottom)

Newlyweds. Toni and I didn't have much money when we got married, but we had a set of golf clubs, a camper, and a cat named Cleo. (Left)

My dad and mom, Ralph and Jean, were my biggest supporters when I began playing. Dad is a retired air force navigator, and Mom is a championship golfer in her own right. (Below)

Lifting one of my most precious trophies, my daughter Josie. (Left)

Sarah Jean helps me to line up a "critical" putt at the Hartford Pro-Am. (Right)

I won the 1992 Tour Championship, which meant I'd won a tournament every year for six straight years. As often as possible I like to have my family along with me at tournaments. (Below)

©David Perkiewicz, Republic

©Associated Press, Wide World Photos

©Frank Christian, Augusta, Georgia

©Frank Christian, Augusta, Georgia

Chipping in on the 18th hole to win the 1989 Hartford Open. (Opposite page, top)

Lining up a putt at the 1991 Ryder Cup, Kiawah Island, South Carolina. Every putt is crucial in Ryder Cup play. (Opposite page, bottom)

At Kiawah Island, Chip Beck and I played against Seve Ballesteros and Jose Maria Olazabal in a spirited match. Chip's caddie and I had plenty of advice on Chip's putt. (Left)

Ryder Cup Captain Dave Stockton discusses strategy during 1991 Ryder Cup. We stayed with the Stocktons in 1994 during my radiation treatments. (Below)

©Frank Christian, Augusta, Georgia

©Frank Christian, Augusta, Georgia

I won the 1993 Memorial in Columbus, Ohio, by holing a bunker shot on 18. My victory was my friend Payne Stewart's loss, but he handled it like a real champion. (Top)

Here Payne and I hold the Ryder Cup after our 1991 victory. (Right)

The victorious 1991 Ryder Cup Team. Top row (left to right): Lanny Wadkins, Fred Couples, Paul Azinger, Raymond Floyd, Hale Irwin, Dave Stockton, Payne Stewart, Mark Calcavecchia. Bottom row (left to right): Chip Beck, Mark O'Meara, Steve Pate, Corey Pavin, Wayne Levi.

Diane Hires,©Toledo Blade

The 1993 PGA Championship at Inverness. Showing the intensity of the final nine holes on number 15, I went down on one knee after just missing a 35-foot putt by inches. I am much quicker to show emotion when I miss a shot than when I sink one. (Opposite page)

By the end of the match I was doing deep-breathing exercises, trying to control my emotions and my heartbeat, as I walked the fairways. (Opposite page, inset)

It was official. I had won my first major. I didn't realize how heavy that trophy was. As I lifted it, an old friend made its presence known—the pain in my shoulder.

The 1993 Skins Game in Palm Springs. Payne Stewart, Arnold Palmer, Freddie Couples, and me. (Opposite page, top)

The wind was howling the last day of the 1993 Ryder Cup. (From left) U.S. Captain Tom Watson and I stand with Nick Faldo and his captain, Bernard Gallacher, before playing the match everyone wanted to see. (Opposite page, bottom)

Chemo treatments couldn't keep me away from fishing and this fifteen-pound tarpon, which I later released unharmed.

A copy of the bone scan. (Below)

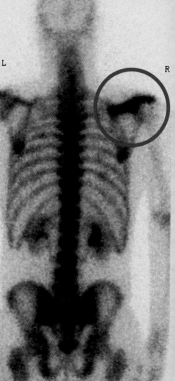

Shots with some living legends of golf. Walking with Arnold Palmer at the U.S. Open Qualifier at Bay Hill in 1986. (Right)

At the 1994 Memorial, where I returned to the public eye, Jack Nicklaus asked for a pair of sunglasses to protect him from the glare off my head. He and Barbara were incredibly supportive during my treatment. (Below)

Defending my title at the 1994 PGA Championship in Tulsa, Oklahoma. This tournament and the 1994 Buick Open in Michigan marked my return to golf after my battle with cancer. (Opposite page)

People keep asking me how I am feeling. I am cancer-free and healthy. Golf is still important to me, but it now ranks after my faith, my family, and my friends. And helping others. From now on, I want to live every day as a gift from God.

© Frank Christian, Augusta, Georgia

Sam Greenwood, © PGA Tour

No one takes Ryder Cup competition any more seriously than Seve Ballesteros ... except possibly Paul Azinger. At the Ryder Cup, he was no longer my encourager. We were on opposite sides. Now I was his nemesis, not his pal.

The tension began to build on Saturday when Chip Beck and I were in an incredible match with Ian Woosnam and Nick Faldo. Chipper and I were psyched up because that pair had never been beaten in Ryder Cup competition. Of course, nobody wanted to beat Nick more than I did. On the first tee I told Chip, "I don't know about you, bud, but I'm taking this match personal!"

Chip and I made a great team. We complemented each other's game. I birdied the first three holes; Chip birdied four. I birdied five, and Chip came right behind me and birdied seven and eight. I birdied nine, and he birdied ten. We couldn't believe it!

Faldo and "Woosie" weren't doing so badly themselves. They were chipping in from everywhere, holing out of bunkers, and making sensational shots look easy. At times I almost wanted to sit back and watch this match as a spectator. This was golf at its finest.

On number ten, a drivable par 4, Chip put his first shot right on the green. Woosie was off the side of the green in two. But then Ian hit another incredible shot and holed the chip for a birdie. Chip was putting for eagle, but when Woosie made his chip shot, it may have thrown off Chip's concentration a bit. He missed the eagle putt, but sank a five-footer for birdie and a tie on the hole.

The English gallery roared its approval of this intense match. As we walked off the green, Chipper called to me above the din, "You gotta love it! You gotta love it!"

"What do you mean?" I asked.

"They've chipped in three times and we're still 1-up!" That's Chipper for you. Chip Beck is one of the most positive people I have ever met. Once he hit a twenty-foot putt ten feet past the hole and said, "It didn't go in, but I really hit it solid!" The world needs more people with Chip's great attitude.

Of course, this match was fraught with the usual friction that accompanies Ryder Cup play. On the next hole I was way off the green, but Chip was on, just twelve feet from the cup. Nick and Ian were both about fifteen feet away, on opposite sides of the green.

It was my turn, but I said, "Chipper, why don't you go ahead and putt first? If you make it, that will put the pressure on them." Chip agreed, and we walked over, knelt down, and started reading his putt. Meanwhile, Nick ambled around and squatted down behind Chip's ball on the other side of the cup from us. I didn't care for that one bit, so I walked over to Nick and said, "I'll read my partner's putts, if you don't mind."

Nick stood up to his full height and said, "Just trying to offer you a helping hand."

Chip drained his putt without extra help.

We battled right down to the end of the match, but Chipper and I finally defeated Faldo and Woosnam, 2 and 1. We were 11-under for seventeen holes, and they were 9-under and still lost. That's what you call a great Ryder Cup match.

● ○ ●

As the Ryder Cup captains planned their playing order for singles matches, near the close of the competition, the American team was two points behind the Europeans. Our team captain, Raymond Floyd said, "We are going to send our two hottest players out, one and two; and we will win those two points, and we will be even with them. And then we are going to beat them!" Raymond selected Chip Beck and me to begin the battle against the Europeans on the final day of play.

I was to go first, so I wasn't surprised when I drew Seve in singles. The Europeans' strategy was to put Seve on the course early so he could hopefully win his match, then spend the rest of the day cheerleading the other European players. I knew from experience what a powerful factor Seve can be, whether he is winning or not.

I found out the night before that I had drawn Seve for the first match, and it made me more than a little jittery. After all, I would be playing the King of Ryder Cup Match Play. Curtis Strange did nothing to calm my nerves when he approached me with a clue about Seve.

"I want you to know that he prides himself in being a great match-play player. Don't let him pull anything on you," Curtis said with a twinkle in his eye. I had heard of Seve's reputation for doing little things to distract opponents, but I wasn't worried about it. He had never done anything to bother me. Quite the contrary, he had offered great encouragement whenever we played together. Nevertheless, I assured Curtis that I would keep an eye on Seve.

The next morning Curtis said again, "Don't let this guy pull anything on you."

"Okay, Curtis."

My mind-set as I mounted the first tee box was, *I am not going to let this guy pull anything on me.*

The first tee at the Belfry was swarming with people for the start of the singles. A raucous European crowd, flying their various national flags, surrounded the tee area and lined both sides of the fairway, standing six deep behind the ropes. Thirty thousand people were on the golf course that morning, and it seemed that at least twenty thousand of them were on the first hole. The two team captains and at least thirty press photographers were there, too.

It is impossible to describe adequately the kind of pressure a player feels when he steps up, in those circumstances, with nothing more than a piece of metal or wood on the end of a shaft, to attempt to hit a little white ball perched on a splinter of wood.

My nerves were jangling as I hit my first drive. My ball found a bunker, I hit a great shot out to within five feet of the cup, and I just missed my birdie. Fortunately, Seve got off to a sluggish start, and we tied the first hole.

On number two both Seve and I hit irons off the tee; then both hit wedges to the green. I hit a pitching wedge to within three feet; Seve put his pitching wedge shot twelve feet from the hole. When we got up to the green, Seve surprised me by saying, "I want to take this ball out of play. It is damaged."

That year, Ping Square Groove clubs were shredding golf balls like crazy, and players had gotten in the habit of taking them out of play on the fringes of the greens. As a result, an old rule was enforced that said a ball must be visibly cut before it could be taken out of play. It was not necessary to receive a referee's ruling before removing a ball from play, only the permission of your opponent.

When Seve made his request, I immediately thought, *He hit two perfect shots. There's no way his ball is cut.* As I thought it over, I concluded, *No way! I am not going to let him do this.*

Seve had already placed a new ball on the green and had given his old ball to his caddie. I approached the caddie and said, "I need to see Seve's ball." The caddie reluctantly retrieved the ball from his pocket. I had to admit, it had several groove marks on it, but the ball was not visibly cut. My ball had similar groove marks, too. In fact, my ball was in far worse shape than Seve's, but I knew I could not legally ask to remove it from play.

I said, "Seve, I don't think you can take this ball out." I walked over to where he was already squatting and lining up his putt with a new ball. He looked at me incredulously.

I had his grooved ball in my hand. "Seve, in the United States the rule says the ball needs to be visibly cut before you can take it out of play. And I don't think these groove marks merit taking it out of play."

Seve said staunchly, "European rules say this ball is unfit for play."

"Well, my ball looks just like that, or worse, so I think we should ask the referee."

Seve stared back at me. "Is this the way you want to play today?"

"I just think we need to ask the referee—"

"Okay," Seve answered curtly, and we called for the referee.

When the referee looked at Seve's ball, he said, "I'm sorry, Seve. You must play this ball. It needs to be visibly cut to take it out."

I said, "Hey, man, I'm sorry. My ball looks just like that—"

Seve waved me off with his hand. "No, no! It's okay. This is the way you want to play today, we can play this way."

The crowd had been buzzing throughout our discussion. One guy shouted at me, "Come on! What are you trying to pull?"

Seve lined up his putt from every angle. He was in no hurry. This was his game, and these were his people. After spending a long time studying his twelve-foot putt, Seve stood up, stroked it, and sank it.

The roar of the crowd was deafening! A European gallery in Ryder Cup competition is unlike anything American players encounter at home. The European fans are into the game, and as in their soccer matches, they really let loose when they want to express their approval.

When the noise finally settled enough for me to get set, a guy in the gallery yelled out, "What would you have done with a good ball, Seve?"

I tried not to pay any attention to the howling gallery as I put my ball down where I had marked it and squatted to read my putt. I was looking at a slightly downhill, left-to-right three-footer. I had missed a similar putt on the previous hole. I hit the putt right into the center of the cup, yet amazingly it did not go in. It did a 360-degree turn around the cup and popped out.

Unlike the galleries in the U.S., which would quietly gasp, "Oooh" or "Oh, no!" at such a shot, the crowd exploded in applause. I think they were cheering louder than when Seve made his putt.

At that, I went from really nervous to really angry.

● ○ ●

The fourth hole was a par 5, and I hit my tee shot into the water. When we got to the green, I made a bogey, and Seve had a five-footer for birdie. He would have had to three-putt here for me to be tied with him on this hole, so I gave Seve his putt. Ordinarily, when one player gives another his putt, he picks it up and they go to the next tee together. Not this time. Seve stepped up and drilled the putt into the center of the cup. Again the gallery erupted. Seve was 2-up on me.

We didn't say another word to each other for the next several hours.

At the fifth tee I told Raymond Floyd, "I don't think Seve is hitting it all that great, so I think I'll be able to get a couple of holes here eventually." I was right. Seve bogeyed number five, and I parred the hole. I was still one-down. At number six I had a fifty-foot putt for birdie, and I made it. A smattering of applause filtered through the gallery. Seve had a ten-footer for birdie, and he missed. Now we were even.

Seve bogeyed the next hole, and I birdied number nine, so at the turn I was 2-up on him.

Number ten at the Belfry is a par 4 that I felt I could drive. It had a creek on the left side of the fairway, and a big hill on the right. The fairway was lined with people all the way to the green and all around it.

I selected the correct club—a 3-wood—but misfired just enough to get myself into trouble. My shot landed about twenty yards to the right of the green. Seve hit his tee shot onto the green, and once again the gallery went wild.

When we got up to the green, it was bad enough that I had to hit my next shot over a bunker. Making matters worse, my ball was sitting on a woman's jacket! We had to call for a referee and clear people away.

I asked the referee, "What should I do?"

He said, "You need to drop your ball right here, at the nearest point."

I dropped my ball, and because of the severe slope of the hillside, my ball started rolling down closer to the hole. I dropped it again, and the same thing happened. The referee was standing there, and he instructed me to place my ball rather than drop it. I attempted to place the ball in the grass, but still it would not stay. It kept rolling toward the hole, as though drawn by a magnet. At last I moved the ball about three feet up the hill and placed the ball on a nice clump of grass. The ball sat up beautifully, almost as if it were sitting on a tee.

I looked at the referee, and he nodded and said, "That's fine."

I turned to my left, and Seve and I were standing almost nose-to-nose. "I want to know where his ball was," Seve said to the referee while looking at me.

"It was right here," replied the ref.

"How come his ball is not there?" Seve asked.

"Seve, it wouldn't stay," I tried to explain.

Seve ignored my explanation, squatted down, and tried to place his ball all around on the hillside where he thought mine should be.

I thought, *I sure hope his ball doesn't stay!* It never did. Try as he might, his ball kept rolling toward the hole, just as mine had done.

Disgusted, Seve said to me, "Now you have a perfect lie." That was the only time we had spoken to each other since the second hole. The entire conflict over the placement of my ball seemed rather pointless anyhow, since Seve's ball was sitting on the green. Unless I hit an incredibly lucky shot off that embankment, I didn't stand a chance of winning this hole. But Seve wanted me to know that he was not taking anything for granted. Nor was he giving anything away.

I chipped to within twenty feet of the pin, but that was not good enough. Seve two-putted for a birdie to win the hole.

By the time we reached the thirteenth tee, I was still holding onto a one-hole lead. I hit first, then Seve teed up, just inside the tee blocks. My caddie, Billy Poore, was standing right next to the tee blocks before Seve placed his tee. Seve said to Billy, "Caddie, you need to move, a little bit, you need to move."

Billy moved about one inch.

"You need to move," Seve said again, clearly irritated.

Billy moved about two inches.

Some guy in the crowd bellowed, "Come on! Get out of the way!"

I grabbed Billy and pulled him down the hill. As soon as Seve hit, Billy and I took off down the fairway. I turned to Billy and said, "That was great! But don't do it again. I think it really made him mad!"

Suddenly I heard footsteps running behind us. To my surprise, it was Seve. As he neared, he slowed down a bit and reached us at a walk. I thought, *Oh, no! This is going to be brutal!*

But Seve surprised me again. Seve said, "I was not trying to pull something on you there. I needed you to move."

"No, it's okay. Don't worry about it," I replied, hoping to calm him down. Off he went.

When we got to the green, I had a two-foot putt. Usually, in Ryder Cup play, if a putt is that close, your opponent will offer a gimme. I looked over to Seve as if to ask him, "Is that good?"

Seve didn't move a muscle.

I thought, *All right, fine!* I slapped the putt into the hole.

We were tied after fourteen, but I went 1-up on fifteen, and we stayed that way until the final hole.

The eighteenth hole at the Belfry is not one of my favorites. It became less so after my next infamous escapade with Seve. The hole has a rather strange layout; it has water lying on the left side, which cuts all the way around in front of the green. You can't see the green from the tee, and because the hole doglegs almost ninety degrees to the left, it is difficult to tell how much a ball will carry.

Seve drove his shot through the fairway into the right rough. I hit a pop-hook that landed in the water on the left. A European Tour referee accompanied me as I walked down to determine where my ball last crossed the hazard. A marshal was standing right there, pointing to a spot in the lake. "This is where the ball splashed," he said.

The referee and I were looking back and forth from the tee to the water, trying to determine where the ball crossed, so I could take the penalty and drop another ball. Just when we thought we had figured it out as well as possible, Seve walked over and said, "Your ball crossed right up there," pointing fifteen to twenty yards ahead of the location the referee and I had settled on.

I said to the referee, "I think it crossed further back here."

Seve was adamant, "No, no, no! Right by that tree. It crossed right there by that tree." The place where Seve was indicating would provide me with a much better lie than the spot where the referee and I originally planned to drop it. With Seve's drop, I would be able to keep a line between the hole and me and walk backward to find a spot from which I wanted to hit. If I dropped it where the referee and I had suggested, I would be in a much tougher jam.

I looked back at the referee and asked, "What do you think?"

Finally the European referee shrugged his shoulders and pointed to the tree Seve had indicated. "Right up there, then."

I marked the spot Seve had indicated with a tee, then backpedaled until I felt I could hit a 3-wood and carry the grass sticking up on the banks of the lake. I asked my caddie what the yardage was from this point, and Billy gave me a number. I discovered later that he had no idea of the actual yardage. He explained, "I just gave you a number; I thought you would make a confident swing." Thanks, Billy.

I dropped my ball, and it caught a nice, clean lie. I crushed my 3-wood shot, hitting a big hook and clearing the water, but landing in the green-side bunker.

Seve was having troubles of his own. He hit a 3-iron out of the right rough, but he must have stood up a bit, because he topped the ball. His ball squirted out of the rough and rolled across the fairway right into the water. Now Seve had to take a penalty and drop a ball. He responded by hitting a beautiful pitching wedge shot that cleared the water, but landed on the third tier of a three-tier green. The pin was on the second tier. He was pretty upset.

I hit a sand wedge out of the bunker, leaving myself a five-foot putt for bogey. Seve was already lining up his twenty-five-foot, downhill, nightmarish putt for bogey. I did not envy his position. He just barely tapped the ball, but it began gaining speed as it rolled down the tier, breaking ever so slightly toward the hole. I couldn't believe my eyes! The ball raced faster and faster and slammed into the back of the cup. He made it for bogey. It was truly a sensational putt.

A huge roar went up from the gallery. As I walked by him, I slapped him on the backside and said, "Great putt!" It was the only time I had acknowledged his play in any way—good, bad, or indifferent—since the second hole.

Now I was looking at my testy little five-footer. If I miss it, Seve wins the hole and we tie the match. If I make it, we tie the hole, but I win the match because I was still 1-up. I carefully lined up my putt . . . and sank it! I had beaten Seve Ballesteros, the "King of Match Play." Seve and I shook hands in

a cursory fashion and quickly vacated the green. This was no time for celebration. Ours was only the first match of the day. There was still much work
to be done in deciding who took home the Ryder Cup.

I hadn't noticed at the time, but a television commentator said later that
it looked as though Seve had tears in his eyes as he came off the eighteenth
green. I would not be surprised. As I said, nobody takes Ryder Cup play more
seriously than Seve except. . . .

● ○ ●

By the end of the day, despite my victory over Seve, the U.S. team only tied
the European team, 14 to 14. We did not beat them. Since the Europeans had
won in 1987, they retained the Ryder Cup in 1989. Although I'm sure the
Europeans would have preferred an out-and-out victory, they celebrated the
tie as though it were a win. The Americans, however, viewed the tie as a loss
because we did not bring home the cup.

After the Europeans' jubilant celebration, all the players went back out to
the course for the closing ceremonies. Tradition mandates that the players
walk out side-by-side with the opponent they faced in singles competition.
Golf is, after all, a gentleman's game.

I walked out, in front of the cheering crowd, with Seve Ballesteros. I didn't
say a word; my face was as steel. It really wasn't my place to say anything. He
was the elder statesman of the Ryder Cup, and I was the new kid.

When the ceremonies were completed, Seve approached me. He extended
his arms, put both of his hands on my two shoulders, and looked me directly
in the eyes. In an almost apologetic voice, Seve said, "We were very hard on
each other today."

I said, "Yep, we sure were!"

Seve spoke softly, still looking at me, like a parent to a child, "But it's
okay." He had a slight smile and a twinkle in his eye.

I just can't help loving the guy . . . except for one week every other year.

CHAPTER NINETEEN
Between a Pebble and a Hard Place

Confidence is a crucial factor in playing winning golf. It can sometimes make up for less than perfect play on the course. The confident golfer will make the risky shots when the golfer suffering from a lack of confidence won't even be willing to take the risks. For me, few events in my career have bolstered my confidence more than beating Seve Ballesteros in the 1989 Ryder Cup singles, and few have devastated me more than my 1990 experience at Doral.

After beating Seve, I went on a roll. I finished third or better in seven of ten events following the '89 Ryder Cup. One of my wins was the prestigious 1990 Tournament of Champions at La Costa, California, featuring a field consisting entirely of PGA Tour winners from the previous year. The Tournament of Champions is the *crème de la crème,* and to win it was a tremendous triumph.

Ian Baker-Finch and I had left the field well behind, so it turned out to be a two-man battle as we knocked heads down the stretch. I hit my fairway shots extremely well, but I wasn't putting very well, and as every golfer knows, putting is nearly half the game. "Finchy's" putting, by contrast, was fantastic that week. That one tournament, as much as any other, gained for Ian a reputation as a great putter.

Nevertheless, we were dead tied on the eighteenth tee in the final round. Ian drove his ball into the left-hand bunker, then hit it out to about thirty yards short of the green. Meanwhile, I hit my drive down the middle and then placed an excellent, punchy, knock-down 5-iron within twenty feet to the right of the pin on the back of the green. Ian chipped outside me, leaving himself a twenty-five-footer. The way Ian was putting, that distance was almost a gimme! He hit a great putt that eased right up to the lip of the cup— and simply stopped.

After that, all I had to do was two-putt from twenty feet to win the Tournament of Champions. But this was the first tournament of the year. Nothing comes easily at that point in the season. I thought, *I'll just tap it so it will trickle down the hill, and I will leave it short.* I did only tap the thing, all right, but it went two feet past the hole. It was a good thing I hadn't hit it any harder! I made the two-footer to win, but that was a much tougher two-putt than it should have been.

● ◯ ●

Winning the Tournament of Champions got me off to a great start in 1990. I played with strong confidence in the Hawaiian Open and nearly won that, too. I was the leading money winner through the first part of the season. Then we went to Doral.

I played great at Doral, too—for the first seventy-one holes. It was the final hole on the final day that did me in. At the time, I was leading the tournament by one stroke, just ahead of Mark Calcavecchia, Tim Simpson, and Greg Norman. All I needed was a par on eighteen to win.

With the tournament at stake, I missed the fairway, hitting my tee shot into the left-hand rough. I decided to take a big chance and try to hit a 6-iron out of the Bermuda grass, over the water, and onto the green. I hit the ball well coming out of the rough; it cleared the water nicely. Had the shot made the green, it would have rolled to within ten feet of the hole. But it didn't. Instead, it lacked about a yard, so it stayed short of the green. I was still okay. I had a beautiful lie, with a relatively easy chip shot to get up and down to win Doral.

It should have been easy—it really should have been—but for some reason I chipped it eight feet by the hole. That left me with a difficult eight-foot, left-to-right putt. Those "short" eight-footers—the kind of putt that every professional golfer and most amateurs make several times a day—suddenly seem as though they are forty feet away from the cup when you are in contention and putting on the final green in the final round of a tournament.

Again, I stroked it too hard. I pulled the ball past the hole and had to tap in for bogey. That virtually handed Calcavecchia, Simpson, and Norman an invitation to a playoff.

On the first hole of the four-man playoff, Greg Norman hit a sensational chip shot from twenty-five feet away. The ball skidded onto the green, took two skips, and gently rolled toward the cup. As it did, Greg raised his wedge high in the air. Instinctively, I raised my own wedge above my head as well. Greg's ball glided into the hole for an eagle and the tournament win.

When I saw Greg's shot slip into the hole, my heart sank with it. I angrily slammed my club into the Florida turf, driving the club face several inches below the surface. I wasn't angry toward Greg. I was frustrated with myself for even allowing Greg and Tim and Mark to be there.

Losing that tournament that way really shook my confidence. Again, it made me question whether I wanted to put myself into a position to fail in front of so many people.

●   ○   ●

Toni and the kids and I packed up and headed for the Florida Keys, one of our favorite vacation spots and ordinarily a place where I can "get away from it all" and find some peace and solace. Not this time.

We had no sooner gotten onto the dock than some guy who was a golf fan said, "Hey! I saw you choke off Doral yesterday."

Without thinking, I lost my temper and cursed at the man. Later I felt horrible about it. The man's buddy apologized to me for his friend's insensitivity, but I really owed him an apology as well.

I feel awful whenever I lose my cool, whether on the course or off. I am known as an emotional player, and I make no apologies for showing my feelings. I truly attempt to keep my emotions under control, although in the past I have stuck clubs in the ground, thrown clubs, or blurted out cuss words in the heat of the moment. When I allow something like that to happen, I feel that I have disappointed people who expect me to be a positive role model; I feel that I have failed my family and also myself; most important, I feel that I have failed the Lord.

I can just imagine someone seeing me bury a club or spit out an expletive and then saying, "Oh, yeah, Paul Azinger. And he's supposed to be a Christian?"

I am a Christian, and I take my faith and its responsibilities very seriously. But I am not perfect. I like the little bumper-sticker slogan, "I'm not perfect, just forgiven." That's me. I don't claim to be perfect—there has only been one perfect person, and our world crucified him—but I do want to be a positive role model and maintain a consistent Christian testimony. Nevertheless, I know that I am on my way to heaven, not because of what I have said or done for Christ, but because of what he has done for me. When you see or hear me mess up, I am not being hypocritical; I am being painfully human.

Just that fact—that I am only human and not an automaton—caused me to be deeply affected by my loss at Doral. Not since losing the British Open in 1987 had I been so profoundly affected by a defeat. But losing the British Open was actually easier to handle. Back then, I was young in the game and regarded as an up-and-coming player. But the British Open elevated my status in the golf world, and as a result my confidence went up. After my loss at Doral my confidence went way down.

Despite Doral, 1990 was a good year for me in many ways. I had twelve top-ten finishes and earned $944,731 to place fourth on the money list. That was just slightly less than I had won in '89. But after Doral I did not win another tournament the remainder of the year.

● ○ ●

I might not have won in 1991, either, had it not been for Mac McKee. Good old Mac! Although he had died in 1989, his words continued to inspire me to break through to the top of the leader board.

I was playing in the AT&T Pebble Beach National Pro-Am near Monterey, California. Pebble Beach Golf Links is my favorite course in all the world—not because it is an easy course by any stretch of the imagination, but because its natural beauty and challenging features make it a pleasure to play. I putted poorly at Pebble several years in a row. I tell myself I am not going back there every year, but the course draws me like a magnet. It is so picturesque there, it is one tournament I don't want to pass up.

The 1991 AT&T was played on three of Monterey Peninsula's seaside courses: Spyglass Hill, Pebble Beach, and Poppy Hills, a new Robert Trent Jones, Jr., venue that none of the pros were familiar with. I shot two great opening rounds—67 at Pebble and 67 at Spyglass—and led the tournament after the second round. But on Saturday I played Poppy Hills and had a horrendous day, hacking out a 73.

As we started the final round, I was two strokes behind the leader, Rocco Mediate. I was playing with John Cook, the winner at Pebble Beach in 1981, and his amateur partner, Jack Wagner, a TV soap-opera heartthrob with a 4-handicap. Wagner had not only made the third-round cut, but threatened to win the tournament! I had never before heard of Jack, but the women in the gallery, including my mom, were crazy about him.

My amateur partner, Larry Colson, had also made the cut and was part of our foursome. Larry is Mac McKee's son-in-law, so it was special just to have him playing with me, let alone having him help our team get into contention.

Early in the round John and I served notice that we were out to win. After the first four holes we were tied for the tournament lead. I had eagled number two and sunk a forty-five-foot putt on number four. Davis Love III was playing well, too, only one stroke behind us most of the day. John bogeyed the fifth, but our team played quite evenly as we tiptoed through Pebble Beach's infamous killer holes on the front nine. On ten John three-putted for a double bogey, and because Rocco Mediate had bogeyed both eight and nine, I moved into sole possession of the lead.

● ○ ●

The eleventh tee was a turning point for me, in more ways than one. I hit my tee shot and immediately hurried up the fairway. I was already anticipating some of the more difficult shots I would be facing as I moved down the stretch toward Pebble's seaside eighteenth green. My mind was racing, my heart was pounding, and my whole system was in overdrive.

Suddenly I stopped. I thought, *Wait a minute! Here I am, playing with Colson, the son-in-law of the guy who taught me how to calm down and concentrate, and I am doing just the opposite of everything Mac taught me.* I knelt down on the fairway and pretended that I needed to tie my shoestrings. My shoes were fine, but I purposely took my time, undid both of them, and then slowly retied them as everyone in our group walked on by me. I stood to my feet and took some deep breaths before continuing up the fairway.

From that point on, I made a conscious effort to slow my walk and calm my emotions. Golf is not like other sports, in which you can feed off the adrenaline in your system. In golf the adrenaline has to be controlled.

● ○ ●

I must have done a good job of keeping things under control, because I managed to make a par-saving putt on twelve and a really difficult twenty-foot putt on thirteen for birdie. For the first time in my career I was feeling that I could accurately read Pebble Beach's greens.

I was pulsating with confidence on sixteen, when my tee shot landed in the left-hand rough, with a dry hazard positioned between the hole and my ball. Now I had a tough decision. I was only one shot ahead of the pack. I could play it safe and try to lay up short of the green, which would mean a certain bogey and the loss of my lead. Or I could try to launch the ball over the dry hazard, straight to the green. If I missed, I would probably bogey the hole, but I felt it was worth the risk.

With my 7-iron I hacked the ball out of the rough, over the hazard, and into the tall rough right in front of the green. From there I hit a pitch to within two feet of the cup and tapped it in. My risk had paid off. But there was no chance to relax and enjoy the scenery. We were going to Pebble Beach's terrifying seventeenth tee.

I hit a 4-iron off the tee to the left pin placement. My shot soared straight and landed two feet from the cup. But when we got to the green, I quickly realized that my putt was no gimme. That little two-footer had a nasty break—true, only two or three inches, but at Pebble Beach that's enough to pull a putt toward the Pacific Ocean. When I hit my putt, I thought sure I had missed it. The ball hung lazily on the lip for a long moment and then dropped into the hole, as if to say, "Okay, I'll let you have this one."

I looked at the leader board and discovered that I was four shots ahead of the closest contenders, Corey Pavin and Brian Claar. Larry Colson and I gave each other knowing looks as we stood on the eighteenth tee. We didn't have to say it, but we both knew in our hearts, *This one is for Mac.*

I played the eighteenth hole relatively safely. I hit a 1-iron off the tee, and we coasted down that scenic fairway. I hit two more careful iron shots, then two putts, for a 67 finish, and the tournament win was mine. It was an extremely satisfying win. Not only had I broken through to the top for the first time in nearly a year, but I had done it with Larry, Mac's son-in-law. Back home in Blackshear, I knew, Mac's wife, Juanita, would be very proud of Larry and me, and had Mac been alive, I'm sure he would have been, too.

● ○ ●

I really wanted to win the Doral Ryder Open in 1991. Memories of my 1990 demise at Doral haunted me. The only way to overcome them was to play well.

On Thursday, the first day of the tournament, I played well all the way to the eighteenth hole, where my ball found the water hazard. When I arrived at the spot, I discovered that my ball had landed about eighteen inches into the lake, and the top of the ball was visible above the water level. I felt sure I could get that ball out of there without its costing me a penalty stroke, so I sloshed into the water and attempted to take a stance.

I was able to find some firm footing under my right shoe, which was almost completely submerged, but I couldn't find a comfortable position for my left foot, which I had to place in the wet gravel and water along the lake's edge. A small rock was lying under my left foot when I tried to settle into a stance, so without even thinking about it, I pawed the stone with my spikes and flipped it out from beneath my shoe.

I took a hard swing, blasting through the water with my sand wedge, and the ball splashed out of the hazard. I went on to par the hole, shooting 68 for the round, and went into the clubhouse feeling wet but satisfied.

The following morning I was striking the ball well again. I started on the back nine and was crawling up the leader board. I shot a brilliant 65 for the day and was only one shot behind. When I walked off the last green, I noticed the Tour officials sitting in a golf cart. *Uh-oh, somebody's in trouble,* I thought.

Somebody was—me!

They called me into the CBS television trailer, and one of the officials said, "Paul, you have a problem."

"What? What is it?"

"We'll show you."

The officials replayed a videotape of me hitting out of the water on eighteen the previous day. I watched the tape intently, but I didn't see that I had done anything wrong.

"I didn't see a thing," I said. "What did I do?"

They said, "Watch it again."

I watched the tape again and still didn't see anything unusual.

"Watch your left foot," one official said, as we watched the scene for the third time. This time I saw my left foot paw the rock.

"So?" I asked.

"You moved a loose impediment in a hazard, Paul, and that is against the rules."

"I what?" I was incredulous. "I was just trying to take a stance. I'm allowed to fairly take a stance."

"Yes, but you can't move a loose impediment in a hazard."

"I was trying to take a stance!" I protested. "I don't even remember moving that rock under my foot, but I was trying to get some good footing."

"You cannot move a loose impediment. That should have been a two-stroke penalty, but you did not mark your scorecard that way. We are going to have to disqualify you from the tournament."

"You what?" I could not believe my ears.

"We're sorry, Paul. You are out of the tournament."

● ○ ●

It was bad enough to be "DQed," but the manner in which I was disqualified made it difficult to accept. A club pro from Colorado who had been watching Thursday's round on television saw my foot move the stone. Being a stickler for the rules, he telephoned the tournament officials to notify them that I had committed an infraction. Upon reviewing the videotape of my shot the officials deemed the caller's information accurate and decided to disqualify me from the tournament.

Technically my infraction was signing an incorrect scorecard—a card that did not include a two-stroke penalty added to my score on eighteen. But why would I give myself a two-stroke penalty if I was not aware I had done anything wrong? It was ridiculous.

I never spoke to the television fairway sheriff, nor did I care to. But he apparently broadcast his "coup" to the wrong people: Someone slashed the tires on his car in the parking lot at his club.

● ○ ●

Back at Doral, when Toni and I emerged from the CBS trailer, I quickly discovered that just about everyone at the tournament knew about my disqualification before I did. Players on the driving range knew about it. People in the gallery, all over the golf course, had heard about it already. And of course, the media were waiting for me the moment I showed my face.

I put my arm around Toni, put my head down, and walked quickly through the crowd of reporters, TV camera operators, and curious onlookers.

"Can you give us a comment?" the reporters shouted. "Paul, what happened? What do you have to say?"

I didn't say a word; I just kept walking with my head down, eyes on the ground. I couldn't have given them a comment if I had wanted to; I was so upset, I was on the verge of tears.

One pesky cameraman hopped along in front of Toni and me, holding his camera down low, almost scraping on the ground, as he tried to get a picture of my face. I couldn't believe the media frenzy over my disqualification.

Toni and I went straight to our hotel room. I knew I would eventually have to address the press, but I needed some time to sort out my feelings, cool down, and get my thoughts together. After about a half-hour, someone knocked on the door. It was Tom Place, the head of the press liaison for the Tour. Tom and his wife, Jean, have been like surrogate parents to Toni and me on the Tour. Tom had helped me through several tough situations already in which I needed to explain my actions or words to the media. He has been an invaluable friend.

Tom's first words were, "Paul, I am really sorry."

"You know, it is not fair. This is not a fair ruling," I said.

Tom nodded and said, "Well, let me give you some advice. Don't challenge the rule. You just need to accept it."

"What do you mean, Tom?"

"Simply this: I would encourage you not to challenge the rules of golf. Challenge the ruling on your shot if you want to, but don't challenge the rules of the game."

I thanked Tom for the advice and said, "I'll see you in about fifteen minutes." After Tom left our room, I sat and thought about what Tom had told me. He was right. For me to challenge the rule under which I had been DQed would only make a bad situation worse.

When I went to the press room, my attitude, thanks to Tom Place, was one of acceptance rather than antagonism. I said, "I don't like it. All I was doing was taking a stance. I believe what I did was an infraction. But I also think it was a trivial thing. Moving that rock had nothing whatsoever to do with the shot. There was no intent upon my part to improve my situation. But I am not going to challenge the rule. I'll accept it."

● ○ ●

Most people in golf circles rallied around me, and I attribute that to the goodwill engendered by my heeding Tom's advice. One of the golf magazines took a survey and found that nearly 98 percent of the respondents felt that I had been given a raw deal.

My fellow players also rallied to my side. Curtis Strange, for instance, defended my integrity by saying, "Paul wouldn't do anything to gain an advantage." Other players were equally supportive. "Since when do we have rules officials making calls from the television audience?" they asked. My intent was never in question. No official on the course had cited my infraction. Nobody in the group with which I was playing pointed it out. The sole factor leading to my disqualification was the TV viewer's call.

For the next several months the Tour experimented with having an official in the broadcasting booth, similar to the NFL's dalliance with "instant replay officials." Yet it seemed almost ludicrous to have an official making calls on action taking place in eighteen locations at once! Fortunately, the PGA Tour decided the video official was an intrusion into the game.

My disqualification at Doral greatly affected my mental attitude. I didn't win another tournament for the remainder of 1991. But if the television disqualification and the video officials' pictures upset my game, they could not compare with the effect that the images showing up on Dr. Frank Jobe's X-ray machine would have on my life.

CHAPTER TWENTY

THE SHOULDER BIOPSY

Since the mid-eighties, the PGA Tour has provided a hospital fitness trailer for the benefit of the professional golfers at each tournament site. Besides receiving basic medical attention, Tour pros visit the fitness trailer for physical therapy and injury-preventing exercises. When the trailer first started showing up on the Tour, I stopped in one day to introduce myself to the staff. "Hi, I'm Paul Azinger. Nice to meet you guys. Oh, by the way, you will never see me in here."

The guys there laugh about that one to this day.

I felt that the fitness trailer was a crutch. I figured anyone going in there was probably looking for an excuse or "babying" an injury. Obviously, I had the wrong attitude about that.

By June 1991 I was ready to retract all my negative thoughts about the medics. The pain in my shoulder was killing me, and a visit to the fitness trailer was sounding more and more inviting.

At the U.S. Open in Minnesota, I played a practice round Tuesday, after which I went to hit balls on the driving range, as I usually do at tournaments. I interrupted my practice long enough to give an interview for a national television show. Then I returned to the range, though feeling a little stiff, and hit some more balls.

The next morning my shoulder hurt so badly I could not reach out far enough to put my hand on my knee, not even from a sitting position. Besides the pain, the shoulder felt hot to the touch on the bone. I decided it was time to visit Dr. Jobe, who was also present for the U.S. Open.

● ○ ●

Dr. Jobe was the head of the Kerlan-Jobe Center of Sports Medicine at Centinela Hospital in Los Angeles, under whose auspices the Tour fitness trailer is operated.

When I went to the trailer, I couldn't even take my shirt off. Dr. Jobe had to gently help me remove it. He gently probed the shoulder area, just barely touching it. But oh, did it ever hurt! Dr. Jobe said it might be something as simple as tendinitis or bursitis, due to overuse, but he was really concerned about the pain I was experiencing on the bone. He ordered an MRI at a hospital for later that day, Wednesday. The first round of play was scheduled for the next day.

I returned to the house that Toni and our family and some friends had rented for the week. For the trip to the hospital I borrowed a car from the owners of the house, a tiny, convertible MG sports car with no top. It had a four-speed gearshift on the floor, which I could hardly maneuver because my shoulder hurt so much. I had to shift left-handed, or let my mom, who was with me, shift the gears from the passenger's seat. We drove that way for more than an hour.

After registering at the hospital, we sat in the MRI center waiting room. I had no idea then what an MRI is. I looked in the room and saw two large machines that looked a bit like washing machines with tubes extending from them. Whatever an MRI was, it seemed rather ominous.

● ○ ●

An MRI, I was soon to find out, is a magnetic resonance image, similar to a fancy X-ray. A technologist explained that I was to lie face up on a special scanning table that is then inserted into the tube. Instead of radiation, the "tube" machine creates a magnetic field, then shoots radio waves into your body and measures the response with a computer. The result is an extremely accurate, three-dimensional image or picture of the inside of your body. The technique allows doctors to look inside your body while avoiding surgery, X-rays, and pain.

A little girl about seven years old took her turn in the MRI room ahead of me. I figured, *If she can do it, I can do it!*

I was next. The doctors slipped me onto the table and instructed me to remain as still as possible. Everyone then left the room. Slowly the scanning table began to move me into the MRI unit. As I entered the tube, I could feel a fan blowing on me and could hear whirring, clicking, and light thumping noises. The technologist had warned me not to be alarmed at these strange sounds, but they still sounded eerie.

The procedure itself didn't hurt, and except for having to remain completely still for about twenty-five minutes, I felt no discomfort other than the pain in my shoulder. When the MRI was all over, the table slowly moved me back out of the tunnel.

I watched as the radiologist examined the pictures right there. He seemed particularly interested in a dark spot on the acromion, the bone on the end of the shoulder. Dr. Jobe looked at the MRI results and became seriously concerned. He said, "I need to biopsy this right away."

I felt panic. *That's cancer!* I thought. Outwardly I tried to maintain my composure and asked, "Why do you want a biopsy?"

"Well, we just want to make sure," Dr. Jobe replied. "We want to know what it is." I didn't know a lot about biopsies, but I knew enough that this was something to be concerned about.

● ○ ●

On the way back to the golf course Mom and I again negotiated the stick shift in our topless convertible. To make matters worse, it started pouring down rain.

I had an eleven o'clock tee time on Thursday morning. My shoulder didn't hurt quite as much as it had the day before, but it still caused me to cringe when I pulled my shirt on. I played the first round of the U.S. Open with a very sore shoulder and a very heavy heart and mind. All I could think about was that biopsy. I couldn't concentrate on the tournament; as a result, I missed the cut by one shot. Little did I know that it would be nearly three months before I could play golf again.

A week later I checked into Centinela Hospital in L.A., where Dr. Jobe performed surgery on my shoulder. He extracted some bone matter for the biopsy, then also removed some scar tissue that he found in the shoulder area. Finally, he removed the bursa sac, which contains the oily substance that reduces the friction between the muscle and the bone. When the bursa sac becomes inflamed, the result is known as bursitis; Dr. Jobe and other doctors whom I had consulted in the past thought that this might be the cause of my shoulder pains.

● ○ ●

Payne Stewart, who ended up winning that 1991 U.S. Open, called me at the hospital to see how I was doing. Payne understood how serious biopsies can be, because he had recently lost his father to cancer.

When the biopsy report came back from the pathologists, two of the three doctors who had attended to me said they thought there might be cancer in my shoulder bone. But they weren't sure. The report was reviewed by a battery of bone specialists, and they overwhelmingly came to a different conclusion:

It was definitely not cancer, although they could not say for certain what it was. One doctor, however, did encourage Dr. Jobe to watch me, because he had seen this sort of cell develop into cancer.

Dr. Jobe promised to keep a sharp eye on me and my shoulder. He never mentioned that doctor's concern to me, but he emphatically ordered an MRI for me every six months between the summer of '91 and the summer of '93. It wasn't until December 1993 that he told me of the lone doctor's dissenting opinion.

After the operation in June of '91, the pain completely disappeared from my shoulder. I felt great! Dr. Jobe was confident, too, that whatever the problem, the surgery had helped alleviate it. He said my rehabilitation required six to seven weeks of healing and therapy. It actually turned out to be ten weeks before I could play golf again.

I wanted to play in the '91 PGA. I committed to play in that tournament and even made the trip to the golf course. When I arrived there, however, I realized I was not yet ready and had to withdraw. A new player was ripping drives down the fairway during the '91 PGA; his name was John Daly, and he won his first tournament—a major—that week.

● ○ ●

A few weeks later, I went to the Fred Meyer Challenge, a tournament started by Peter Jacobsen as part of his personal crusade to bring professional golf back to the great Northwest. I played for the first time in more than two months. It was a good tournament for a comeback, especially because there was no cut to make. I played well and felt my confidence returning. Ben Crenshaw and I were partners in that event. Ben put on a putting exhibition, of which I was the main benefactor. We won! Thanks, Ben. It was great to be back.

The next challenge, however, promised to be much more intense. Despite my abbreviated season, I still qualified for the U.S. team in the upcoming Ryder Cup matches.

CHAPTER TWENTY-ONE

HAZARDS ON AND OFF THE COURSE

After the disappointment of tying the Ryder Cup matches in 1989, which allowed the Europeans to retain the trophy, Captain Dave Stockton needed no extraordinary pep talks to get our U.S. team motivated and ready for the 1991 "War on the Shore." We wanted to beat those foreign boys badly and take back the cup. In addition, we were playing the matches on our home turf, at the Ocean Course on Kiawah Island, South Carolina.

My shoulder had healed well, and I was feeling healthy for the first time in longer than I could remember. It was great to be able to go to sleep at night without the nagging pain in my shoulder. It felt even greater to be able to hit a golf ball without having to worry about arc pain.

I was taking the Ryder Cup matches as seriously as ever, right from the opening ceremonies. This was my second Ryder Cup in succession, so I knew what to expect and was aware of the intensity of the play. For whatever reason, I put my "game face" on early. I didn't talk much or smile a lot. My mind was already on the golf course, imagining some of the best golf of my life.

● ○ ●

It was only fitting, after my conflict with Seve Ballesteros in 1989, that Chip Beck and I should draw Seve and Jose Maria Olazabal for our first alternate shot match. There's nothing like taking on Europe's best first thing in the morning! Seve and Jose had never been beaten in Ryder Cup action when they played together. Chip and I were hoping to end their streak.

Nor was it any surprise that before the end of the second hole, we were embroiled in another conflict over what I considered to be a controversial drop of their ball. We had another question over their lost ball on number four. It went like that all day long, just one bit of controversy after another. By the ninth hole I was livid. When Jose hit his drive way off to the right, I was right there to help spot the drop. The referee was intimidated by Seve and Jose, so he simply stood aside and waited to see how we would settle things. Seve and Jose wanted to drop the ball much farther up the fairway from where I thought the ball had gone into the water. We argued over it for a while, and finally Seve looked at me with disgust and said, "Okay, where do you want us to drop the ball?"

"You need to drop it right back here," I said as I pointed to the original position I had indicated. Reluctantly Seve dropped the ball at that spot.

I walked over to Chip "Mr. Positive" Beck, and said, "I am not saying another word to these people. If there is another problem, you are bringing it up."

We didn't have to wait long before the next problem arose. On the tenth tee Seve and Jose accused Chip and me of hitting the wrong compression balls. In truth, we actually had hit the wrong compressions earlier in the match. But we had not intended to deceive anyone.

In alternate shot play, one player gets the odd-numbered tees and his teammate the even ones. Today Chip had the odd holes. I was playing a 90-compression ball and Chip was playing a 100-compression. Because a 100-compression ball is wound more tightly, it should fly farther.

When we got to number seven, which is a par 5, Chip was going to hit my 90-compression ball off the tee in the hope that I could put our second shot with the 90-compression ball onto the green. Looking at the distance, however, I was a little skeptical. I said, "Chipper, I'm not sure we can reach this green. If you hit your 100-compression ball, then I can lay up, and you can hit your 100 onto the green."

Chip said, "That's a good idea; I like that." Chip teed up his 100 and blasted it out the fairway.

Now we had made a mistake. Chip was supposed to hit the 90. Seve and Jose overheard us talking about this, and red flags started waving in their minds.

On number eight, a par 3, I hit the correct compression ball off the tee, as did Chip on number nine. And after nine holes we were 3-up on Seve and Jose. Then on number ten tee, they called for an official and charged us with playing the wrong balls.

I was furious! I could not believe this was happening, especially after all the other questionable incidents we had endured during this match. The four of us and the official engaged in a heated discussion right in front of the huge gallery around the tee, with television cameras recording it all on tape for the whole world to see. Finally the official ruled in Chip's and my favor, because Seve and Jose had not brought up the infraction on the hole in which it had occurred. No penalty was assessed.

Although Seve and Jose had not received a favorable ruling, they had succeeded in breaking our momentum. That's no excuse, of course, but Chip and I were so shaken by all this commotion that we three-putted the next green. Our game went downhill from there. Seve and Jose turned theirs around, coming on strong in the back nine to beat us 2 and 1.

Later that day Chip and I played Seve and Jose again. I played the match of my life, making eight birdies, and they still beat us! We lost 2 and 1 again. That loss was really heartbreaking for Chip and me.

Throughout our matches—throughout the entire '91 Ryder Cup, actually—Seve continued to pull little stunts that helped me better understand why, prior to the '89 Ryder Cup, Curtis Strange had warned me not to let Ballesteros pull anything on me. During these '91 matches Seve seemed to come down with a severe case of sporadic throat-clearing. It usually struck just as a player was approaching his ball. Seve later blamed the problem on allergies to sand and dust.

● ○ ●

For my finale I drew Olazabal in singles. Jose was playing the best tournament of anyone on the European team, so I knew this would not be an easy match. Moreover, the U.S. team had suffered a disastrous Saturday in which the Europeans had come close to sweeping all four better-ball matches in the afternoon. Even our stalwart captain, Dave Stockton, later admitted that Sunday morning was the first time he even considered the possibility that we might not win.

Day three of the Ryder Cup got off to a rough start for the U.S. team. Raymond Floyd fell to Nick Faldo; Payne Stewart lost to David Feherty; and Mark Calcavecchia tied with Colin Montgomerie. As one after another of our guys bit the dust, the pressure for me to beat Jose increased accordingly.

When Jose and I teed off, we didn't say a word to each other. We were both still smarting from our opening matches. Besides, words were not necessary in this match. This was war. It was the most incredible match I have played in Ryder Cup competition. It was not my best golf ever, but the seesaw battle with Jose made it an extremely exciting day.

Jose was brilliant. I never felt as though I had him beaten. We tied four holes of the eighteen. I had to save par on sixteen with a huge sand wedge blast, followed by a twelve-foot putt that slammed into the hole to keep me even with Jose. I finally went 1-up on Jose on the seventeenth after I sank an eight-footer. When I won eighteen as well, I let out a shout that must have scared people as far away as the clubhouse!

Now the entire Ryder Cup match came down to one man, Bernhard Langer, on the last hole. As Bernhard lined up his six-footer, the pressure was enormous. If he makes the putt, we tie again, at 14 to 14, and the Europeans take the Ryder Cup back home with them. If he misses, the cup resides in the United States.

The thousands of spectators surrounding the green at Kiawah fell silent. Millions more, watching on television, stared intently at Langer's ball lying motionless on the green. In the background the multicolored flags of the nations represented in the Ryder Cup flapped loudly in the wind. Bernhard stroked his putter toward the ball. The ball rolled toward the hole ... and missed by an inch. The U.S. had reclaimed the Ryder Cup!

Our celebration was like no party I had ever attended. Golf doesn't have the tradition, like NFL football, of dousing the coach at the end of a super performance. Instead, we simply tossed our captain, Dave Stockton, into the Atlantic Ocean, as part of our congratulations.

● ○ ●

Sadly, back in Europe, Bernhard took an awful pounding in the foreign press because of that final, missed putt. It was unfair. What his critics conveniently forgot was that Bernhard had sunk a crucial eight-foot putt on sixteen to keep the match alive and then poured in another one of equal distance on the seventeenth green. Although I was happy for our U.S. team when Bernhard missed that last putt on eighteen, I was just as delighted for him when he won the next two tournaments he played on the European Tour.

Seve Ballesteros was especially upset by the U.S. victory in 1991. Once again I was the object of his wrath. Following the '91 Ryder Cup, Seve told the press, "The American team has eleven nice guys ... and Paul Azinger."

During the matches I had told reporters that I considered Seve the "King of Gamesmanship." I was referring to his "allergies," his habit of walking while other players were hitting, and some other distractions. I wasn't saying anything that most of my colleagues hadn't said numerous times in the locker room, but now I was saying it publicly.

Eventually, I feel, Seve went too far. During an interview he accused me of taking an improper drop during our singles match in the '89 Ryder Cup at the Belfry. That comment really got under my skin, but I kept quiet about it. I knew Seve was wrong, and I could prove it. I had the videotape of the tournament, including Peter Kostis's comment, "A strange thing has just happened. Seve walked across the fairway and told Paul where to drop the ball." I felt vindicated.

Finally, at the end of the year, at Tryall in Jamaica, I approached Seve on the putting green. I said, "Seve, we have to put an end to all this gossip. What is this about me taking a bad drop?"

"No, no, no, I never said this," Seve replied defensively. "I said the referee gave you a bad drop."

"Seve! You told us where to drop it!"

Seve stared at me sort of quizzically for a second. Then we went on to talk about some of the other times when we had grated on each other.

Seve said, "You say to me, I am the King of Gamesmanship. This hurts me. This hurts me deeply."

"Seve, I'm sorry," I said sincerely.

He said, "It's okay. I say some things sometimes just to hurt you, just to let you know how much you hurt me. But you know, this is like old toilet water. We'll flush this."

And we did. We have gotten along well ever since.

● ○ ●

The Ryder Cup matches in which I have played hold deep meaning for me. Part of it is that the Ryder Cup has been a real stepping-stone in my career. Raymond Floyd once said, "You usually don't win a major until you have played a Ryder Cup," and that adage holds a lot of truth. If a player can deal with the pressure there, he can deal with it anywhere in golf.

There is also the sense of American pride I feel during those matches.

In that spirit of patriotism, one exciting fringe benefit of being on the Ryder Cup team is a visit with the President at the White House. Before I made the team, the closest I had ever gotten to the White House was driving by the grounds on my way to the Kemper Open, which is played near Washington. Imagine how awed I was when the kid who grew up saluting sergeants on a military base actually got to stand in the Oval Office!

George Bush was the President during my first visit to the White House with the '89 Ryder Cup team. I was thrilled just to meet him and his wife, Barbara, but I was amazed when the President called me by name. I may never get over that simple fact: He knew me.

The former President loves golf. He had a synthetic-grass putting green out of public sight on the lawn behind the White House. I have an artificial turf putting green on my back porch, and when I told him mine was made of the same kind of material, we got to talking.

The entire team and our wives were invited to join President and Mrs. Bush at the putting green to have some photographs taken. After the formal photo session, the President and I hit a few chip shots to his "green." There we were, the President of the United States and the professional golfer, acting just like a couple of guys practicing our chipping out on a driving range—except that we were both wearing coat and tie.

A White House photographer snapped a picture while the President and I were chipping. President Bush later sent me the picture of him hitting while I was "studying" his form. He signed the photo: "Paul, stop laughing. This is a new, improved technique. Watch and try not to copy." You just have to love a guy like that!

The team got to see the Bushes again in '91.

● ○ ●

My visit to the White House as a member of the 1993 U.S. Ryder Cup team took a totally different twist. As has happened before in my career, some of my unguarded comments created quite a commotion. I jokingly told Payne Stewart that the election of Bill Clinton was great motivation for me. Payne was puzzled.

"Yeah, my goal is to play well enough to make the Ryder Cup team so if they ask me to visit the White House, I can say no."

Payne understood my joke and thought it was rather funny.

I did ask my father about the matter, and he said emphatically, "You should definitely go. I want you to go."

At the U.S. Open at Baltusrol, when a reporter asked me about the pending visit, I replied, "I don't want to do anything to disrupt the team before, during, or after the matches. If Tom Watson [the team captain] wants us to go to the White House, I'll go."

I was not the only member of the team who was reluctant about meeting the Clintons, and the press knew it. Later in the week the same reporter asked Payne Stewart about his feelings, and Payne jokingly replied, "Well, I know Azinger doesn't want to go. He told me his dad fought in the Vietnam War, and he doesn't want to shake hands with a draft dodger." Payne was trying to be funny, and the reporter knew it. Besides, the reporter had already talked to me and had my quote on the record.

Overnight the story became big news on sports pages, with headlines like AMERICAN TEAM SAYS NO TO CLINTON.

Payne and I were shocked the next day when we saw the newspapers. On the putting green the next day, I commiserated with Payne about it. I said, "What were you thinking about, man?"

"You said it, didn't you?" Payne answered.

"Sure, I said it to *you,* but I didn't say it to the press! I wasn't saying it to the whole world!"

Payne hung his head and said, "I'm sorry, buddy. It was a bad joke."

"Payne, I don't think you realize what a mess this is going to be."

I was right. The night the '93 Ryder Cup team arrived in Washington, everyone was fairly uptight. Julius Mason, who runs logistics for the Ryder

Cup, met us at the airport. Julius is the "go-to" guy, the person team members go to when they don't know where to go or what to do. Julius was concerned. He said the White House staff had heard about players sounding off about the President and had asked him whether we really wanted to be there. Julius assured us that he had diffused their agitation. "I told them, 'Why, yes! Of course, the team wants to visit with the President.'"

"So you basically lied to them, didn't you, Julius?" I deadpanned.

Julius didn't know me well at that time and wasn't accustomed to my sense of humor. Finally he caught on and bellowed, "Aw, you're funny, Paul. You're so funny!"

● ◯ ●

The team was scheduled to have dinner that night with our families and officials of PGA of America, then meet President Clinton at the White House early the next morning. The dinner was to be a semiformal, coat-and-tie affair. Before leaving for the dinner, I told Tom Watson that a friend of mine had two masks, one of the President himself and one of Hillary Rodham Clinton. I asked Tom whether, as the team captain, he minded if I wore the masks at the dinner as a joke. Tom said he didn't mind.

I talked Lee Janzen into wearing the "Hillary" mask, and I wore the "Bill" mask. When we arrived, the room was full of people, and there were more chatting outside on a little porch deck.

Lee and I put on our masks and barged through the room and out onto the deck, where I raised my voice in my best imitation of the President and said, "May I have your attention, please?"

It was a horrible impersonation. I cracked a couple of really dumb jokes about Arkansas and said a bunch of other silly stuff.

To Lee's surprise and mine, nobody laughed. Everyone just stared with a look somewhere between stark terror and absolute embarrassment. Several team members rolled their eyes at me as if to say, "Shut up, Zinger! Shut up!"

Although they maintained their professional golfers' cool demeanor outside, our teammates were panicking inside. They knew something Lee and I did not—that a top member of the Clinton Administration had joined us for dinner.

Finally Lee and I learned what was going on. We felt terribly humiliated at the time.

The administration official didn't seem upset at all. Later in the evening, when he stood up to speak, he began by saying, "I didn't realize my boss was going to be here tonight." He thought it was really funny. Apart from Lee and me, he seemed to be the only one there who did.

● ○ ●

When President Clinton walked out onto the White House lawn the next morning to greet the team, he headed straight toward me. I wasn't sure how he would react to me—or I to him, for that matter. *What will he say?* I wondered. *Worse yet, how should I respond?* I assumed that the President was aware of my comments and Payne's that had been in the press. Perhaps he had heard about last night's dinner debacle as well. I honestly expected him to say to me, "I didn't dodge the draft!"

Instead, the President looked me right in the eye, and in his soft, southern drawl, he said, "I need to take a bunker lesson from you."

He really caught me off guard with that. "Heh, heh," I laughed politely. "Yeah, I guess so." I mean, what do you say when a President says something like that to you? Agree with him, and let it go. I mustered the "brilliant" comeback, "You know I'd be happy to give you one if you wanted it." And there went my ambassadorship!

President Clinton moved down the line and shook hands with everyone on the team. Then Tom Watson presented the President with a golf club and gave him a lesson on the grip. In mock seriousness, Tom instructed, "Mr. President, if you grip it too far to the right, you'll have trouble with the left. But if you grip it too far to the left, you'll have trouble with the right. So the idea is to grip it somewhere in the middle...."

The President finished the line. He quipped, "I know, I know. You're supposed to grip it right down the middle. I've been trying to do that my whole political career."

● ○ ●

As much as I love talking about politics, my true love is the game itself. All of my Ryder Cup experiences have been exciting, but the 1991 matches were especially meaningful to me.

Being a part of the winning Ryder Cup team helped me finish 1991 on a positive note. I followed that with a sensational 1992, but ironically did not win on the Tour all year long until the last tournament of the season. I did win the BMW Open in Germany, but that was not part of the PGA Tour.

I started the season with a near-miss at the Hawaiian Open, coming in second at Waialea Country Club, two strokes behind John Cook. I had several other brushes with victory early in the year. I finished among the top-ten money leaders in three of my first four tournaments. Of the twenty-three Tour tournaments I entered in '92, I had ten top-ten finishes.

I had at least one win on the Tour in each of the past five years. But as 1992 was slipping into the record books, I realized that I had only one more chance—the Tour Championship—to stretch my streak to six years in a row, the longest current consecutive-year victory streak on the Tour.

The 1992 Tour Championship was played at Pinehurst Resort and Country Club in North Carolina. A tough course under any circumstances; it becomes impossible if a player is not hitting the ball well. Coming into Pinehurst, I had had trouble with my putting, so I wanted to make a change. Most players fall back on the tried and true when the pressure is on. I usually do, too, but not this time.

I decided to switch putters for the tournament. I chose a putter called "The Thing," which was anything but the usual for me. It was one ugly-looking stick. When Greg Norman saw me using "The Thing" on the putting green, he laughed and said, "Is that a practice tool, or what?"

I said, "No, this is what I'm using this week."

Greg shook his head and said, "No way!"

Despite the appearance of "The Thing," my putting improved. I turned in a 5-under, 66 for the second round and moved into contention. A third-round 69 gave me a three-stroke lead over John Huston. Then in the final round I played par golf, shooting 71, which was enough to beat Lee Janzen by three strokes and bring home $360,000, the largest purse on the Tour that year. Besides the money, I did keep my consecutive-year victory streak alive. I finished 1992 seventh on the money list, earning a total of $929,863. Not bad for winning only one tournament!

I was now a highly visible player, winning big money. I was a prime candidate for endorsement deals of all sorts. Many businesses wanted to pay me to put their logo on my clothing or have me play using their equipment. Other companies wanted to use my name on their products. Endorsements are a normal part of professional sports today. Pro sports probably could not survive, as we now know them, if it were not for corporate sponsorships and television contracts, all of which are involved in the scene to get the biggest bang for their advertising buck.

Similarly, some sports celebrities will advertise just about anything for whoever puts up the most money. But from the very beginning I have tried to be involved only with products I could believe in. I have turned down lucrative deals when I could not honestly endorse the product or when the company ethics violated my value system. My first endorsement deal with a nationally known company or product was with Tropicana, makers of orange juice and other citrus-related products.

I also endorsed a local Cadillac dealership. In return, I was given a brand new Cadillac to use, free of charge, every year I was under contract with them. I gave each car to my mom and dad. It only seemed right, since Mom and Dad had given up their Cadillac to help Toni and me get started in the motor home. Now it was our turn to give back to them.

Early in my career I was too busy playing golf to worry much about endorsements, so I simply turned over all my business dealings to my father. Dad poured himself into the job of looking out for my interest, and it was nice to have someone I could trust handling my financial affairs. But as the level of my success rose, my business dealings became more and more complicated.

Dad had retired from the air force and was now also retired from his position as president and co-owner of the Gulfwind Marina in Sarasota. It wasn't fair for me to expect him to have to constantly compete for my interests in the intense, high-stakes, lawyer-saturated world of big-money sports contracts. I knew I needed a management company.

I had met Robert Fraley back in 1987. Robert was the founder of Leader Enterprises, a management company in Orlando that specializes in handling sports figures. Both he and his wife, Dixie, were extremely gracious, down-home folks. I liked Robert right away, but in 1987 I was just starting to make a name for myself in professional golf and Dad was taking care of business matters. I didn't see any need for an agent or manager.

By the end of 1991, however, whether I wanted to or not, I had to take more of an interest in my business dealings. I called Robert Fraley for help.

● ○ ●

One of the first projects in which Leader Enterprises helped advise me was a difficult one. A few years earlier, I had naively signed an endorsement deal with a company that sold golf equipment. The deal looked great on the surface. I would be a one-third owner of the company. That was the positive side of the deal. The negative side was that I had virtually signed my life away to this company. Without the advice of an attorney, I had unwittingly signed over all licenses to my name for golf-related activities.

I now know I was extremely foolish ever to sign such a deal. At the time, however, I was naive and preoccupied with trying to win tournaments, not sell golf equipment.

Not long after I signed on with Leader, Robert Fraley and I were discussing my business ventures with the golf equipment company. Robert asked me straightforwardly, "How are you going to make money in that deal?"

Just as directly, I replied, "I don't know. I don't like it. I want out." Robert did some investigating and discovered that the chances of my ever making any money with this company were slim.

About the same time, the most prominent partner in the company besides me walked away from the deal. That put me in a 50-percent ownership position, but I still felt as if I was locked up for life.

One of my first sponsors when I turned professional as a golfer was a friend and lawyer. I asked him to examine my contracts with the company. He couldn't believe his eyes. "Do you realize what you have signed?"

"I have no idea."

"You are bound for life!" my lawyer friend said with a horrified expression on his face.

"But what can I do about it?"

The lawyer recruited two other attorneys from his office, and together with the help and advice of Robert Fraley and Rick Neal from Leader Enterprises, they set about the task of renegotiating my contract to one that was less restrictive.

Extended negotiations took place over what seemed like an eternity. Finally a settlement satisfactory to both parties was worked out, and my freedom to pursue other business opportunities was restored.

What a relief to get this behind me! I realized now more than ever that I had not been a good steward of my business dealings. The Bible teaches us that we are accountable for how we use our money, abilities, and influence, and I was beginning to understand the potential hazards and enormous responsibilities that go along with being a more highly visible player.

The next sand trap I faced would be on a golf course.

CHAPTER TWENTY-TWO
A BUNKER MENTALITY

When I first started on the Tour, all bunker shots terrified me. Hitting a ball out of a sand trap was the weakest part of my game. I recognized the weakness and determined to do something about it. I knew I would never be a good player unless I learned to get out of bunkers and got over my fear of them.

I spent countless hours practicing bunker shots, with no significant results. Finally, with the help of Marc Arnette, who was taking some lessons from Davis Love's dad, I came up with my own style of hitting bunker shots out of the sand.

I created my own simple, but effective system, basing my entire bunker game on what is "normal" for me. Once I learned how to get out of the bunker with a normal full swing, I established that as my standard of "normal." I studied how far my "normal" shots went, then established the sand on my home course as my standard of "normal" sand. No matter where I played, I compared the texture and depth of the bunker sand to the sand at home.

I also noted that my "normal" weight distribution during my swing was 50–50 on each leg. I started to experiment: What would happen if I made a normal swing with 70 percent of my weight on my left leg? How about the opposite? I noticed that if my weight is on my right leg, the ball goes farther than if it is on my left leg. Moreover, with my normal swing, the less sand there is in the bunker, the further the ball goes. Now, when I get in a bunker, I am digging, not to get footing, but to see how much sand is in the bunker. If there is more sand than my normal, I know I have to swing a little harder than my normal.

I worked hard to establish my system, hitting literally thousands of balls out of bunkers in practice. I would stay in the bunker for three hours at a time until every aspect of my "normal" bunker shot was ingrained in my mind. This system can work for any amateur—but you must be willing to work hard for two or three hours at a clip as you try to establish your own standards of "normal."

When I committed myself to becoming a better bunker player, I also changed slightly the path of my swing during bunker shots. I got farther away from my ball, squatted down closer to a sitting position, and tried to take the club back a little bit lower. I try to fully release the club with my hands, with my club face very open, but I never let the club face turn over.

Another bunker secret I have learned has to do with the follow-through after the swing. My normal follow-through is about hip-high without turning the club face over. But when I have a close-in shot, when the ball has to hit the green with one hop and plenty of backspin, I will pull the club right back after contacting the sand, almost like a shotgun recoil. The ball comes out with a bang, but then backspins to a nice, slow roll.

On the "fried-egg" bunker shot—when the ball is buried in the sand so deep you can scarcely see it and it looks like the yolk on a sunny-side-up—I position myself with the ball back a little farther than my normal, and when I hit down on the back of the "egg," I don't ever follow through. I explode the sand beneath the ball and recoil immediately, and the ball pops up nice and softly. I am a pretty good fried-egg bunker player now; before I went to this technique, I could barely get the ball out of the bunker without its costing me strokes.

To me, the time-honored, inviolable principle that you have to hit a bunker shot two inches behind the ball is a farce. That condition has no bearing on the shot. Yet, for years that was all I had ever heard, and I was the worst bunker player you can imagine. As in most other aspects of my game, I decided to ignore what everyone else said and go with what works for me. Consequently, I went from being scared to death when my ball landed in a bunker, to being one of the top five bunker players in the game.

Like most players, I used to regard bunker shots as the toughest shots on the course. Now hitting out of a bunker is really a whole lot of fun for me—usually. I wasn't so sure at the 1993 Memorial.

● ○ ●

I did a lot of tarpon fishing during the spring of '93 and used my fly rod quite a bit. Maybe it was all the fly-casting I did in the Florida Keys, or maybe it was the excessive ball-beating I was doing on the golf course, but around April I began to notice a slight pain in my shoulder. I thought, *Oh, no! Not again!* I found, however, that if I took it easy for a few days, the pain would disappear. I decided to take a break for a few weeks and skip several tournaments before the Memorial.

As a result, coming into Muirfield Village, I was feeling terrific. The pain had receded, and I was hitting the ball superbly. During the first three rounds I played my way to the top of the leader board. As we began the last round, only one guy was ahead of me—my good friend, Payne Stewart. Since Payne was leading the tournament at 14-under-par and I was in second place at 11-under, we were paired.

On the first tee I wished Payne luck and then repeated a comment that Larry Nelson had made to me one time at the Atlanta Classic. I said, "Look, if I go bad today, I don't want you to worry about me. You mind your own business and play your own game." I thought that was an appropriate comment to make to Payne because he had a good shot at winning the Memorial, and if I stumbled, I didn't want my buddy to feel bad about me. (Later I made the same comment to a good friend, Bobby Clampett, at the New England Classic, and he really appreciated it.)

As it turned out, I was hitting the ball great, but Payne made some early mistakes. He hit it in the water on number five when he was trying to lay up. I eagled number seven with one of my best 3-woods ever. Right after that Payne hit it in the water again on number nine. When we finally got to eighteen, Payne was still one shot ahead of me. Corey Pavin had posted, and I was tied with Corey.

Payne hit a 1-iron off the eighteenth tee. The ball went straight up the right side of the fairway, hit the ground, and took off—perfect. My 1-iron went up the left side, hit the ground, and stopped dead—plugged. I had 212 yards to the hole, with at least 194 yards to carry the bunkers. I decided to hit a 5-iron, which landed in the green-side bunker. I am usually a positive person—hitting out of bunker is fun, right?—but since I was one shot behind, I thought, *I can't win this tournament.*

Ironically, Payne's second shot ball landed in the same bunker where my ball was lodged. Payne is a great bunker player, but his ball was buried.

I stood to the side of the bunker and watched Payne hit his shot. I was almost sure he couldn't get that thing within twenty feet of the pin, but he hit the greatest plugged, fried-egg bunker shot that I have ever seen under those conditions. He hacked the ball to eight or nine feet from the hole. What a shot!

I needed to get this bunker shot close.

I closed my eyes and pictured the bunker shot I wanted to hit, going through the motions. I cocked my wrists, wielding an imaginary sand wedge, feeling how I needed to nip it and how I needed the ball to land. I played the entire shot in my mind before I picked up a club.

I stepped into the bunker, settled into my stance, and swung the club as hard as I could—considering how short the shot was—trying to get as much spin on the ball as possible. The ball popped up and out of the bunker beautifully—just clearing the edge—hit the ground about ten feet from the pin and started to trickle. It also started to break toward the hole. At the same time, I lowered myself back down into the bunker, with both of my arms straight up in the air, with my left hand gripping my sand wedge down near the club face and my right hand raised with palm outstretched like a traffic cop.

A friend later asked me, "Did you know that ball was in the hole early or what? As soon as you hit it, your arms went up."

I wasn't celebrating. I wasn't saying, "Yes, it's in!" I was saying, "Whoa! Whoa! Stop!"

The farther the ball rolled, the lower I squatted in the bunker, peering over the edge almost as if I were afraid that if the ball caught me watching, it would suddenly change direction. I felt like a parent who sees a child doing something cute, but you don't want the kid to know you're watching or she will stop doing it. My arms were still up in the air, and I started to lose sight of the ball as it curled and disappeared into the back of the hole.

I yanked off my visor, dropped to my knees, shut my eyes, and shouted to the heavens.

Suddenly it occurred to me what had happened: I had holed the shot, and now Payne could lose. Strangely, I was no longer as concerned about winning as I was about Payne's losing. Payne had been through some grueling, close defeats recently. Remembering how I had felt losing at Doral when Greg Norman chipped in on the first hole of a playoff, I didn't really want to hand Payne one more tough loss.

Payne was visibly stunned as he stood over his putt. He missed the eight-footer, which would have taken us to a playoff. Instead, I had the victory. Worse still, he blew his remaining two-footer and dropped to third place in the tournament.

● ○ ●

I had mixed emotions when Payne missed. I didn't know whether to laugh or cry. Certainly I was glad I had won. But I felt bad that my friend had lost. I went to him immediately, while we were still standing on the eighteenth green.

"Payne, I am really sorry."

"It's okay, bud," Payne replied. "That's part of it. That's the game."

We walked down to the Tour tent, and again I tried to console him as we signed our scorecards.

Again Payne said, "Hey, don't worry about it."

There was nothing else to say. Payne Stewart has had some great victories in his career along with those tough defeats. He handles both with grace. True champions don't make excuses. They accept the good with the bad; they can hold their heads high in victory or in defeat because they know they have done their best.

Payne Stewart is a true champion.

● ○ ●

Winning the Memorial kept my consecutive-year winning streak alive. I had now won at least one tournament in each of the past seven years, the longest such streak on the PGA Tour. Little did I know that I would soon be battling, not to keep my streak alive, but to keep myself alive.

If timing is everything, God's timing must be perfect. I won the Memorial Tournament in May, and by June the pain in my shoulder had returned full force. Anytime I threw my fishing net too long or tossed a baseball too hard, I could hardly lift my arm the next day.

The pain continued to intensify, but I tried to ignore it. I see now that I was being naive, but at the time I was playing some of the greatest golf of my life. I wasn't about to let the knotty areas that I felt on the bone of the scapula slow me down. To the contrary, I was having a stellar year.

A few weeks after the Memorial, I played in the U.S. Open at Baltusrol. I was still hitting the ball well, but the shoulder was bothering me more. Almost on a whim, I stopped in at the Centinela Hospital fitness trailer. Dr. Lewis Yocum, Dr. Jobe's colleague, was there, so I told him about the knotty areas in my shoulder. He said, "Let's have a look."

I removed my shirt, and Dr. Yocum began feeling around my shoulder. He found the hot spot on my scapula and said matter-of-factly, "I think we need to do an MRI."

I readily agreed. I wanted to find out what was happening inside my shoulder so I could get it fixed and get on with my game. Besides, doctors had been doing MRIs on me every six months since 1991, when Dr. Jobe had performed arthroscopic surgery on the shoulder. Doctors had done a biopsy at that time as well.

Although the biopsy reports had been negative, I must admit that just having one done had made me nervous. Almost everybody knows what doctors are looking for when they do biopsies. Undoubtedly, a biopsy can tell a doctor a lot about a body, but the one disease on everyone's mind is usually the unmentionable. "The Big C." Cancer.

In 1993 I had another MRI and a bone scan after the U.S. Open. When Dr. Jobe viewed the results, he didn't like what he saw. The MRI, according to Dr. Jobe, showed some abnormality in the bone. He wanted to do another biopsy right then and there, but I refused. The doctor reluctantly agreed to wait until after the New England Classic. I won that tournament, but the pain was becoming excruciating. The antibiotics and anti-inflammatory medicines I was on by that time helped, but only a little.

Then came the PGA Championship at Inverness and the Friday night phone call. Seeing the results of my latest MRI, Dr. Jobe again insisted on doing a biopsy. No doubt, the words of that lone pathologist in 1991 were ringing in Dr. Jobe's ears, reminding him to keep an eye on me. Once again I managed to stall the good doctor.

● ○ ●

This is where God's timing comes into play. Had we done the biopsy at the time of the PGA Championship, Dr. Jobe later told me, we might have missed the cancer in my shoulder. The cancer cells may not have been developed sufficiently to the point of showing up in the biopsy. I would have gone on my merry way, thinking I was okay, and the bone cancer cells would have continued to grow. I don't even like to think about what might have happened then.

We did another MRI after the 1993 Ryder Cup matches, but there was no significant change in my condition. Throughout the entire summer and fall of 1993, I was experiencing severe discomfort, yet the pain always seemed to subside after taking the anti-inflammatory medicine. Had my back not gone out at Greg Norman's Shark Shoot-Out, I might have continued to simply endure the pain.

I wasn't about to complain. I was thirty-three years of age, was feeling fairly bulletproof, and was having a great year. I had won a major for the first time in my career plus two other impressive tournaments. I ended the regular season number two on the money list, winning $1,458,456, just $20,000 less than Nick Price, who took top honors and the Arnold Palmer Trophy.

I never mentioned the soreness in my shoulder to members of the press or to my fellow players. No one except my doctors, my caddies, and, of course, Toni, knew that nearly all my PGA Tour victories had been won in the presence of pain.

Then came that fateful day in December when the truth was discovered, and the whole world found out what I did: Paul William Azinger had cancer.

CHAPTER TWENTY-THREE

DID THE CANCER SPREAD?

P aul! Paul?" I heard Toni's voice calling me.

I was still holding my head as I stepped out of the restroom, where I had gone to throw up shortly after Dr. Jobe told me that I had cancer.

"Paul, are you all right?" Toni asked as she and Dr. Jobe hurried down the hallway toward me.

"I'm fine," I answered, rather unconvincingly. We walked arm in arm back to Dr. Jobe's office. His secretaries had taken Sarah Jean and Josie somewhere, so Toni and I sat down and listened quietly as Dr. Jobe explained what would happen next. He mentioned that my treatment may require six months of chemotherapy and possibly some radiation treatments, too, but we wouldn't know for sure until the oncologist, Dr. Lorne Feldman, reviewed my tests. Dr. Feldman was the codirector of oncology at Centinela Hospital and was one of the best oncologists in the business, Dr. Jobe assured us. The first step was to determine whether the cancer had spread to any other areas in my body.

Toni, the girls, and I walked across the hospital parking lot to the oncology center. Dr. Jobe was to rejoin us later. When we entered the lobby of the center, the reality of cancer struck us once again. I stood there and just cried on Toni's shoulder. We held onto each other for dear life.

By the time Dr. Feldman came down to meet us, I had already been directed to the X-ray room. He explained briefly to Toni what was to happen. They would take some blood, shoot some X-rays and another MRI, remove some bone marrow, and wait. It would take three days to assess the extent of the disease in my body with any certainty. That assessment would dictate the regimen of treatment.

Meanwhile, I sat in a small room where I put on a hospital gown and submitted to giving blood samples. I was then sent to the waiting room for X-rays.

A half-dozen or so other people were already sitting there, so I sat down to await my turn. Toni joined me there while some secretaries and nurses entertained Sarah Jean and Josie.

At last a nurse called me into the X-ray room. In the dark, windowless room, a technician helped me onto a sheet-covered, but ice-cold table, where I immediately began shivering, partly from the cold temperature in the room and partly from sheer fright.

The technician adjusted the machines, went behind a barrier, and started taking pictures, periodically coming out to reposition me on my side, my stomach, my back. The X-rays, which should have taken only ten or fifteen minutes, seemed to take forever. The technician kept making mistakes; his machine wasn't working right, he said. All the while, I was shivering.

As I lay on the table in that cold, dark room, stripped of all the elements everyone associated with my supposed success, the thought struck me, *I could die from this cancer!* And suddenly the reality hit me: I am going to die eventually anyhow. Whether from cancer or something else, I am definitely going to die. It is only a question of when.

When you are thirty-three years of age, hardly sick a day in your life, and sitting on top of the world, you rarely think about dying. Now death was staring me right in the face. Worse still, I sensed that I could die soon. And I was downright scared.

Beyond that, I suddenly realized that I was not the one in charge. I had long prided myself on steering my own destiny, calling my own shots, and being in control of my life. Now, with just a few puffs of air from a doctor's lips, control was wrenched away from me.

In that same moment, I recalled some words spoken to me many times by Larry Moody, my spiritual mentor, who directs a Bible study on the PGA Tour. Larry always said, "Zinger, we are not in the land of the living going to the land of the dying. We are in the land of the dying, going to the land of the living." In a much deeper way than ever before, I began to understand what Larry was talking about.

My PGA Championship, the ten other PGA Tour victories, my house, the boat, the cars, my bank accounts—all the material things of this world suddenly became meaningless to me.

All I wanted to do was live.

● ○ ●

After about forty-five minutes the X-ray technician finished his job and escorted me to the door. I got dressed again, and by that time Dr. Jobe had returned. I was being summoned to the other building to get an MRI. Over there, Toni and I were the only ones in the waiting room.

The whole ordeal was turning into a surrealistic blur. I sat there, almost dumbfounded, watching a newscast on a television in the waiting room. I thought, *How trivial so many events in the world suddenly seem!* It was a weird feeling.

About that time I encountered another strange, new sensation. I realized that everyone who was working on me and with me knew that I had cancer. I became extremely self-conscious. I was certain that anybody who looked at me was thinking, "Hey, this guy has cancer."

I felt sympathy from them. They knew I was shaken up; they could see it in my tearful eyes. The staff at Centinela had a way of being extremely professional, yet compassionate. That was something different for me. I was not accustomed to receiving compassion. Scrutiny, admiration, nit-picking observation, analysis, yes; but to be the object of this sort of compassion was a new experience, and it made me even more uncomfortable.

Before the MRI, a nurse injected me with sodium fluorescein, a fluid that looks like iodine but is actually an enhancement agent to help make the details of the magnetic resonance image show up more clearly. The technologists laid me on the scanning table and then left the room. I had been through numerous MRIs, but this one seemed interminable. Actually, it took only forty minutes—but every minute of my life was now precious to me.

Dr. Jobe was waiting when Toni and I left the MRI center. He led us to the room where I originally had some blood work done before my shoulder surgery. Here the doctors would remove some bone marrow to check for the presence of cancer cells. Again I waited. Phlebotomists hurried back and forth, in and out. I thought, *They must be drawing blood from patients all over the hospital!*

Three doctors wearing lab coats—two men and a woman—came into the waiting area. I noticed that one of the guys had on blue jeans, and for some reason it struck me as odd. I wondered, *Is that guy a real doctor or just someone off the streets?* They took me into a small but brightly lit room in which there was only one piece of furniture, a table against the wall.

One of the doctors said, "We're going to draw some bone marrow."

I nodded in understanding.

"It's gonna hurt," the doctor continued. "It's going to feel like somebody punched you, but it is only going to hurt for a second."

"Okay."

"Just unbuckle your pants."

I unbuckled my pants.

"Get up on the table."

I got on the table, and the guy pulled my pants down. He said, "I want you in the fetal position." Talk about going back to the womb! I lay motionless with my back to the woman, who was busy preparing all kinds of test tubes and small rectangular pieces of glass on which she was ready to smear blood and whatever other samples they needed.

The doctor said they were going to numb my hip, and they injected me with two shots. Within minutes my hip was numb.

The doctor said, "Okay, now you're going to feel this needle hit the bone, and it's going to break through the bone into the marrow."

"Okay," I replied compliantly. I watched as the doctor injected the needle into my hip, but I couldn't feel it break the skin. Nor could I feel it go through the flesh. But I did feel it when the needle hit the bone. The needle was stout and thick, and the guy was really pushing hard, and I felt it break through the bone. I could hear it crunching, but it didn't hurt. It only hurt as they were sucking out marrow. Wham! I felt as if a boxer had just slugged me as hard as he could. It hurt terribly, but it was over that fast, too. One second. It left a nasty little bruise on my hip, and I limped for two days.

I zipped up my pants and got out of there. By then, it was late afternoon, and Dr. Jobe wanted me to see Dr. Feldman. Would it never end? Dr. Feldman checked me over, top to bottom, examining lymph nodes all over the neck, all around the arms.

Technically, he said, I had a disease known as *lymphoma,* a form of cancer that is eminently curable. But they had to determine the extent of the disease in my body. He wanted me back at the hospital on Saturday morning to do another test, a CAT scan. He instructed me to drink a "contrast" several hours before coming to the hospital and gave me a bottle. I had to drink two ten-ounce cupfuls of the stuff—the colder the water, the better.

Toni and I thanked the doctors, went to gather up the children, and drove to our hotel.

Back in our rooms, we were still operating in a daze. The kids were hungry and tired, so we hurriedly fed them and put them to bed. We didn't try to explain anything to them at that point—we were barely grasping things ourselves. We merely told them that Daddy had an early morning doctor's appointment and that Mildred Henderson was coming up from San Diego again to stay with them. When Mildred arrived, Toni and I retreated to our own room.

● ○ ●

Toni and I didn't say much. It had been a long day, and we were physically and emotionally exhausted. We collapsed onto the bed and tried our best to sleep.

My appointment for the CAT scan was at eight o'clock on Saturday morning. I got up at five o'clock to drink the "contrast." I didn't have any really cold water, but I tried to drink it anyway. It tasted awful. I wasn't able to keep very much of it down.

Toni heard me struggling with the "contrast" and came to my rescue. For the first time, I began to open up my feelings to Toni about being diagnosed with cancer. I cried on her shoulder as I told her I didn't want to have to go through all this. I couldn't even manage the "contrast," and that was only the beginning of this nightmare. I just didn't know if I could make it through this.

Toni wrapped her arms around me. "We're going to make it, Paul," she kept saying as she buried her head in my chest. "God is going to help us."

Toni had not allowed herself any emotional outbursts on Friday, not when Dr. Jobe had told us the horrifying news, not while I was having my tests done, not even during the bone marrow removal. She felt she had to be strong for me, so she somehow kept herself from falling to pieces. But on Saturday morning, she shut herself in the bathroom and opened up to God. She poured out her heart in prayer and asked the Lord to help us.

Now, as I was pouring my heart out to her, she kept encouraging me just to trust the Lord. I nodded in understanding. Then I attempted to drink the "contrast" one more time. This time I was able to keep it down.

CHAPTER TWENTY-FOUR
CHANGING MY TOP PRIORITY

A weekend goes by quickly when you are relaxing around the house or casting a fishing line out on the water or playing eighteen holes. But when you are waiting to find out if a deadly disease has ravaged your body, three days seem like an eternity. Yet, in many ways that three-day period of uncertainty was a life-changing experience for me. It was a time to collect my thoughts, to sort through my feelings, and to realize what is truly important in life.

We arrived at Centinela early on Saturday morning to prepare for the CAT scan, now known as a CTT scan—computerized transaxial tomography. Dr. Jobe was already there. He explained that the CTT scan is used to detect tumors, blood clots, or other abnormalities in a body. The CTT scan is similar to an MRI, except that it focuses more on one "slice" of the body at a time rather than the overall image. Unlike regular X-rays, in which dense tissues such as bones can block the view of body parts behind them, the CTT scan "sees" all.

Once I was able to get the "contrast" down, the actual CTT scan was a relatively simple process. It meant more time lying still and quiet on a scanning table, which was inserted into another giant washing-machine-type ring. While I was in the tube, the technologist and radiologist were examining the computer generated images on a screen in another room.

The technologist invited Toni to sit in the screening room, but she declined. Toni later said everything looked like a tumor to her, and she decided she did not want to subject herself to watching the screen while not knowing what anything meant. Her nerves didn't need that extra stress.

After the scan, the technologist said it did not look to him that the cancer had spread. The oncologist would have the official word, of course, but we were nonetheless encouraged by these words.

Dr. Jobe stayed with us all morning until the completion of the scan. He, too, seemed cautiously optimistic, even though the definitive test results would not come until Monday.

We were all the way across the country, thousands of miles from home, from close friends and family. In some ways that increased our sense of insecurity, considering all the decisions to be made and the details with which we had to deal. In other ways, it may have been a blessing in disguise. We had little time to sit around and brood on my condition; and there were many distractions involved in living out of a suitcase.

We had been away from home for more than three weeks, and most of the clothing I had with me in my suitcase was "golf course clothing." I decided that if I had to stay in California any longer, I wanted some casual clothes. Since there was nothing else medically to do until Monday, Dr. Jobe recommended we visit a nearby mall.

● ○ ●

It sounds like a Gary Larson *Far Side* cartoon caption: "On Saturday, after all my tests were completed, not knowing if the cancer had spread, the Azinger family filed to a shopping mall." But that's what we did. The mall excursion proved good for me. It took my mind off blood tests, bone marrow, CTT scans, and the myriad medical details, the meaning of which we were still trying to absorb.

Our first stop at the mall was a restaurant to have lunch. I took one look at the menu and immediately ordered only healthful food. Then we went shopping for some new clothes. The mall was decorated for Christmas, and the girls got to see Santa Claus, which to their young minds was a lot more fun than hanging around a hotel waiting for Mom and Dad to return from the hospital.

When we returned to the hotel later that afternoon, Toni and I decided that our emotions were stable enough to call home and inform everybody what was going on. The first call was the toughest—to my mom and dad. Mom and Dad had been out west to attend the Grand Slam of Golf and the Shark Shoot-Out, so they were aware that I had seen Dr. Jobe and was having another biopsy. So in one sense they were prepared to receive the news. Nevertheless, no parents want to believe that their child has cancer.

I was afraid of falling apart emotionally, so we agreed that Toni would talk to Mom and Dad first. When she dialed my parents' telephone number, it was about 9:00 P.M. in Florida.

When my mom answered the phone, Toni started as gently as possible. "We have bad news. Paul has cancer." Toni talked briefly to my mom, and then I got on the line. I wanted to sound as positive as I could.

"Dr. Jobe told me that this is the most curable cancer I could have," I told Mom. She assured me that she and Dad would be on a plane to California as soon as possible.

My mom is a strong woman, but when she got off the phone and told Dad, she broke down and wept. Dad was crushed by the news, and held Mom. "He's going to beat that," he said soothingly. "No doubt in my mind, kid. I know our boy is strong. Paul is going to beat that." Mom and Dad consoled each other for about an hour before they called the other family members. By then, Dad had raised Mom's spirits.

Dad knew well the debilitating effects of cancer. His father had died from cancer at the age of fifty-eight, when Dad was only twenty-four. Dad had attended his bedside and had given him pain medication every two hours for three years as he watched his father's life slip away. Now, with the news that his boy had cancer, Dad maintained a firm attitude that I was going to beat this thing.

My next call was to my agent, Robert Fraley. Robert and Dixie were good friends, and they had always been there for us in the past. They didn't fail us now. As my agent, Robert had the unenviable responsibility of preparing a press release, informing the world that I had cancer.

● ○ ●

Sunday morning we awakened bright and early, not because we wanted to, but because the hotel fire alarm was going off! People were running every which way in the darkened hallways, looking for the fire escape. No doubt, visions of *The Towering Inferno* and other high-rise building fires filled many minds. It was bad enough that I had cancer—now I had to rescue my family from flames!

We called Mildred's room, and there was no answer, so we assumed she had already headed for the stairwells. Toni and I gathered the kids and hustled outside onto the fire escape. We stayed out there until the "all clear" report was given by the fire officials. It had been a false alarm.

Once the elevators were functioning again, Toni went downstairs to get something. Passing through the hotel lobby, she noticed a sign announcing a Sunday morning church service to be held in one of the ballrooms. A group of believers was meeting there each week while their own sanctuary was under construction. When Toni returned, she asked me if I wanted to go. She sure didn't need to twist my arm! If God had been trying to get my attention lately, he had definitely succeeded.

Toni again helped me to get ready. She had to help me bathe, wash my hair, and put on my clothes during this entire ordeal because I still couldn't move my right arm as a result of the surgery that had been performed less than a week earlier. My shoulder was still bandaged, so I couldn't get it wet, and of course, I was not able to lift anything yet. We got through it, and finally I was dressed for church.

● ○ ●

We had been attending church services back home as a family, whenever I was home, and lately I had been reading some of Toni's Bible study notes. But as soon as our family, and Mildred with us, entered the ballroom, we could sense something different about this group of people. Everyone seemed happy! They were smiling as they greeted us and made us feel like smiling, too.

Nobody recognized me as we slipped into a row of chairs, took our seats, and waited for the service to begin. Soon the place became electrified. The people sang so enthusiastically; they prayed so sincerely. When they talked of Jesus Christ, it was not simply as a historical figure, but as a person with whom they had a deep, personal relationship. Many of the songs and much of the talk that morning was not simply *about* God, but *to* him.

There was so much faith and commitment being expressed in that tiny congregation that morning, it was astounding! It was obvious that God was there. I don't mean in some vague, ambiguous, generic sense; I mean God was *there!* I could sense his presence in the place, and so could Toni and Mildred and the kids.

● ○ ●

I had considered myself a believer in Jesus Christ for more than eight years, and I was sincere in my faith. But it is one thing to believe in him and quite another to trust him completely with your life. My Christian experience to that point had been inconsistent at best, and at times a total washout. Jesus was not the Lord of my life—I was. God was not my top priority—golf was. Winning tournaments and improving my standing on the money list were most important to me. Most of my decisions, often including those regarding my family, revolved around golf, golf, golf.

As I sat in the hotel church service that morning, I realized how trivial many of my priorities were. I began to see recent events as a cumulative "wake-up call" from God.

When things happen to us that we don't understand, we can scream, "Why me? Why me, God?" We can allow circumstances to drive us away from God. Or we can do an about-face and run to God and cling to him and find in him our security and our hope. I decided I wanted to run to God, and that's what I did.

In Dr. Jobe's restroom I had cried out to God to save me. On that cold, metal table in the X-ray room, I realized that one day, perhaps soon, I was going to die and that God was the One really in charge, not me. Now, at that hotel church service, I committed my life totally to the Lord. I decided that I was going to trust Jesus Christ, not only in this struggle against cancer, but with my life, all of my life, completely, for as long—or as short—a time as he gave me. I made up my mind that from this day forward, Paul Azinger belonged to Jesus Christ, not just for the remainder of my life, but for all eternity.

● ○ ●

Mom and Dad arrived later that afternoon. We all met downstairs in the hotel lobby. It was an emotional reunion, but I think they were surprised at my positive outlook and my sense of peace. Mildred returned home, now that my parents were there. We all turned in early that night.

Tomorrow we would find out how we were going to treat the cancer that we all knew was there in my shoulder, and we would find out whether the cancer had spread. With the renewal of my relationship with the Lord, I felt that, regardless of the report, I was ready.

CHAPTER TWENTY-FIVE
CHEMO NIGHTMARE

Monday morning dawned as another bright, beautiful California day. We slept in a bit and ordered breakfast in our rooms. We didn't dare leave the hotel for fear we might miss a call from Dr. Feldman's office. The call didn't come until early afternoon.

Thanks to my renewed spiritual strength, I was handling things much better by Monday, but I was still an emotional wreck. Prior to finding out about the cancer, the last time I could recall crying was when Mac McKee died in 1989. Now the least little thing opened up floodgates in my eyes. One such incident really struck me.

Toni and I were on our way out of the hotel to keep our appointment with Dr. Feldman. Someone in the elevator recognized me. "Hey! I just saw you on CNN!" he said.

"Oh, really?"

"Yeah, yeah!" the man gushed. "The volume was turned down on the set, so I didn't really get to hear the report, but you must have won Player of the Year. Congratulations!"

When the elevator reached the main floor, the man went his way and I held onto Toni as I led her to a corner of the hotel lobby. The tears streamed down my face. What the fellow had seen, but had not heard, on CNN was the announcement that Paul Azinger has cancer.

● ○ ●

By the time we reached the doctor's office in the oncology center at Centinela Hospital, I had regained my composure. Dr. Feldman took us to a small examination room, where we sat down prepared for the worst but hoping for the best.

181

"I have good news for you," Dr. Feldman began. "The cancer is localized, and there is no evidence of any spread beyond the right scapula."

Toni and I wanted to shout! We squeezed each other's hands. The cancer had not spread to the lymph nodes; it was not in my bone marrow or any other part of my body. *Thank you, Lord!*

Dr. Feldman was still speaking. "Lymphoma in the bone is more rare than in glandular tissue, occurring in only about 5 percent of the cases, but the statistical cure rate is about 90 percent. Our treatment plan calls for six chemotherapy injections, once every four weeks, followed by five weeks of daily radiation therapy. Most patients resume their normal activities soon after completing the radiation therapy. In your case, our expectation is for a total cure."

The doctor further explained that this plan of action was not his decision alone. He had consulted with specialists in New York and Houston and at UCLA, and the entire team of doctors had concurred that the disease could best be treated this way. Feldman said there was even a possibility that I may not need the radiation treatments, but he would wait and see.

Next Dr. Feldman explained how the chemotherapy would be done. It would be an intravenous injection, administered right there in his office. Each treatment would take about ninety minutes. Chemo is a systemic treatment, he explained, that went wherever my blood traveled in my body. It would kill off the cancer cells in my shoulder and also any rogue cells that may have broken off and were hiding out somewhere else.

He looked at my hair, which fell softly down over my forehead, almost to my eyes. "Your hair will definitely fall out," he said matter-of-factly. "You will wake up some morning and find a few strands on your pillow case, then the next morning there will be more. Many chemotherapy patients lose all body hair within the first month or two of treatment. Others take longer, but inevitably it will happen, so expect it." Dr. Feldman smiled. "But don't worry; it will grow back after we're done."

Almost everyone gets sick after a chemo treatment, he said, but the degree of sickness and nausea varies greatly from patient to patient. I would also be on a steroid and a medication called neupogen. They were necessary to help prevent infection, because the chemo thwarts the growth of healthy new cells at the same time it is killing the bad ones.

Finally he asked, "Any questions?"

Toni and I had a zillion questions, but none of them seemed to matter right at the moment. We shook our heads.

"All right, then," said Dr. Feldman, "let's get started."

● ○ ●

We entered the room where the chemotherapy was to be administered, and I received a pleasant shock. I guess I expected to find such a powerful, serious treatment administered in a stark, very sterile environment. Instead, what we saw were several patients receiving treatment at the same time, all seated comfortably on chairs and couches and looking extremely relaxed. One person was reading the newspaper; others were laughing and telling jokes.

Dr. Feldman introduced me to Dede Gallagher, the clinical nurse specialist assigned to my case. She was to play a very vital role in our lives over the next six months. Dede and Toni had met on Friday while I was receiving my diagnostic tests, and they had already struck up a fast friendship.

I was then led to a more private room, and Dede began hooking me up to an IV of clear liquid and explaining the procedures. Suddenly she stopped and looked me right in the eyes. "This chemo that we're giving you is going to just eat that cancer up. If you had a tumor the size of a baseball or a softball—which you don't—this chemo would still melt it away. You'll get better." I was encouraged by Dede's confidence.

Dede hooked up another bag, this one filled with a red liquid. "This is the stuff that will make your hair fall out," she said sprightly. It was obvious that she liked her work.

Finally Dede got everything arranged, and the chemotherapy began. I received a thirty-minute bag of antinausea medicine and then a forty-five-minute bag of the red liquid. The IV was pouring the stuff into my system, but I did not really feel a thing. I simply laid my head back and shut my eyes.

I was on a regimen Dede referred to as C.H.O.P., consisting of four drugs: cyclophosphamide; doxorubicin, also known as adriamycin—the red stuff; vincristine; and prednisone, which is basically a steroid. Actually, as long as they killed the cancer in my shoulder, I didn't care what they called the IV components. I referred to them as "red drip" and "clear drip."

● ○ ●

While this was going on, Dad arrived and cornered Dr. Feldman in the hallway outside his office. "Doctor, I know you said Paul has a 90 percent chance of recovery, but tell me about the 10 percent that are not cured."

Dr. Feldman replied, "I don't think Paul falls in that 10 percent. He is so physically sound, I think he is way above the 90 percent."

"Thank you," Dad responded. "That's what I was hoping to hear."

I finished the treatment around four o'clock in the afternoon and walked out of the hospital feeling great. Toni and I gathered up the family at the hotel and went out to eat. I ate well that evening, downing a good-sized portion of lemon chicken.

When we were back in the hotel, Payne Stewart called me to see how I was doing and to encourage me. He sounded surprised to hear how buoyant my spirits were. I described a few details about our weekend and said, "This is a cakewalk, Payne. Chemo is a piece of cake. I'm going to smoke this thing, buddy. The doctor says this cancer is beatable, the most curable kind. Chemo was easy. It was a snap."

Payne was delighted to hear the good news. Too bad it was a bit premature.

I was mentally prepared not to be sick. I had even prayed that God would prevent me from getting sick. But about eleven o'clock that night, I woke up in bed with a headache. I got up for a few minutes, then laid back down, wide awake. Before long I began to feel a quiver in my stomach, like butterflies flitting around inside me. It got worse. Around midnight I awakened Toni and said, "I think I'm going to be sick."

I was right. Ten minutes later I threw up for the first time. Twenty minutes later I threw up again. From then on, for the next nine hours, about every fifteen to twenty minutes, I was spitting up. After the first few times, there was nothing left inside me to come out except yellow bile. Nevertheless, my body continued to convulse with "dry heaves" all night long. Each session lasted anywhere from five to seven minutes. Afterward, I would collapse onto the bed or a chair, gasping for air, and then suddenly it would start all over again.

The children were sleeping in an adjoining room, and we hoped they would not hear the frightful sounds emanating from their father. But they did.

At one point I thought I could go into cardiac arrest. So around four o'clock Toni called Dr. Feldman, who told her that nausea was normal for some patients after chemotherapy. He suggested we come in first thing in the morning, when office hours began. We felt he had no idea how bad my condition was.

Toni called my parents, and they promised to meet us at our hotel room. When my father saw me there, he was horrified. When he last saw me, I had looked perfectly normal. Now I looked more like an emaciated prisoner of war—and in a way, I guess I was. My body was so weak, I could barely walk down the hotel corridor. I shuffled along, carrying a wastebasket in my hand, for obvious reasons.

Once outside the room, smells started to bother me. The hallway smelled awful; the parking lot, terrible; the car, horrible. Even the fresh air was repulsive to me. Because my olfactory nerves were playing tricks on me, everything in my life stunk . . . literally.

I rode all the way to the hospital with the wastebasket between my legs. When Dr. Feldman saw me, he immediately recognized that my postchemo response was not normal. I had what is called intractable nausea. I could have told him that much!

Dede quickly injected me with antinausea medicine and then hooked me up to an IV to replace the fluids and electrolytes in my system. Then they gave me medicine to put me to sleep. I slept in the doctor's office until after five o'clock in the afternoon. When I awoke, we returned to the hotel. Apparently the antinausea medicine worked, and I was much more comfortable that night.

● ○ ●

We stayed in California a few more days. I slept for most of Tuesday, and Dr. Feldman checked my electrolytes on Wednesday to make sure I was not dehydrated. I was injected again to replace the lost minerals in my body.

After each chemo treatment I was to receive a daily shot of neupogen for ten days to prevent infection, but I was too weak on Tuesday to handle much of anything, so they started on Wednesday. Dede gave me the first one and taught Toni how to give the shots. Because she had worked her way through college as a phlebotomist, Toni caught on quickly. Her college line—"You've got good veins! I'd like to stick those veins!"—was coming to pass.

The neupogen shot was just a tiny needle, injected into my thigh. My bones ached for days afterward. I felt as though I had a mild case of the flu, which was ironic since that was exactly the kind of thing the neupogen was meant to prevent.

Finally, on December 9 we packed our bags and prepared to leave our California home. We checked out of the hotel, but not before someone had stolen our telephone credit card numbers. For the next few months, every time we received our telephone bill, we found expensive long-distance calls to various locations around the world.

Going through the Los Angeles airport sapped me of what little strength I had been able to recoup. I looked a mess and felt a mess, but it was great to be going home. I had been gone since mid-November, when I made the trip to play in the Grand Slam of Golf. I couldn't wait to see the turquoise waters of the Gulf Coast of Florida once again.

When we finally arrived home and pulled the car into the driveway, we saw an amazing sight. Our outdoor Christmas lights were up and turned on. Our home was completely decorated, including a large *Z* in the window facing the road.

Our neighbors and friends, the Geigers, Steve and Scott Pleis and their dad, Bill, and my brother Jed had wrangled a house key out of Janet, our babysitter, and had dug through the storage room until they found our Christmas decorations. When I saw this beautiful sight, I could not hold back the tears as I realized how much these friends cared for my family and me.

It felt good to be home.

CHAPTER TWENTY-SIX
WILL I GET BETTER?

The first few days we were home, I would spend hours in our backyard, just walking around, looking at the flowers and the trees, or watching birds through binoculars. I wanted to buy a camera and film wildlife. I was getting so mellow, it was beginning to scare me! I thought that perhaps the chemotherapy had damaged my brain and had transformed me into some sort of politically correct, left-wing, liberal nature lover. Whew! Happily, that sensation wore off relatively soon.

It was different for me, however, being home with no golf tournament to prepare for and no prospect of playing golf for a long time. Fortunately, it was December and the 1993 golf season was drawing to an end. Under ordinary circumstances, I would have been off for a few weeks at this time of year anyhow.

Our days were quite busy just answering the telephone. It would start ringing early in the morning while I was still in bed and would keep on ringing all day long, every day, when we were first home. Some days we received more than forty calls. Among the well-wishers were President Bush, Senator Sam Nunn, and NFL football coaches Bill Parcells, Joe Gibbs, and Dan Reeves. Bobby Bowden, the football coach at my college alma mater, Florida State, sent a football along with his best wishes. Jack Nicklaus and just about every other player on the Tour called. Greg Norman called me several times.

Many of the people who called weren't sure how to approach me now that I had cancer. But I was still the same Zinger. I was a little weaker, but I had not suddenly turned into some unapproachable person who had to be pampered and handled with kid gloves. I quickly discovered that when people called to encourage me, it was an ideal opportunity for me to be an encouragement to them. In every conversation I would tell the caller, "This cancer is beatable. We're gonna beat this thing."

● ○ ●

Then the cards and letters started pouring in, even though in a press release I had tried to encourage people to support their local Cancer Society rather than send cards to me. Still they came. At first I planned on answering each one personally, but then they started coming by the hundreds, then by the thousands. The outpouring of love, support, and encouragement I received was truly amazing, and I will always be grateful for it.

Besides all the wonderful cards and letters, I also received more than fifty health and nutrition books within the first month of being diagnosed with cancer. I appreciated people's kindness in sending us these books, but for the most part my diet was already fairly decent before I got cancer. You can't survive the Tour lifestyle for long eating junk food. On the Tour as well as at home, I ate a lot of fruits and vegetables with a good bit of salad and very little red meat. My one vice when it comes to food is sweet stuff. I love my desserts!

I also received numerous letters suggesting alternative treatments for cancer to replace the chemo and radiation I was scheduled to undergo. Some letters said, "There is this place in Mexico that can treat cancer...." Others said, "There is this doctor in France who has found a cure...." Still other letters were critical of the nation's health care system, saying, "The U.S. doesn't really know what it is doing in the area of cancer treatment."

Some of the letters were hilarious. One letter is indelibly impressed upon my mind—unfortunately. It was three pages long and had a heading: GUARANTEED CURE FOR CANCER. That got my attention right away, but I soon realized I was wasting my time. The "highlights" of the writer's suggested regimen were the following:

- For three hours, sit three inches higher than your normal sitting height; normal dining room chair height. (I guess I was supposed to sit on a telephone directory or something similar.)
- Drink one glass of carrot juice while sitting up. Then go immediately into a hot bath for thirty minutes, as hot as you can stand it. When you get out of the bath, vigorously pat yourself, every inch of your body from head to toe; don't forget the ears, don't forget the genitals.
- Eat a banana. Then massage the anal wall with your finger....

By the time I got to that point in the letter, I was convinced the cure was worse than the disease! I was nearly rolling on the floor laughing.

I disregarded most of the homemade cures for cancer that I received from friends, relatives, and well-wishers. It wasn't that I thought I knew so much, but I had confidence in my doctors, and I knew that God had given them the wisdom and knowledge to help me get well.

● ○ ●

One aspect of my having cancer that Toni and I hadn't anticipated was the impact it would have on Sarah Jean when she returned to school. Many of her friends and even some well-meaning adults said, "We're so sorry your dad has cancer."

Toni and I had avoided using the word *cancer* around Sarah Jean and Josie because they knew people who had died of cancer and we did not want to frighten them. We simply said things such as "Daddy is sick" or "Daddy's medicine is making him sick." Sarah Jean knew I had lymphoma, but I'm not sure she really understood what that was until she was back in school.

After Sarah Jean's first day back at school, a teacher who was a friend of ours, said, "Sarah Jean was visibly upset today because some of the children were saying that Paul has cancer."

That night Toni and I decided we needed to have a talk with Sarah Jean. Sitting on our bed, we explained as best we could that Daddy was sick right now, but that I was going to get better.

Sarah Jean looked at us with her "big-girl" expression and said, "Well, as long as he is going to be okay, I am not going to worry." After that, she was fine.

For me, acceptance didn't come quite so easily. Once I got over the sickness from the chemo, life became fairly normal. Yet the time I spent alone was different. Often I would be lying down and wonder if I was really getting better. Was the chemo doing what it was supposed to do? Would this cancer go away?

Although I had a new appreciation for life, every morning when I looked into my bathroom mirror, the reality of my situation would hit me afresh. I'd think, *Boy, you have cancer.*

● ○ ●

After I had been home about seven days, I was in the bathroom, going through my normal routine and sort of praying, when suddenly I sensed an unusual feeling coming over me. That's the only way I know how to describe it. It was as if God revealed to me that I would get better. There were no lightning bolts, no thunderclaps, no voices out of the sky—just a calm, peaceful assurance that I was going to get well.

After that, whenever I felt down or depressed, I would recall that feeling and that unspoken word. Whenever I started wondering and questioning, I recognized that it was the Devil putting doubt in my mind, and I treated it that way and rejected it. In my heart and mind I would continually go back to that revelation I had received that I was going to get better.

I don't want to suggest that God said that the cancer would never come back, or that he said I would never suffer any further hardships in life; but he did say that I would recover from this. I would get better. None of us are promised tomorrow, so I made up my mind I was going to live every day God gave me to the fullest.

From that point on, my struggle was not to face the fact that I had cancer. The difficult thing for me was dealing with the fact that everyone's perception of Paul Azinger had changed. I thought of Gene Littler, the great golfer who had suffered a much more severe case of lymphoma than mine. I had to admit that I never regarded Gene Littler quite the same after his bout with cancer, even though he survived the disease more than twenty years ago—when the odds were definitely against him—and went on to win tournaments on the PGA Tour and play well on the Senior Tour. But he was no longer simply "Gene, the great golfer." From then on, Gene was always: "Gene Littler, who survived cancer."

I thought, *That is the way everyone is going to look at me now. Paul Azinger has cancer. He is not healthy.*

When all the pressure to win a major was placed on me, I had always responded, "My goal is longevity. If I can stay healthy, I will have a great career." Now, almost overnight I was not healthy, and I felt that everyone who knew me, or knew about me, was looking at me differently from the way they did just a month before. Now they regarded me with a sympathetic eye. People who called or who saw me personally during the early stages of my treatment were likely to say, "I am so sorry for you." I greatly appreciated their sympathy and compassion, but I wanted to shout, "I am not dying! I'm getting better."

Rather than reinforcing negative thoughts, however compassionately expressed, I would return to that revelation I received from God that I would get better. At times when life seemed to be going in slow motion, I would ask myself, "Is this really happening to me?" I would get better. When I became discouraged or started giving Toni a hard time about my treatments or my shots, I would go back to that assurance God had given me, and Toni and I would talk about things and pray through them.

● ○ ●

Ironically, one of the first calls I received during the early stages of my treatment was from Gene Littler, and I will always treasure that phone call. He was a tremendous inspiration to me. After that call I began to consider that perhaps part of the reason God had allowed me to undergo my experience with cancer was so I could encourage and inspire other people who were fighting the disease.

I decided that I should keep some sort of record of my experience. After I had been home about two weeks, I began to write down my thoughts and feelings in a journal. I started by recording some of my initial reactions to the discovery that I had cancer:

> From Friday till Monday, I cried like a baby several times. I felt like I had no control of my life. No more golf. When can I go home? When will I get better? Am I going to die? What about my kids, my wife, parents, brothers, sponsors? I couldn't think straight. I was so scared.
>
> I love Toni so much. She is so strong and was there for me when I needed her most. I don't know what I would have done without her.

I went on to describe the spiritual transformation I had experienced. I was not easy on myself:

> My life has completely changed. In desperate times, people run to God. I am no different. I knew immediately that I wanted and needed God's help through this.
>
> My Christian walk had been weak, at best. In the past, I'd thank God after all my tournament wins, but that's about all I would do. My life itself has never been totally committed to Christ, only to myself and my desires. I've been a hypocrite for years.
>
> This experience has caused me to do an about-face to Jesus. I have asked Christ back into my life again, and this time, with all my heart. I pray for a complete renewing of my mind, and for my commitment to God for the rest of my life. God's grace is so good and salvation is a great thing, as well. Lord, I am totally committed to You forever and ever.
>
> I know there are thousands, maybe millions, of people praying for my recovery and that is such a great feeling. I know that God answers prayer, and I am so blessed by Him. To have that many people praying for me is overwhelming. I can feel their prayers working in my life, no doubt.

CHAPTER TWENTY-SEVEN
"CHARLIE BROWN"

As we approached the week of Christmas, my hair started falling out. True to Dr. Feldman's word, I woke up one morning and found some on my pillow. When I took a shower, even more hair came out. Nevertheless, I was not about to let cancer destroy our celebration of Christ's birth.

Right after Christmas I got together with some of "the guys" in our neighborhood for what was supposed to be an informal gathering at a friend's home. Unbeknownst to me, it was actually set up as a prank at Payne Stewart's expense. Gary Geiger, formerly the club pro at River Wilderness, had received a package from the superintendent at Muirfield Village allegedly containing sand taken from the "exact spot" where I had holed the bunker shot that beat Payne in the 1993 Memorial. The sand was supposed to be a gift for me, and a short note addressed to me had been attached. When Gary and the guys saw it, they couldn't resist pulling one on Payne.

Payne was coming over from his home near Orlando. Another good friend, Bob Delaney, is a referee in the National Basketball Association. Payne is an avid fan of the Orlando Magic and spends most of a game screaming at the referee about his officiating. It seemed only natural to bring Bob in on the joke. Payne and I were the only two people who did not know what was going to happen.

"Bobby D." intentionally arrived late, after Payne. And Bobby came bearing Christmas gifts for everybody—everybody except Payne.

"Hey, Bobby D.," Payne playfully protested. "Where's my Christmas present?"

"Payne, I'm really sorry. I didn't realize you were going to be here or I would have brought a gift for you, too."

Meanwhile, the rest of us were busy unwrapping our presents: great-looking NBA T-shirts. Payne's jaw dropped even lower.

Suddenly Bobby D. "remembered" that he had one more present. "You know, Payne, on second thought, I do have a gift for you."

Bobby D. pulled from behind his back another brightly wrapped package similar in size and shape to all of ours. "Here you go, Payne. Especially for you."

"Hey, thanks, Bobby D.!" Payne exclaimed. "I love T-shirts." He quickly tore open the wrapping paper and found the sand from the Memorial along with a note Gary had doctored to read, "Payne, Thought you might like to have this sand, from the very spot where Paul Azinger holed the bunker shot in the 1993 Memorial."

For a moment Payne sat speechless. He could hardly believe that someone would be so rude and callous as to rub in his defeat in such a way. It was one of the only times I have ever seen Payne Stewart speechless in all the years I have known him.

When I saw the sand—and the expressions on the other guys' faces—I figured out immediately that they were pulling one on us. We all burst out laughing. I jumped from the table and started whooping it up and running around the room.

That's when I really noticed my hair. As I ran around the room, I was leaving a trail of flying hair behind me. It was worth losing my hair just to see the expression on Payne's face. Payne had a good laugh about the episode later.

● ○ ●

A day or so before Christmas, my hair really started feeling kind of dead. When I washed it, I would just barely get it wet and then pat it dry. No shampoo, and no hairbrush. But all the care was to no avail. Each morning a bit more hair was showing up on my pillow and my shoulders.

On December 28 we had a party to celebrate Sarah Jean's eighth birthday. After the party was over, I was playing with about six or eight of the girls out on the front porch, just down the steps. I noticed some strands of my hair flying away, so I thought it might be fun to open the opportunity for all.

"Who wants to pull out some hair?" I offered.

"I do! I do!" squealed Sarah Jean. Once the birthday girl expressed an interest, the other kids wanted to join in, too. I lined up the girls and let them take turns pulling my hair out. It didn't hurt a bit, and the kids loved doing it.

They didn't get it all; they just got chunks. When I washed my hair that night, I soaked and scrubbed it. Down by the drain, an area about seven inches across was covered with hair. I came out of the shower, dried my head, and looked in the mirror. That was the first time I felt I really looked sick.

I wrote in my journal for December 30:

I'm almost bald. Hair is all over the house. I didn't think it would bother me to lose my hair, but it does. I feel like I'm looking sick, even though I don't feel sick. I guess it makes me realize that in reality, I am sick.

I started wearing scarves on my head, not necessarily to hide the appearance, but to keep my scalp warm. Even though we live in Florida, when I was lying down at night, my head got cold.

The kids thought my bald head was wonderful, and after a while I adopted their attitude, too. Sarah Jean got into the habit of calling me "Charlie Brown." Some mornings she would come into the bedroom and whisper in my ear, "Time to get up, Charlie Brown." Other times, I would awaken to find both girls kissing my bald head. They would coo "aah, aah, aah" as they kissed me. Occasionally they would just rub my head. It was quite a funny spectacle.

We watched a video of the musical *The King and I,* and the girls started calling me after the name of the leading man, Yul Brynner. I think it became one of their favorite movies.

● ○ ●

Apart from these episodes, life carried on in a relatively normal fashion after I was diagnosed with cancer. Except for the nausea caused by the chemotherapy and the throbbing pain I felt for four or five days after taking the neuprogen shots, I was functioning fairly well.

It did feel strange the first time I watched golf on television, knowing that I would not be playing for at least seven months. I watched the Johnny Walker World Championship from Jamaica. Toni, the kids, and I had at one time planned on attending that tournament.

It was close to Christmas, and my body was just shaking off the effects of the last neupogen shot in the first battery. My hair was beginning to fall out. I saw Colin Montgomerie chip to within about four feet and then miss his putt. Colin is a great guy, and he has a look about him that makes it hard to tell whether he is happy or unhappy with a shot. But on this occasion there was no doubt; Colin was definitely not pleased with his performance, and the TV camera caught it all.

As I watched Colin grimacing and grieving over a missed four-foot putt, I thought, *Look at that guy! He ought to be so happy he's able to be out there playing golf. He's complaining because he's missed a four-footer. Big deal! If he knew what I was going through, he wouldn't be complaining.*

I wasn't really criticizing Colin or feeling sorry for myself. As much as I was looking forward to the holidays, the calendar on the wall reminded me that it was only a few more days before I would have to return to Los Angeles for another chemo treatment. I was already anxious about it. I wrote in my journal:

> I am very nervous about going to LA for my next treatment. I'm kind of scared, I guess. I don't want to get sick again. I'm trying to change my frame of mind, because I know that the chemo will kill the cancer.

Soon it would be time to relive the nightmare.

CHAPTER TWENTY-EIGHT
A TURNING POINT

In some ways my second chemotherapy treatment was worse than the first. I didn't experience the intractable nausea, but my bodily systems were shocked by a violence that seemed as strong as the earthquake that shook Los Angeles a few days after we left town.

Our wedding anniversary fell during our stay in California. Because the kids were back in school, we left them with my mom and dad, but our trip was not exactly a romantic getaway. What a way to celebrate twelve years of marriage!

"Did you take your wife out for dinner on your anniversary?"
"No, I took her with me to my chemotherapy treatment."

Dede Gallagher was in rare form when she greeted us again. She loved my new "hairless" look so much that after I was done with my treatment, she went out and bought me a hat that said, "Having a bad hair day!"

I was determined not to allow things to get out of hand, as they had during the first treatment. Consequently, Dr. Feldman's office recommended some stronger antinausea medicine to take before the chemo rather than waiting until I got deathly sick and then trying to slow things down. In addition to the chemo, I received antinausea medication intravenously for two days, plus other shots to make me sleep. When nausea struck this time, it was not as bad as before.

We had made arrangements for Dede to stay at the hotel in a room next to ours so that she could give me more medications should I get sick. The sleeping drug knocked me out cold. I went to sleep about nine o'clock Tuesday evening and didn't wake up for twenty hours.

Waking up was as hard as coming out of surgery. I was in a haze; I had no idea how long I had slept or what day it was. Toni was stretched out next to

197

me on the bed, and instantly I could tell she had eaten Italian food. The chemo-heightened sense of smell was back. I asked her to please roll over and get on the far side of the bed.

I was really perturbed that I had slept so long and, worse yet, still got sick anyway. In fact, the nausea lasted five whole days, and it took a full eight days for my head to clear. I felt extremely weak during that entire time.

What's more, my back went out again. We had to summon a chiropractor to the hotel to snap my back into place.

I did try to go outside one day. I covered my head with scarves, and Toni and I went for a walk around the marina in Los Angeles. It was a beautiful day, but everything seemed ugly to me—the marina, the stagnant water. Nothing appealed to me. The sun was bright and hurt my eyes and my head. The nausea returned.

● ○ ●

When it was time for us to fly home to Florida, I was looking and feeling quite haggard. We were just getting comfortable in our seats when who should board the plane but Jay Leno, host of television's *Tonight Show*. Jay was casually dressed in blue jeans and a denim shirt and was being friendly to everyone who said hello to him. He walked down the aisle and sat in the seat catty-corner from ours. If he recognized me, he gave no indication of it.

An elderly woman was sitting next to him who obviously did not know Jay was a television star, and I doubt she would have cared if she had recognized him. She was a typical "Grandma Moses" kind of senior citizen who could probably get away with murder just because she was so old, rickety, and cute.

"Young man, young man," she kept badgering Jay, "can you help me with my luggage?" Jay cheerfully complied. He had no sooner sat back down than she was asking him to do something else. "Young man, young man, can you do this, can you do that?"

All the while, Jay Leno was just as polite as could be.

During the flight I was able to eat for the first time in five days, although all I cared to eat was a couple spoonfuls of yogurt and some croutons. I was very weak and emaciated, having lost twenty pounds since the first treatment. I weighed less than 160 pounds, and my face was drawn, with prominent cheekbones. My clothes did not fit anymore; both my jeans and my shirt seemed to hang on me. I had a black bandanna on my head, and a very long scarf that came across my shoulders. I looked nasty—really tough!

Midway through the flight, I got up to go to the bathroom. On the way back to my seat, just as I was passing by Jay Leno, the plane lurched a little. Weak as I was, I fell off balance—right in Jay Leno's lap!

Jay looked up with an expression that said, "Oh, this guy is really sick-looking!" and, "Help! There's a sick guy falling all over me!" Obliging as ever, though, he caught me and helped me to my feet. I shuffled back to my seat and sat down. I was too sick to talk. But I did laugh a little about it.

Leno was probably thinking, "Man, is this great material for next week's *Tonight Show!* Some derelict falls all over me in a plane." I was just happy I wasn't holding a glass of orange juice at the time.

● ○ ●

Back home, my own house smelled awful to me. For the next six or seven days, every smell made me nauseated—even Toni's hair, which I had always found fragrant.

The dizziness and headaches persisted. I was so weak, I could barely unscrew the cap from a jug of milk. My bones ached terribly from the neupogen shots.

I hated that neupogen! It must have worked, because I caught only one cold the entire six months between treatments. Nevertheless, the neupogen affected my mental outlook. It got to the point that I was in a bad mood all day when I knew I had to receive a shot. Once I got the shot, I couldn't sleep all night. Finally I decided I might as well get the shots early in the day so that we'd all be less miserable.

Since Toni was responsible for administering the shots, we had some good fights over her technique. Trying to coach her, I'd say, "Now, lift the skin up. Lift the skin up now. Get it up high. All right, now. Just stick it in there."

"Just hush up," Toni would say. "I'm doing it my way."

"Can't you just stick it in there like this?" I tried to show her. And we'd start fighting about it.

"If you can do it any better, do it yourself."

Toni tended to allow the skin to be too thin, and I would get impatient and disgusted. Once, because she didn't get enough flesh, she stuck me and poked the needle right out the other side of my skin. Toni was squealing and the neupogen was squirting out of the needle, so she jerked the needle out of my leg and promptly stabbed me with it again. Consequently, I really didn't have sixty shots. I got sixty-one shots, because Toni gave me one shot twice!

My bones would ache for four or five days after each series of shots. After one shot I jumped in a golf cart and wanted to drive down to the river, just to go sit by the water. But the road was a bumpy, dirt road that caused the cart to vibrate, which made my back hurt so much I had to go home.

The whole cancer ordeal reached its lowest point after that second chemo treatment. Much of my melancholy could be attributed to the medicine, but in part it had to do with the realization that the 1994 golf season was starting without me. Many players and golf personnel sent me greetings over the airways. It was touching, but tough to receive. After watching a tournament on television, I wrote in my journal:

> Monday, the 10th of January. I cried several times with Toni today. I was upset about the way I felt watching the first golf tournament of the year. I was really bad. It was really hard. Just not being healthy and unable to do the things that I'm used to doing anymore is the reality I face, but I couldn't take it.

The next day I became very angry and took my frustration out on Toni all day long. Toni hadn't done a single thing to deserve such treatment, but she was the only target available. Sometimes we lash out unjustly at those we love the most, and that's what I was doing.

For the next two days we really struggled. All my frustrations came pouring out. I didn't want to look at any mail. I didn't want to talk to anyone on the phone. I didn't want to get out of bed or take a bath.

I continued to cut Toni down for no reason. And finally she broke down.

Suddenly I realized how wrong I was. I apologized to Toni and asked her to forgive me, which she did. That was an emotional time for both of us. I was sorry for the way I treated her and sorry for her sake for being sick.

Slowly I regained enthusiasm and regard for the basic responsibilities of life, but I had help in doing it. I talked to Robert Fraley for over an hour on the phone one night. Then Larry Moody came to visit and spent the night with us. With Robert and Larry's help I came to realize that I did not have to be Superman. I didn't always have to say I'm all right. Certainly I didn't want anyone to see me looking sick or think I was down mentally and therefore get down themselves. But I had to recognize that there would be days of discouragement and that that's okay. I also had to accept that my life and my family's had changed and that none of us would ever be the same.

● ○ ●

The real turning point came when I received a phone call from a friend whom I had not heard from in a long time. He is a club pro, but he has always been a negative guy, easily upset on the course. When he called, I expected him to ask all the usual questions about my cancer treatment.

I said, "How you doing?"

He said, "Terrible." He told me how he had lost his job and had a multitude of other problems, and I said to myself, *I thought he was calling to see how I was doing!* All I could think about was what a selfish, insensitive jerk this guy was. Five minutes went by, and he never asked me how I was doing.

I felt like saying, "Hey, you jerk. You think you got problems.... I have cancer, for crying out loud. I don't want to hear about you losing your crummy job." I really said, "Hey, you're a good club pro with a lot of experience. You won't have any trouble getting work."

He snarled back, saying, "I don't know how you can say that. There are over two hundred pros looking for work as we speak." Meanwhile I was thinking, *Talk about a negative attitude. He still hasn't asked me how I'm doing.*

He then asked me to write a letter on his behalf, and I was thinking, *Wow, this guy really has a problem!*

Finally he asked me how I felt.

"Well, I feel great," I told him. Sure, I had been through the wringer recently, but I was doing fine now.

Suddenly I found myself expressing a new, positive attitude. I realized I had been wrapped up in my own little world and acting out of the same selfishness of which I was accusing him. I also realized that this was an opportunity I had been waiting for, a chance to be an inspiration to others. So I talked about drawing peace and strength from the Lord. I offered him encouragement. I sensed that when he hung up, he felt better. I know I did.

I had tried to be positive every time I was on the phone with a well-wisher, but many times I was just mouthing the words they wanted to hear. This time I felt my positive attitude was real. That phone call helped me to start taking my eyes off me and seeing the needs of others. However much I might have helped my friend, little could he know that his call had helped me even more.

I wanted be more useful to God and more usable. I prayed that I would be more thankful for every day God gives me to live.

In a very real way, that phone call helped me to get well ... truly well.

CHAPTER TWENTY-NINE
STILL ZINGER

After the second chemotherapy treatment Toni, Dede, and I established a system. Chemo was simply more of the same—IVs and nausea, shots and soreness. I looked for the landmarks: third treatment, I'm halfway through; fourth treatment, over the hump; fifth treatment, only one more to go!

As far as the national media were concerned, I was a recluse. I dropped completely out of sight from December 1993 until May 1994. Many members of the media called and said, "Paul, you are making a mistake. You are missing a great opportunity here. People want to know how you are doing. They need to hear your story."

"Maybe so," I replied, "but I do not want to give a weekly report or a monthly blow-by-blow description of where I am in my treatment. There are people who are really suffering with this disease who are not famous and are not getting the attention you are willing to give to me. They are the ones we should be talking to. For now, just tell your audience that I am doing fine."

For the most part, that's what the media did, although my name was frequently mentioned on television as people expressed their get-well wishes. I greatly appreciated their expressions of concern, encouragement, love, and prayers.

Cards, letters, get-well wishes, and assurances of prayer continued to pour in from around the world. I couldn't possibly answer them all, and many I had difficulty even reading because they were so moving. Many of the letters told stories of people who had faced cancer and won.

After the Masters I received touching letters from Seve Ballesteros, Jose Maria Olazabal, and Nick Faldo. All three of the guys greatly encouraged me. Jose said the Masters just wasn't the same without me. They let me know they were looking forward to facing me again in the Ryder Cup in '95. Now that was a challenge I could not ignore. It made me even more determined to conquer this cancer.

One call I received early in my treatment was from Lanny Wadkins, the captain of the 1995 U.S. Ryder Cup team. Lanny assured me, "Paul, if you are playing even halfway decently in '95, I'll pick you for the team. I love your spirit. I love your attitude about the Ryder Cup. If you are back out there and hitting the ball at all, I'll pick you."

I said, "That's a sympathy call . . . but I'm gonna hold you to it!"

Another of the many inspiring phone calls came from Johnny Miller, the 1973 U.S. Open champion. He called just as I was beginning the third month of treatments, and I needed a little boost. Johnny told me something I will never forget: "Zinger, it's not what we accomplish in life that matters, but what we overcome." I thought, *Johnny, you are so right.* Johnny continued, "And Zinger, you have to overcome something far greater than what most people have to overcome."

● ○ ●

During the spring of '94 I had a lot of time to think about my life. Once I regained my strength after each chemo treatment, I enjoyed just going out on my boat on the Manatee River. The water was good therapy for me—to hear nothing but the birds chirping and the gentle lapping of the waves against my boat, to feel the warm Florida breeze that lightly caressed the mangroves along the shoreline. It calmed my anxieties and helped me relax.

Out there on the Manatee I resolved that if the doctors told me, "Zinger, you can't play golf anymore," I would be all right. Consequently, as difficult as this may seem to some people, I began to regard my entire ordeal with cancer as one of the greatest experiences of my life. It brought me closer to God, to my family, to myself.

I already had a great appreciation for nature before I got sick. But having the time to drift along the dark waters of the Manatee made me esteem the intricacies of the Lord's handiwork in creation even more. At times I felt like shouting his praises; at others, I was awed by his majesty.

● ○ ●

As one might expect, I did some good fishing during the spring. I could not cast with my right arm, but I was learning how to handle a spinning rod fairly well left-handed. A friend, Doug Hall, helped me lift the gear I couldn't lift alone. He and I spent many hours together on the river in January and February, supposedly the best time to fish the Manatee. It didn't matter to me whether I caught anything or not; I just loved the anticipation of hearing the sound of my line spinning off the reel.

Toni and I also found time to take a fishing excursion to the Florida Keys. There I caught a baby tarpon that weighed about fifteen pounds and photographed it as a special reminder of these moments in our lives.

Even though I was avoiding the national media, I wasn't bashful about being seen in public locally. So Toni and I did many things together we rarely had time to do when I was on the Tour—eating out, going to concerts. We even got involved in a political campaign, something new for us even though we had both always taken political matters seriously.

Bald head and all, I stood on the street corners of Bradenton during the Florida primary and passed out campaign literature. It was interesting to see people's reactions as they drove by. Some would yell, "Hey, that's Paul Azinger! How are you doin', Paul? Great to see you!" Then they would notice the placards for the conservative candidates Toni and I were supporting and offer us various salutes with their fingers. Ah, the fickleness of celebrity!

During this time I faithfully attended a men's Bible Study Fellowship group in our hometown. I had been reading the Bible regularly since my first chemo. After recommitting my life to the Lord, I found that the Bible was no longer a dusty book, but a living Word. I knew I couldn't live without it ever again.

My initial meeting of the Bible study impressed me in many ways: the number of men there, the demographic diversity—wealthy and poor, black and white, young and old. But all the guys had a common goal—to discover in the Bible how Jesus Christ could be more real in their lives. My Bible study group became a mainstay in my physical and spiritual improvement.

● ○ ●

Naturally, we attended all of Sarah Jean and Josie's school functions and recitals. One instance near the end of my chemotherapy stands out in my mind. Toni and I and my mother attended the girls' dance recital, held at the municipal auditorium, for students of Georgene's School of Dance. The girls looked incredibly cute. Sarah Jean wore a white sailor's cap and a bouncy blue skirt. Josie looked like the little angel that she is in her lacy white outfit. The girls did their dance routines with their classes, and like all the other proud parents, we applauded loudly.

At the conclusion of the grand finale, I walked up to the stage and the girls ran over to kiss me. As usual, I was wearing one of the many baseball hats from my collection. I tilted my face up so we could kiss, and both girls planted one on me. Then Sarah Jean reached down, grabbed my baseball cap, and lifted it off my head. As she did, she flashed a big smile, leaned over, and kissed my bald head. It was as if she were saying to her world, "This is my bald-headed Daddy. And I'm proud of him!" To me, there's no acclamation on earth any greater than that.

As the reigning PGA Champion, my responsibilities included attending the PGA Media Day, a promotional blitz for the annual event. I refused to set a date with the PGA until after my last chemotherapy was completed. The PGA reluctantly agreed, rescheduling their event so I could attend. Having the Media Day as an incentive helped me through my final chemo, but I got sick as usual. Fortunately, two days after my final neupogen shot I felt like a new person.

I had not been able to touch a club since December except for some light chipping and putting around the house. As odd as it may seem, I can honestly say that after my initial bout with the blues, I did not miss playing golf. Nevertheless, I was excited about the opportunity to speak to the world for the first time about what I had been through since the public had last seen me, and more important, the new priorities I had established, including my relationship with the Lord.

● ○ ●

My "coming-out party" took place in Tulsa on May 16, 1994. It was the first time many of those people had seen me since the '93 Skins Game. I looked quite a bit different. I was totally bald and a little self-conscious because my eyebrows and eyelashes had fallen out and I didn't have a hair on my body. When I walked into the press room at the gorgeous Southern Hills Country Club, there were 120 media people in the room, with another sixty hooked up on a telephone conference call around the world. I had prayed the night before that God would give me just the right words to be an encouragement, not just to the people in that room, but to any who might see, hear, or read about this event in the days ahead.

In commenting on my appearance and my treatments, I tried to strike a balance between the light and the serious. I said I was thrilled when my hair all fell out and kind of liked myself bald. "After all, bald is in," I told them. "Just look at all those NBA basketball stars; they all have bald heads. As a matter of fact, as soon as I lost all my hair, I shaved my head and went out to our basketball hoop in the backyard. Within seconds, I was dunking shots."

The press corps loved it. They could tell that I had been through something devastating and were glad that at least when it came to my sense of humor, I was still Zinger.

I went on from there and related many of the details leading up to the discovery of the cancer. Many of them were shocked to learn that the shoulder pain went all the way back to 1987. They had assumed it had just begun to bother me in 1991 and again in 1993. I wanted the press to know that I had felt fairly bulletproof in my life up until I heard those three devastating words, "You have cancer." But I also wanted them to know that by renewing my faith in the Lord, I had found a peace I had never known before.

● ○ ●

Prior to the PGA Media Day, a member of the Memorial Tournament staff had called to ask whether, since I was the defending champion, I would be willing to send a greeting to the players. I said, "Why don't we do one better than that? Why don't I come see them in person?" The opening ceremonies were to be held two days after the Media Day in Tulsa.

We arranged for David Henchel of the Occidental Company to have me flown in a G-3 private jet to Tulsa for the Media Day and still get back in time for Bible study that night. The men in my Bible study were amazed. "Hey, we just saw you on ESPN an hour ago!"

Then Jack Nicklaus's plane picked me up on Tuesday evening and whisked me to Dublin, Ohio. I stayed the night with Jack and his wife, Barbara, who had been a great support to Toni and me all through my career, but especially during the cancer ordeal. Jack said, "Hey, you look great!" I told him that I knew he was lying, but I appreciated it anyhow.

The next day I attended the opening ceremonies of the Memorial at Muirfield Village. This was the first time I had been near a "live" golf tournament, and the atmosphere was electric. I had not seen most of these players in more than six months. It was great to see all of them, and perhaps, seeing me, bald head and all, they were reminded how thankful we should be for good health.

Many of the guys did double takes when they saw me. I saw my friend and Ryder Cup partner, Chip Beck, upstairs in the locker room. I called out, "Chipper!"

As I walked toward him and extended my hand, I realized Chip recognized my voice, but did not realize who I was. Then I grabbed his hand and looked into his eyes.

"Zinger! You're back!"

● ○ ●

I wasn't exactly back. I still had five weeks of radiation therapy ahead of me. Early in my chemotherapy, Dr. Jobe had told me about a new machine in Loma Linda, California, that was the only one if its kind in the world. The proton radiation accelerator, as it is called, takes a hydrogen atom, splits the proton out of it, and accelerates the proton at the speed of light. The beam can be stopped at the bone so the radiation will go into the bone, but not beyond it.

Rather than blasting the area with a large, scattered dosage of neutron radiation, which often causes arthritis in the joints, this machine can target the proton radiation so specifically it can hit a pinhead. Because of the area of the shoulder in which the cancer was found, Dr. Jobe thought I might be a perfect candidate for the new technology.

I wasn't excited about going back to California for radiation, since I could easily have gotten it at home. But once again, Dr. Jobe's wisdom and extra effort were invaluable to me.

● ○ ●

Ken Venturi is on the board of directors at Loma Linda Hospital, and Dave Stockton is on the board at Loma Linda's Children's Hospital. Both of them recommended that I consider treatment with this new machine.

Dave went one step further. He insisted that if I decided to do the radiation at Loma Linda, he and his wife, Cathy, would move out of their home near the hospital, and my family could live there during the five weeks of treatments. "It won't be any problem at all," Dave assured me. "I will just play those five weeks on the road. We have dogs and cats, and the kids will feel just as if they are at home." We accepted his generous invitation.

My radiologist, Dr. Jerry Slater, examined me and gave me some great news. There was no evidence of any remaining cancer in my shoulder as we began radiation treatments. Therefore they were going to radiate the spot where the cancer had been, rather than an existing cancer.

On my first day I walked into the room where some men were working with a liquid in a machine that looked like a giant blender. They poured the liquid into a green plastic garbage bag, laid it on a table, flattened it out, and instructed me to lay down on my back. As I did, the warm liquid began to rise like dough around my upper body, neck, head, and torso. Then it began hardening into a mold of my body.

I started my daily radiation treatment on May 23. Each day I had to put myself into the mold of my body so the radiation could hit exactly the same spot every time. It took about thirty minutes to get me set up in the mold; the actual process of zapping the radiation into my shoulder lasted about ninety seconds.

Ironically, before the treatments began I had to sign a document agreeing to the procedure and acknowledging that I understood that the radiation could cause cancer.

● ○ ●

Once the chemotherapy was completed and I had received a good report from my doctors, I had set a personal goal of wanting to be strong enough to defend my PGA title at Southern Hills in August. I would have loved to have been able to defend my New England Classic title in July, but I knew that was really pushing it. Nevertheless, during the time I was doing the daily radiation treatments, I hired a personal fitness trainer, Jon Hall, to help get my body back in shape.

Except for my stomach muscles, which were hard as rocks from all the nausea, my body was extremely weak. I had no muscle tone at all, and my right shoulder had severely atrophied owing to my inability to use it. Yet if I wanted to play golf, I needed both my shoulders to be in good condition.

Jon is a strong, forty-two-year-old fitness trainer. From the time we met we hit it off well. Within the first hour we were indulging in good-natured repartee.

Jon said, "All right, we're going to do some leg extensions here, nothing heavy. Your legs look pretty good."

I glanced down at my hairless legs and thought, *Yeah, they do look pretty buffed; not bad, considering what I have been through.*

Jon quickly burst my bubble. "Yeah, most of the girls I work with would love to have legs that smooth."

We were supposed to do twenty-five one-hour sessions, but Jon took much longer with me than the procedure required. Our daily sessions were right after my morning radiation treatment. Once we got started, many of our stints went two or three hours.

When I first met Jon, I couldn't do a leg extension at more than ten pounds. I couldn't stay on a stair-climber for more than five minutes. My weight had dropped to 160 pounds, at least fifteen pounds below my playing weight.

Jon designed a specific training program that he felt would get me back into playing shape in time to meet my goal of defending the PGA title. The exercises he came up with we dubbed "the Zinger Six." Most of them targeted my debilitated shoulder and upper body strength. The program was designed to be fun, not drudgery. We did everything from throwing a Frisbee—to restore my rotary torso flexibility—to jumping rope.

Cancer may not have killed me, but jumping rope came close. Although I have always been athletic, I nearly strangled myself on that jump rope before I got the hang ... er, idea of it.

● ○ ●

By the end of the five weeks, Jon had me doing leg extensions with seventy pounds and doing twenty-minute sessions on the Versa-Climber. My weight had increased to 170, most of the new pounds coming from toned muscles.

My shoulder surgery had healed. I no longer felt any pain there. Dr. Feldman had declared me cancer free. Dr. Slater had done his job pouring the radiation into me. Jon Hall had helped me get my body back to playing strength. The only question left to answer was, Could I still hit a golf ball?

CHAPTER THIRTY
Charging Back

As I stood on the tenth tee at the Buick Open on August 4, I had not played in a PGA tournament in more than nine months. I had played only six rounds of golf during that time, two of which included the practice round and the Pro-Am at the Buick. It had only been within the past few weeks that I had even seriously begun to practice.

During my last few weeks in California, Dave Stockton and I went to Palm Springs to hit some golf balls. I hit my first 5-iron in more than six months, and it was perfect! Stockton couldn't believe it. I was pretty excited about it, too—probably more excited than I should have been, because I hit too many balls that day and my shoulder felt sore afterward.

I had been duly warned not to rush my return. Back before the radiation was completed, I had complained about soreness developing after I had hit a few balls with Dave. Both Dr. Jobe and Dr. Feldman assured me that any discomfort would not indicate a recurrence of cancer, but rather strained muscles affected by a long period of disuse. But I was also given a clear message: Slow down.

During my fourth week of radiation, I had surgery to remove a lypoma from my side. The lypoma was a fatty tumor that had been growing for several years, totally unrelated to the cancer in my shoulder. But when it began to bother me, I grew concerned, especially when the doctor ordered a CTT scan. The test results declared the lypoma benign, but the doctors said, "Let's get it out of there, anyhow."

The lypoma surgery set my recovery time back three more weeks, allowing me only two weeks to prepare for my planned return at the Buick Open in Michigan. Once I was back in Florida, my coach, John Redman, came over to Sarasota, and I went out to hit some balls so he could check out my form. John thought I was doing better than ever and said he wouldn't be surprised if I won a championship or two before the end of the year. John's confident optimism persuaded me to enter the Buick Open.

● ○ ●

The announcement that I would play turned the tournament into a media circus. Tuesday morning, my first official practice round, I was excited to get out to the course. I drove out by myself and dropped off my clubs at the main entrance. I thought I was arriving early, but the media got there first. I was encircled and interviewed from the start. I didn't give formal interviews at that time; I simply answered the questions thrown at me as I passed by. I said, "I'm doing fine. Doing great!"

I walked into the locker room and spoke to the attendant, "Hi, I'm Paul Azinger. Can you tell me which locker is mine?"

"Yes, sir, Mr. Azinger," he answered. He led me to my locker—and suddenly everything was like old times. This was the routine, and I was back in it.

The sun shone brightly in the beautiful blue skies on Thursday. Michigan is gorgeous that time of year, and the summer air felt crisp and clean. By my tee time shortly past noon, I had already answered the "How are you doing?" question hundreds of times. What can you say? As when your kids start asking only three miles down the road, "Are we there yet?" and repeat the same question every three miles thereafter, there are only so many ways to answer. Or you exhaust your energy trying to come up with an original answer. I didn't mind the questions, however, nor the many requests for autographs. But they did make it very difficult to concentrate on playing golf.

By the time I was ready to walk to the tenth tee—my first hole—I felt a nervous excitement from head to foot. The tee area and the fairway were lined solid with people, and the tee box was crowded with media. Press tape recorders and cameras were everywhere I looked.

When a little boy said, "Good luck, Azinger," as I was signing an autograph on my way to the tee, the crowd erupted in a huge ovation. I joined my good friends and playing partners, Corey Pavin and Ben Crenshaw, inside the tee box ropes. Toni was in the front row of the crowd, so I leaned over the ropes to give her a kiss as I passed by.

It was incredibly exciting, and I did a lot of nodding thank-yous and waving to the crowd. Most of all, I was trying to prepare mentally to hit a good shot while taking deep breaths, walking over to the scorer's tent, getting my scorecard, getting my tees, getting my pencil, keeping my head down, trying not to look at anybody.

Corey hit first and he hit a good shot. Then it was my turn.

● ○ ●

I tried to focus on my shot as Randy Hutton, the announcer on the tenth tee, began to introduce me: "Winner of eleven tournaments on Tour, three-time champion in 1993, winner of the 1993 PGA Championship—ladies and gentlemen, please welcome back to the game...."

While Randy was introducing me, I was bending over to put my tee in the ground and trying to avoid eye contact with anyone, lest I break down. And when he said, "Welcome back to the game," it struck me like a lightning bolt. More specifically, it struck my emotions, which were already wired.

Randy had not said, "Welcome to the Buick Open," nor had he said, "Welcome to Warwick Hills Golf and Country Club." He said, "Ladies and Gentlemen, please welcome back to the *game* ... Paul Azinger." And it hit me that he was right. That's what I was doing here; not simply going out for a round of golf; not merely playing in another media event. I was coming back to the game and all that it meant to me. The game I loved. The people, the competition, the beautiful scenery I had always enjoyed but had taken for granted. Welcome back to the game—the game I had missed more than I had realized.

"Ladies and gentlemen, please welcome back to the GAME ... Paul Azinger."

If I had needed to talk to somebody at that moment, I couldn't have. I was choked up, and I knew I was in trouble. My eyes started to tear up right away, and I blinked as much as I could. I thought, *I have to get rid of these tears right now, because I don't have time for this. I've got to hit!*

And then the crowd started cheering and clapping, and I started acknowledging and waving, and they continued to applaud ... and applaud ... and applaud! Players behind me, whom I couldn't see, had stopped what they were doing. They stopped and stood on their tiptoes, to look over the crowd, to watch me hit my first competitive shot in ten months.

I was still sort of nervous but now I was way more emotional than nervous. I'm thinking, *I can't hit it.* I kept saying to myself, *You must collect yourself, and you must do it now.*

I sucked in a lot of air and continued to allow the gallery to applaud, not because I wanted to evoke a larger ovation, but because the tears had blurred my vision to the point that I couldn't see the ball well enough to hit it. I pretended that I was taking a few extra practice swings. Without wiping my eyes, I went through my normal shot routine, picking up a few blades of grass, tossing them into the air to check the wind, and finally addressing the ball. The clapping died down, and the gallery grew silent.

● ○ ●

I felt terribly uncomfortable standing over the ball, but there was no turning back now. I swung my "Big Bertha" driver and ripped the ball right down the middle of the fairway. The ball sailed about 270 yards, past Corey's drive by about twenty yards. I was just glad I hadn't killed anybody off the tee. I had been afraid that I might hit this thing on the heel, line it into the crowd, and take someone out on my first shot back.

I put my hand over my heart, stuck my tongue out, and sort of faked stumbling, pretending I was going to faint. The fans really didn't know how close to being true that was.

A huge gallery, at times five and six people deep, followed Corey, Ben, and me down the fairway. Hundreds of people called out, "Welcome back, Zinger!" and "Go get 'em, Paul." I tried to acknowledge as many as I could and still keep my mind on playing golf. Not an easy task.

I parred my first hole, just missing a birdie when my twenty-five-foot putt rolled two inches by the cup. The crowd roared its approval. I would have been happier with the birdie, but after nine months of not touching my clubs, I was delighted with par.

Around every tee I walked onto that day, there was a huge gallery. At every green, the crowd gave me a hearty ovation. I was beginning to feel like Arnold Palmer or Jack Nicklaus!

I played the first two rounds of the tournament, shooting 74 and 70. My putting was awful, and I missed the cut. But I was not disappointed. In a way, it may have been a blessing in disguise, because one day's play was rained out. As a result, had I made the cut, I would have had to play thirty-six holes on Sunday. Having played only eight rounds of golf—five of them while riding in a cart—a thirty-six-hole finish may have been more than my legs could take. I had done a lot of leg-work with Jon Hall, but those exercises are much different than walking a golf course and squatting and standing to read putts.

In addition, the extra day off gave me a chance to be fresh when I defended my title at the PGA Championship in Tulsa the following week.

● ○ ●

I had thought the media frenzy at the Buick Open was amazing, but the amount of press at the PGA made the Buick pale by comparison. I was especially on display here because I was the reigning champion. As such, I felt an even greater obligation to give time to the media and make myself available for autographs. I signed just about anything anyone put in front of me that week. I sure hope there were no shady endorsement contracts thrust at me in Tulsa!

I also took time to visit Scott Carter's sports collection, which was on display at a local bank. Scott Carter was the spunky twelve-year-old boy who had died of bone cancer on December 2, 1993—just about the time the doctors discovered cancer in my shoulder bone. Scott was an avid Oklahoma State

University basketball fan, and during his last year the team saved a special place at the end of the bench where Scott could sit in his wheelchair to watch the games.

Scott's "Player of the Game" award—a paper certificate scrawled in the twelve-year-old's handwriting and given by Scott after each game to the player "who gave it his best and didn't quit"—became the most coveted prize in the university's sports history. I was honored to meet Scott's parents, Mike and Paula, and was inspired by their son's story.

Because of my experience, I was constantly coming into contact with people who are fighting cancer. I always tried to be an encouragement to those who introduced themselves or told me about someone in their family who was battling some form of the disease. One such person was Wes Edwards, another young man. Wes was sixteen years old when I met him.

I met Wes on Tuesday at the home of Steve Largent, the former NFL star pass receiver. I invited Wes to come out to the course and walk with me as I played my practice round. Wes's eyes lit up. He was dressed in a shirt and tie, so when we got to Southern Hills, I went into the pro shop and bought him a golf shirt so he would be more comfortable, and a hat so his bald head would not get sunburned. I was not trying to exploit Wes's condition or make a name for myself for doing something nice. I wanted Wes Edwards to have an experience he would never forget, an experience from which he might draw a little bit of encouragement the next time he had a tough time dealing with his disease.

● ○ ●

On Wednesday morning I spoke to a breakfast audience of 800 people before my practice round. It was a mixed group of business people and golf professionals. I began by saying, "A year ago this week, I realized a dream, winning my first major championship, the PGA."

As the reigning PGA Champion, I shared with the audience an abbreviated version of the events leading up to my victory at Inverness. Then I related the discovery of my cancer and how it has changed my life.

The room grew still as I related how my major championship and my ten other Tour victories had suddenly grown meaningless when I was diagnosed with cancer. Businessmen, professional golfers, and others in the audience listened intently as I zeroed in on the most important part of what I wanted to say.

> I don't know how successful you are. I don't know how big your house is, how much money you have, or how nice your car is, or how nice your boat is. But I'm telling you, we came into this world with nothing, and we are leaving with nothing. And everything we get along the way is a blessing from

God. If you are finding your contentment and happiness in your accomplishments, or from the amount of money and possessions you own, I am here to tell you, it doesn't last.

I'm not saying that I have more money than I can spend, but I've made a lot of money since I've been on the Tour, and I've won a lot of tournaments. That happiness is always temporary.

The only way you will ever have true contentment is in a personal relationship with Jesus Christ. I'm not saying that nothing ever bothers me, and I don't have problems, but I feel like I've found the answer to the six-foot hole.

I know I will spend eternity with God. And I have a promise that as a child of God, he will help me deal with anything. He promises to give me contentment no matter what life brings—even cancer.

I closed my talk by telling a story that my Bible study leader, Mike Hammrick, had told us one night at Bible study. It seems Mike got on an airplane one day and saw one of the strangest things he had ever seen in his life. The man sitting next to him in first class was dressed in a bathrobe and slippers. The man's seat was a beautiful leather chair, but my friend's was simply made of fabric. The man said to my friend, "I see you have noticed my chair. This chair is made of the finest leathers money can buy."

Then my friend noticed that the man had a mahogany tray table. Again, the man said, "Ahh, you have noticed my gorgeous tray table."

My friend looked up and saw that the guy had a ceiling fan. The rich man was also surrounded by a VCR, a television set, a CD player, and a computer.

My friend was flabbergasted. He asked the rich man, "Why would anyone go to the expense to have all these things installed in an airplane?"

The man replied bluntly, "Because this is my home."

My friend thought, *What a shame! A place that was intended to be a journey, he has made his home.*

Of course, Mike's story was just an illustration, but the audience got the point. I took a deep breath and said, "I'm just here to tell you that God does not intend for this to be the best of all possible places for us. But it is a place where we can prepare for the best of all possible places."

No one stirred as I concluded:

Even though it's great to be called a PGA Tour player, and it's probably even greater to be called a PGA Champion, no greater gift is mine than to be called a child of God, because I place my trust in Jesus Christ. When I talk about contentment, I'm not talking about complacency. I am the least complacent person I know. But I am talking about true contentment. Fame and notoriety won't bring it; money won't bring it. So just ask yourself this question, "Is there another way?"

I thanked the crowd for coming and sat down. The room exploded in applause as the audience gave me a hearty and prolonged standing ovation. In my heart I thanked the Lord for fulfilling two more of my dreams—to be able to inspire people who were fighting against cancer, and to tell them about the One who has already won the victory over death, hell, and the grave.

● ○ ●

When I finally made it to the first tee in the first round at Southern Hills, the gallery gave me a standing ovation there, too. I thanked them, acknowledged everyone, and then addressed the ball. The crowd was just as gracious as the gallery at the Buick, but when they saw that I had come to play golf, they quickly grew quiet. I ripped a good first shot down the fairway and into the left rough. As I had done at the Buick a week before, I parred the first hole. I shot a 75 the first round and a 74 the second. I hit some great shots, with four birdies on the back nine the second day. But once again, my putter let me down, and I missed the cut by three strokes.

Of course, I would have loved to have played better, but I was not greatly disappointed. On the contrary, I was thrilled. My goal was to play in the PGA, to defend my title, and I had accomplished that and much more. Zinger was back.

CHAPTER THIRTY-ONE
PLAYING TO WIN

After playing in the PGA on Thursday and Friday, I awoke Saturday morning with a sore right shoulder. *Oh, no! Not again!*

I soon realized that the pain was not bone-related. It was a dull pain informing me, "Son, despite your best efforts, you're still out of shape!" Most of my body seemed to be in excellent condition, except that I don't think I realized until then how badly my shoulder had atrophied from lack of use during chemo and radiation treatments.

Since then, many people have asked me, "Zinger, did you come back too soon?"

I don't think so. Mentally I was ready to return. I had gone through one of the most difficult experiences of my life and set reachable goals. Looking back, however, I fear that my body might not have been as fit as I thought it was.

I had to withdraw from the Fred Meyer Challenge, which was a disappointment because I received so many kind cards and letters from that locality during my rehabilitation. I had wanted to play as a way to say thank-you to all the people in Portland, Oregon.

I didn't touch a club for three full weeks after that. For a while I didn't even miss not playing. I spent most of my time fishing, although I was getting my shoulder rehabilitated very slowly. Dr. Jobe had advised me to take it easy for a while, and I was happy to comply with the doctor's orders.

Hale Irwin had invited me to serve with him as cocaptain of the first U.S. President's Cup team. I accepted Hale's offer and thoroughly enjoyed my role. Hale allowed me to be very involved in the pairings of our players, and I loved working out the strategies to use against the International team.

Most of all, it was great to be an inspiration to the younger guys who had never played on a Ryder Cup team. I shared with them from my Ryder Cup experiences some of the anxieties I had felt as well as the tremendous honor I enjoyed at being able to stand on that first tee to represent the United States of America. One day I would like to be captain of a President's Cup team or a Ryder Cup team—or both.

● ○ ●

I had to leave the President's Cup on Sunday evening to fly back to Orlando for the first annual "Zinger Stinger." I had been bombarded with requests to play in dozens of celebrity golf tournaments for various causes, especially the American Cancer Society. I could not possibly accept all the invitations, yet in good conscience I could not say no to them all either. David Moorman, my manager with Leader Enterprises, hit upon the perfect solution: "Let's have our own celebrity tournament to raise money for cancer research."

David and his team at Leader put together a top-notch celebrity tournament. We got great cooperation from some of the best professional golfers in the world to play with a strong group of amateurs. The event was held at Lake Nona Country Club near Orlando, and we raised a fortune for the Leukemia Society of America and lymphoma research. Part of the reason why I received such technologically advanced treatment is that people who have gone before me paid the price to work hard at finding cures for cancers of all kinds, including lymphoma. I want to be involved in helping to find a cure so that others do not have to go through what I did.

● ○ ●

Through my experiences I have learned the value of a timely, encouraging word. When I recall the many people who took time out of their busy schedules to call me and attempt to lift my spirits, I am still astonished. I think of former President Bush, who took the time to call this ailing golfer; or Curtis Strange, whom I always regarded previously as something of a "tough guy." They exemplify the kind of encourager I want to be.

It does not take a lot of money, knowledge, or influence to be an encourager. It just takes someone who cares and has a sensitivity to the opportunities that surround us every day. Those opportunities can arise in unexpected ways.

For example, I really wanted to keep my consecutive-year winning streak alive, so in late 1994 I went to San Antonio in the hope that I might win one of the last tournaments of the year. On the practice tee, however, I began to have trouble with my back. I had to withdraw from the tournament.

The following week I attempted to play in the Las Vegas Invitational in a last-ditch effort to maintain my streak. My back was still bothering me. Despite the pain, I persisted right down to the last minute on the practice tees, still undecided whether I should play or not. At the same time, a young man who had just graduated from tour school was sitting there waiting to see what I would decide. If I withdrew, he would get a chance to play; if I played, he would have to go home and hope to qualify the next year.

Finally I made up my mind. As much as I wanted to play at Vegas, I decided to withdraw. It was silly for me to try to play with my back hurting the way it was, especially when this young man had an opportunity for a shot at keeping his tour card.

Mark Jimenez, my caddie, took my clubs back to the car. I was feeling disappointed for so many reasons. I had come a long distance and now felt I had wasted time and money in doing so. I had inconvenienced Mark, who had flown in just to be there with me. And, of course, my streak was now to end at seven in a most ignominious manner. Yet I knew in my heart that the decision to withdraw was the right one.

As I walked back to the car, I heard someone call my name from some distance behind me: "Paul! Paul! Do you have just a second?"

I turned around and saw two women and a man coming toward me. I stopped and waited, figuring they probably wanted my autograph.

When they reached me, one woman said, "I want you to meet Pam. She was diagnosed with breast cancer about three weeks ago. She has to have surgery to have her breast removed."

"Oh, I'm so sorry." We struck up a conversation. Pam was very emotional. She was scared and didn't know what to expect as she faced this surgery.

Pam and her husband, Sam, introduced themselves as big Paul Azinger fans. They had followed me through every hole at the 1993 PGA Championship in Toledo, had a golf ball on their fireplace mantel that had been autographed by me, and had pictures I had signed also. They said they simply liked Paul Azinger.

When I was diagnosed with cancer, they were shocked and hurt, and they kept up on my progress continually. Now Pam is diagnosed right before the Vegas tournament, and I'm back. When they heard I was going to be there, they were determined to find a way to see me and talk to me.

Pam asked many questions about cancer, and I tried to alleviate her anxieties and fears.

"What is chemo like?" she asked.

"Well, it's different for everybody," I said. "I personally didn't really like it very much." I didn't tell her how horrible it was for me. "I got really sick on it at times, but some people hardly get sick at all. With most kinds of chemo, your hair will definitely fall out. But don't worry about it. It will grow back. Just get yourself a nice wig."

I ended up spending about twenty minutes with these three people, just talking and answering their questions as best I could. I was also able to express what a difference my faith in the Lord has made, especially when I was going through the toughest times.

"You know you can 'trust in the LORD with all your heart,'" I said, quoting some Bible verses. "'Lean not on your own understanding; in all your ways acknowledge him, and he will make your paths straight'" (Proverbs 3:5–6). I explained that God tells us not to be "anxious about anything, but in everything, by prayer and petition, with thanksgiving, present your requests to God. And the peace of God, which transcends all understanding, will guard your hearts and your minds in Christ Jesus" (Philippians 4:6–7). We talked a little longer, and I had to go, so I said to Sam, "Please give me your number, and I'll call you." Pam was crying, and we hugged one another. When I walked away, I looked back at them, and they were all crying. I understood. I remembered how frightened I had been when I was told I had cancer.

As I got into the car to return to my hotel, I felt that there was a much bigger reason why I had come to Vegas, and why—as much as I had wanted to play—I was not on the golf course just then. I believe God put me in a certain place at a certain time so that I could encourage Pam and Sam.

I knew Pam was having surgery on Wednesday of the next week, and I called them. They were surprised to hear from me. I reminded Pam of the things I had told her in Las Vegas.

Pam had the surgery, and her husband called me the day after to report that she was doing well. He thanked me for helping her to get through the crisis. He said that brief encounter at the golf course made a big difference in her life.

Strange, it helped me, too. I like being an encouragement to someone else. Before my bout with cancer, I had never done that sort of thing. I never felt comfortable calling someone who was sick, because I never knew what to say. I couldn't relate to that person's need. But now I realize, what is said is not the most important thing. All one has to communicate is, "Hey, I want you to know that I'm thinking about you today." Sometimes that is all it takes to be an encourager. And it makes a difference.

I can honestly say that it was more rewarding to encourage that couple in their anxiety than winning that tournament could have ever been. And frankly, I didn't need to win that tournament, as much as I would have liked to keep the streak going. But maybe Pam and Sam needed me to be there right at that moment.

People often ask me now, "Zinger, is golf still as important to you as it was before you had cancer?"

Yes and no. Yes, of course, golf is important to me. I love the game; it is how I make a living. But no, golf is no longer at the top of my priority list. In fact, it runs a slow fourth. My priorities now are God, my family, my friends, and golf. Golf is no longer my god. Golf is hitting a little white ball. God is my God, and God is a whole lot bigger than golf.

But don't get me wrong. I played some great golf at the end of 1994 and the beginning of 1995, and I plan on playing a lot more. You won't hear me out on the course, saying, "Woe is me. I missed that four-footer, but at least I'm alive."

Oh, no. I'm playing to win. But then, in many ways, I have already won.